Origin of Indian Civilization

Origin of Indian Civilization

Edited by
Bal Ram Singh

Center for Indic Studies
Dartmouth (USA)

D.K. Printworld (P) Ltd.
New Delhi (India)

Cataloging in Publication Data — DK
[Courtesy: D.K. Agencies (P) Ltd. <docinfo@dkagencies.com>]

Origin of Indian civilization / edited by Bal Ram Singh.
p. cm.
Contributed articles.
Includes bibliographical references.
ISBN 9788124605608
ISBN 8124605602

1. Indus civilization. 2. India — Civilization. 3. India — Antiquities. I. Singh, Bal Ram, 1958-

DDC 934 22

ISBN 13: 978-81-246-0560-8 **ISBN 10: 81-246-0560-2**
First published in India in 2010

Published by:
Center for Indic Studies
University of Massachusetts, Dartmouth
285, Old Westport Road
Dartmouth, MA - 02747 (USA)
Phone: 508-999 8588 *Fax*: 508 999-8451
Email: bsingh@umassd.edu *Website*: www.umassd.edu/indic

and

D.K. Printworld (P) Ltd.
Regd. Office: 'Srikunj', F-52, Bali Nagar
Ramesh Nagar Metro Station
New Delhi – 110 015
Phones: (011) 2545 3975; 2546 6019 *Fax*: (011) 2546 5926
E-mail: indology@dkprintworld.com *Website*: www.dkprintworld.com

Printed by: D.K. Printworld (P) Ltd., New Delhi.

Preface

INDIA is over 5,000 year old civilization, and is considered as the only living ancient civilization in the world. It has had its philosophical and literary influences on many world thinkers and philosophers to include Ralph Waldo Emerson, Henry David Thoreau, Albert Einstein, Erwin Schrodinger, Arthur Schopenhauer, Mark Twain, Will Durant, Martin Luther King, Jr., and Nelson Mandela among them. With current trend of international migration, business network, global communication, and diasporic community, including presence of over 3 million people of Indian origin in the United States of America, it has become apparent that culture and traditions of India (both ancient and modern) be made available to students, scholars, and public for better understanding of the world.

Furthermore, there is so much incremental interest in India's traditional practices, such as Yoga, Āyurveda, music, and literature in the Western world, especially in the United States that proper and original information on the diverse culture and philosophies of India is essential to students of world history, sociology, and literature.

Invariably, students and scholars encounter conflicting reports and views on Indian civilization, particularly its origin and current practices. Recently, a controversy arose in California on textbook representation of Hinduism which has serious implications in America and elsewhere for students of Indian origin as well as the general student population. One of the major problems has been very strong scholarship and published work since colonial times, widely carried out by scholars under the influence of British colonialists. Much of that scholarship, particularly related to the Aryan origin of Indian civilization has continued under one pretext or the other.

Today's multicultural world requires new noncombative ways of preventing and resolving cultural mis-understandings. The California controversy involves the portrayal of India and Indian origins in the California education system as well as in various text books. In response to this, the Center for Indic Studies at UMass Dartmouth organized a symposium to discuss and debate the essence of the issue: whether Indian population of today is the product of Aryan invasion or a continuation of indigenous peoples.

This was the first time in a conference on this topic that included population geneticists such as Dr. Peter Underhill of Stanford University and Dr V.K. Kashyap of National Institute of Biologicals, India, share the stage with prominent international scholars on archeology, history, linguistics, and anthropology to try to resolve the vexed issue of Aryan vs. Indigenous origin of the oldest surviving civilization on earth.

Given the list of speakers and topics being covered, the discussions are going to be hard. I hope we can keep it civilö, commented Dr. Petr Eltsov, of Deutches Archaeologisches Institut, Berlin, Germany. The symposium speakers included Dr B.B. Lal, former director of Archeological Survey of India, and Dr N.S. Rajaram, author of *Sarasvati River and the Vedic Civilization* (Aditya Prakashan, 2006).

This was first time for scholars in the fields of linguistics, philosophy, history, archeology, physics, mathematics, and genetics, gathered to discuss the single issue of the origin of Indian civilization. The symposium was part of the Fourth Annual Indic Conference organized by the Center for Indic Studies at University of Massachusetts Dartmouth, June 23-25, 2006.

The topic and timing of the conference was relevant to contemporary conditions. The controversy on California textbooks just provided us an extra impetus to contact scholars in the field to put together a symposium on the topic. I am very grateful for the response of scholars to the symposium. It was not easy to gather scholars of such varying fields, and to keep them in one room for two days trying to make sense to each other. The symposium was attended by many other scholars and interested individuals, including Michael Witzel of Harvard University, and representatives of the Education Society for the Heritage of India.

This book is result of the deliberations at the symposium facilitated by the recordings of the symposium, and chapters submitted by the authors. While not a scholar specializing in the study of civilizations, I am left with the responsibility of collating these contributions to facilitate their reach to interested scholars and students of Indian civilization.

I am grateful to my assistant, Miss Shwetha Bhat, for transcribing a couple of the chapters, and for helping me put together the proceedings. I would also like to thank my administrative assistant, Ms. Maureen Jennings for helping in organizing the Symposium, and to Dr Sitanshu Chakravarti of University of Toronto and Shri Shekhar Shastri of Meru Education Foundation for chairing the sessions of the symposium.

Finally, financial support from the Center for Indic Studies and Education Society for the Heritage of India is gratefully acknowledged.

Bal Ram Singh

Contents

Introduction

Classifying Civilizations

CIVILIZATION is a general term to refer to a variety of features of people to include culture, traditions, way of life, religion, ethnicity, etc. Consequently, there are multiple definitions and perspectives of the term civilization. According to one definition available at www.dictionary.com, civilization is "an advanced state of human society, in which a high level of culture, science, industry, and government has been reached." In modern parlance, the definition is more expanded: "an advanced state of intellectual, cultural, and material development in human society, marked by progress in the arts and sciences, the extensive use of record-keeping, including writing, and the appearance of complex political and social institutions."

Because of socio-political and economic implications and history of the past several hundred years, particularly as it relates to the colonial period and colonized people, the meaning of civilization(s) has become a sensitive issue since late 1940s when many of the former colonies became independent politically. The word civilization itself is an eighteenth-century construct, a period marred with the domination of Western European countries which had colonized the rest of the world.

Samuel Huntington's acclaimed book, *Clash of Civilizations*, depicts civilizations of the world based mostly on religions, such as Islamic, Hindu, Buddhist, Orthodox, and nation-state or political, such as Western, Japanese, Sinic. Religious classification itself is a framework, which is difficult to superimpose on the whole world without compromising the reality. Similarly, nation-state construct is temporary and keeps changing, and certainly not a reflection of human behaviour through natural evolution, a feature that must be considered in constructing rubrics for civilization. Huntington's class is not that of civilization but everything else, and is partly due to mixing of political nation-states, religious identities, and cultural classifications (such as African, Latin American) provided by the manipulators of the global world.

I believe the history is then constructed to suit the systems of world management for the benefit of a few or a group of few countries, nations, or even individuals. In the current context, nation-state has become a dominating feature of the world after the dismantling of the colonial world. Much of what is reflected even in academic scholarship is unfortunately reflection of past colonial scholarship and present nation-state system of dominating powers. Academic scholarship by its nature is built on the foundation of documented knowledge, irrespective of perspectives, and is therefore bound by the past. A lot of this constraint is reflected in the construction of India's civilization as well. In the modern Indian nation-state, it has failed to develop scholarship in framework away from the past colonial scholarship, and the consequence is this class of opinions, backed by strong scholarship on both sides of the argument. India as a nation-state has failed to provide a cohesive construction of its past, primarily due to its complex society which may have had varying narratives. This is happening now in the rest of the world as the diversity takes root in the Western world as well.

Whereas separation of Church and state was devised as a

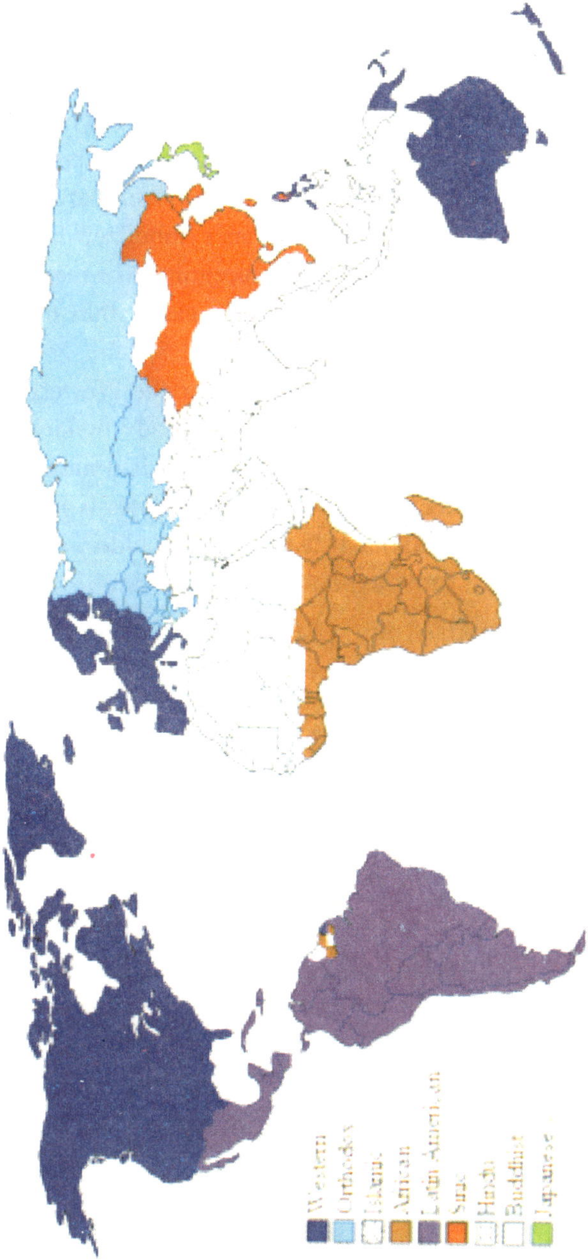

fig. 1: World map showing different dominant civilizations outlined by Samuel Huntington in his book, *Clash of Civilizations*. (http://en.wikipedia.org/wiki/Civilization)

mode to protect state players from religious (many times blind faith) domination as the society had moved to rationality, diversity of culture and even religions within the past half century has forced other steps within the democratic institutions of state — interfaith dialogue, ethnic diversity, multicultural approach, and pluralism. Election of Barack Obama as the President of United States has symbolized this evolution in the Western society, as is the recognition of many traditions — Hindu, Muslim, Buddhist, Sikhs, etc. within the cultural milieu of particularly United States and Britain. This is posing, albeit slowly, a narrative problem for the Western world as well, and right wing political class is already making arguments that United States, for example, is a Christian nation or is built on Judeo-Christian principles. United States is less than 250-year old nation, India is at least 20 times older, and complexities of a society grow exponentially with time.

Today, a new *mantra*, the globalization, seems to undermine even the nation-state concept at its core, and threatens the role of political masters much the same way as the colonial masters or slave masters. The long yearning for freedom from masters may be finally inching towards its final steps.

In a speech entitled "The argument for India" on 23 September 2005, India's then External Affairs Minister, K. Natwar Singh, at Brown University, stated

> . . . as early as 1931, Mahatma Gandhi and the Indian leadership chose to opt for a democratic form of government with universal adult franchise as its basis. . . . Till then, India was considered more an embodiment of a civilization than a definition of a conventional nation-state. It took a democratic construct to bring together its very many languages, ethnicities and customs and provide it a firm binding force.

Why should a civilization take a back seat to the concept of the nation-state? The honourable minister was making brave efforts of salvaging the sinking ship of a nation-state, by somehow constructing a seemingly non-existing cohesion in India where people are totally divided on the basis of languages, castes, and religions, and democracy is used to get even with their perceived adversaries, both historical and modern.

In this game of the control of the nation-state, innocent and ignorant people are almost always the victims, despite the prevalence of a democracy. It should not be surprising given what Benjamin Franklin said about democracy a long time ago. "Democracy is two wolves and a lamb voting on what to have for lunch. Liberty is a well-armed lamb contesting the vote!"

On the other hand, a civilization even by a dictionary meaning is "an advanced state of intellectual, cultural, and material development in human society, marked by progress in the arts and sciences, the extensive use of record-keeping, including writing, and the appearance of complex political and social institutions."

A Case for Modern and Scientific Concept of Civilization

India's civilization seems to have a long narrative of its existence through huge amount of literature, scientific advancements, continuing cultural practices, and millennia old preservation of art and music, all being corroborated by the examination of natural history and scientific data.

While it was possible to construct the origin of Indian civilization from Western colonial perspective at one time that was well supported by academic scholarship, which used a biased paradigm to support the political class of the time, it is impossible today to sustain such a narrow view primarily due to the presence of Indians within the Western societies and due to the globalization. Advancement in scientific technology for examining the past — carbon dating, population genetics, astronomical calculations, and computational linguistics — has opened the door for data-based analysis of the past, and many of the past practices of history and linguistics have come under pressure to conform to more scientific documentations.

Measures other than religion or nation-state could be used to define civilizations. Geography could provide a good prediction of civilizational identity, but in today's globalized world geography can hardly limit flow of information and cultural behaviour. In a recent article on sex ratio in the world, we examined the sex ratio in all the countries, not only at birth but also in different age groups (Singh and Roy, 2010). Our goal was to examine if there was any pattern in the world to preserve the natural sex ratio throughout the age groups. Our hypothesis was that if there was a preservation of the sex ratio then there must be cultural and traditional strengths on a national or civilizational basis.

Our methodology was to collect uniform set of data on all the countries in the world. We also wanted to collect this data for the year in the vicinity of India's census of 2001. Therefore, we collected the data from the world book of facts maintained by the Central Intelligence Agency (http://www.cia.gov/cia/publications/factbook/index.html). Our approach to assess the preservation of sex ratio was to calculate variation in the sex ratio in three age groups (0-14 years, 15-64 years, and >65 years) for which data was available. The variation was calculated in terms of standard deviations in the sex ratios of these age groups.

In this analysis, it was found that while the sex ratio at birth is 1.05 for most countries in the world (*fig.* 2), variation in this ratio is quite rampant in many countries. India has one of the least variation in the sex ratio, among all the countries in the world, and holds third position from the top after Zimbabwe and Taiwan. We divided the variation in sex ratio data in four quartiles to plot them on a colour coded world

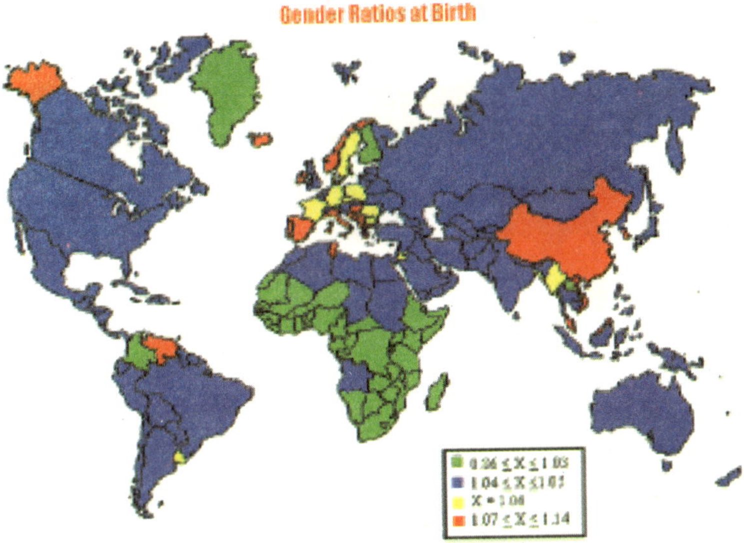

fig. 2: World map showing range of gender (male to female) ratio at birth.

map to represent if there is any civilizational pattern in the preservation of sex ratio. As shown in *fig*. 3, it seems the top quartile of countries with least variation in sex ratio are largely concentrated in Indian subcontinent, and includes Middle East countries such as Iran and Iraq. Most variation in the sex ratio was mostly concentrated in Europe and North America, the so-called advanced countries of the world.

From the data presented, it is quite clear sex ratio preservation (SRP) varies significantly in different countries. Considering the fact that there is a concentration of quartiles to large degree in parts of the world geographically, there

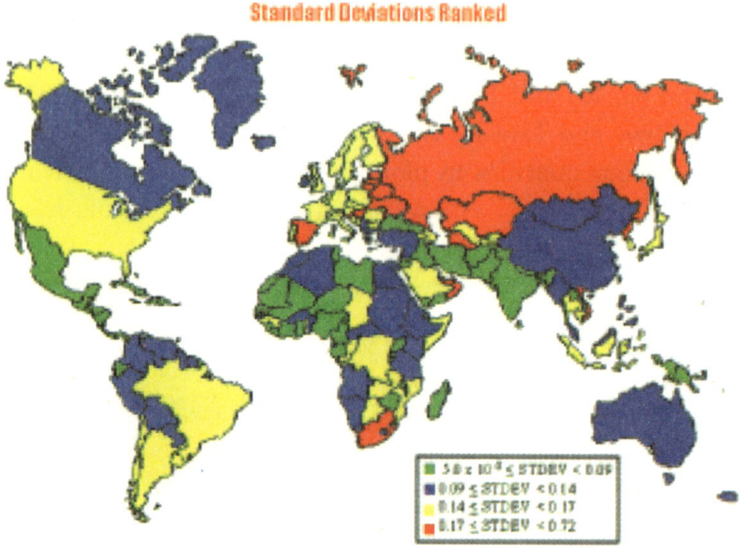

fig. 3: World map showing variations in gender ratio among three age groups.

seems to be a civilizational role in SRP. The civilizational role seems to be more cultural rather than religious, as countries with the best SRP in the top quartile are located in Indian subcontinent, and part of the Middle East that is contiguous with the subcontinent, do not belong to a religiously homogeneous group. This observation is also noted within India where there is little evidence that sex ratio at birth is affected by religious beliefs and practices of the families (Khanna et al., 2003; Jha et al., 2006).

It is interesting that most of reports on sex ratio published in the newspapers and journals (Clark, 2000; Sharma, 2003; "Declining Sex Ratio in Himachal Causes Concern", *Hindustan Times*, 27 June 2004) have mostly focused on unpleasant stories on India and countries in its vicinity on girl foeticide blaming mostly on the traditions and culture either due to son preference or poor treatment of women and girl child. Such media reports and scholarly works have failed to critically examine the population data. This is not to say that sex ratio has not been altered in certain parts of India drastically due to sex selected abortion. There is clearly a strong feeling for son preference in the Indian subcontinent and most of East Asia. However, that feeling is also true in the United States of America (Dahl and Moretti, 2004). In Asia, it is considered that sons may be preferred for family lineage and economic reasons, sons are preferred in the USA for reducing the chances of divorce.

Thus cultural practices that maintain the natural sex ratio from birth to death is not based on son or daughter preference, and are indicative of civilizational features irrespective of region or religion. Such objective data-based analyses are better parameters to describe cultural practices than artificially created features such as religion and nation-state, both of which are primarily means to control people rather than making them free.

History and Indian Civilization

History of Indian civilization has been particularly contentious for many decades even after India's Independence in 1947. The old scholarship on Indian civilization has been comprehensive, mostly from literature and linguistics, providing ample research material to build a strong modern academic scholarship. However, several other tools have become available within the past few decades related to archaeology, astronomy, and more recently population genetics and computational linguistics. In addition, there is a growing assertion by nationalist scholars in India that the continuation of the colonial scholarship on Indian civilization is biased and untenable.

The academic discourse has been marred with accusations and counter-accusations to the extent that both the camps exclude each other from their conferences, meetings, and symposia. Most Western scholars, mostly represented in American universities and colleges, have decried attempts by nationalist scholars as amateur, non-academic, and outright fascists. This characterization has been extended to even Western scholars who may question the traditional Western scholarship with new or more balanced data from either modern research tools or re-interpretation of old linguistic and literary data. The basic narratives of the two camps remain as follows:

(a) There was an invasion/migration/movement of a group of people from Central Asia or south-eastern Europe into north-west India via Persia in the vicinity of 2000 BCE. This group is considered Aryan who brought and developed language, literature, and philosophy, including Vedas in India.

(b) Indian languages, literature, philosophy are indigenous, developed by people who lived there for millennia. Vedas and Indian civilization is much older than the 2000 BCE period.

The population in India from north to south and east to west is largely same ethnically and culturally, and any similarity of culture or language between India and Central Asia or parts of Europe is due to outward migration of Indian people over thousands of years and other interactions between Indian civilization and Persian and Greek civilizations.

These are obviously diametrically opposite positions, even considering the same piece of data. History is always written from a perspective. It is difficult if not impossible to make it an objective field of knowledge, despite assertion to the contrary by many historians. Once in 2002 I had invited a prominent history professor, Dr. Sumit Guha, who was initially trained in Jawaharlal Nehru University (JNU) before getting his PhD from Cambridge University, and was the Sant Purandara Das Distinguished Professor of South Asian History at Brown University. He being from my *alma mater* I took some liberty to ask him frankly why historians in JNU bring such a scorn to the university when they describe Indian history which does not sync with the country's cultural memory and traditional view. He gave a very pertinent answer which I have been cherishing since then. He said that the history he and many of his colleagues at JNU and other liberal and leftist campuses advance is from Marxist point of view, nothing more nothing less. That makes perfect sense as I feel quite comfortable with scholars being able to employ different perspectives to examine issues of interest to public. Marxist perspective is certainly a valid scholarship, even as I have had many disagreements with my communist-oriented student friends while I was in JNU during 1977-2003 when I even served in the student union.

Professor Guha presented a seminar on "Religious Authority and Political Power in Medieval India." The text he provided for the introduction of his seminar included the following.

> Many of the knottiest political problems of the modern world have arisen, and continue to arise at the contentious interface of religion and politics. This is true not only of Asia but, after a brief twentieth-century intermission, also of much of Europe, East and West alike. The interaction of State power and religious institutions in the continent that coined (and bloodily implemented) *eius regio, cuius religio* has been much studied, and I wish to offer a perspective from medieval South Asia. This is a subcontinent in which it has often been assumed that the relation between power and religion was at once closer and more remote than elsewhere — closer in that religious authority encompassed political power, and more remote in that spiritual leaders maintained a conscious distance from secular rulers. We shall see that

> both these ideas are substantially inaccurate as depictions of real behaviour.
>
> I would propose by way of perspective that power derived from access to what we now term "the supernatural" was simply one of the recognized forms of power, and as politically and economically significant as any other form. As Max Weber pointed out "religious or magical behaviour or thinking must not be set apart from the range of everyday purposive conduct, particularly since even the ends of the religious and magical actions are predominantly economic." Since power had isomorphic effects, political authority and success also conferred on terrestrial potentates a charismatic aura not dissimilar from that possessed by holy men. This was true of Islam, Hinduism as well as other cults and religions.
>
> This point has, I think, been lost sight of because much study of Hinduism (in particular) has in fact adopted the clerical doctrine that the religious encompassed and controlled the secular, and that therefore hereditary religious specialists were superior to hereditary warriors.

In his presentation, Professor Guha meticulously outlined many court documents, and propounded a thesis that there was a well worked out collusion between kings and religious groups for their mutual benefits of keeping people loyal to the king and obtain financial support, respectively. This was of course a classic Marxist analysis of events, and showed both religious and ruling classes in bad light, in which religious and ruling class colluded to control the masses.

During my conversations before the seminar, Professor Guha had emphasized the scientific nature of history research by collecting data and deriving conclusions. During the question-answer session I reminded him that assertion of his. I showed my appreciation of the comprehensive research data he had collected from court cases where it was established that property and funds were used by rulers to influence religious authorities to gain loyalty of masses through religious justification of the king's power and authority.

I asked him a question that in science we consider views and evidences opposed to our hypotheses, and whether he has considered any positive roles of the religious institutions. His first and embarrassing response was "no, I have not considered that." It obviously showed that he was totally committed to the Marxist theory, and did not even consider other perspectives. After a few more questions from the audience, he came back to answer that question of mine again, and said, "well, the religious institutions were the keepers of the knowledge, preserved manuscripts and books, and imparted knowledge and education." To which I responded rhetorically that even though we are a state institution (University of Massachusetts), and not a religious institution, we are also the keepers of knowledge, maintain a library of books, and obviously impart education, for students to evolve into good citizens, and we also go out to lobby for funds from the state rulers. How is that different from what was done by those religious institutions?

I give this example to show how seemingly a valid academic exercise can lead to misleading conclusions about scholarship.

In Indian contexts, it is important to be careful when casting the system in Western framework, especially if that is the only framework being considered. Disciplinary training and limitations, and the professional race that academic scholars undergo make us all educators vulnerable to reject or at least ignore other perspectives. While this problem is less acute in sciences, humanities and social sciences are more affected by this vulnerability. Scholars in such fields more commonly respond by excluding other points of views by excluding them from conferences, meetings, seminars, and even publications.

The Center for Indic Studies being a multidisciplinary entity at the University of Massachusetts offering courses in language, history, civilization, culture, philosophy, business, and sciences, naturally provides a platform for cross-checking and cross-breeding of ideas on a variety of issues.

The Conference of the Origin of Indian Civilization

To understand the origin of Indian civilization, it is necessary to assemble scholars from all the fields which shed light on the history, philosophy, literature, traditions, and practices. A conference, fourth in the series of the Indic Conferences, to discuss the origin and practices of the Indian civilization was held by the Center for Indic Studies at UMASS Dartmouth on 23-25 June 2006. Many firsts happened at the conference — for the first time the centre was able to bring together in one room experts from genetics, archaeology, physics, linguistics, anthropology, history, and philosophy to discuss various arguments on the origin of Indian civilization.

Dr Piotr Eltsov, a young scholar, gave an interesting analysis of city-states from the Haṛappan and Ganges civilization using archaeological and literary data to compare and contrast the two. Prof. Michael Witzel of Harvard University, who attended the conference and interacted with several panelists, raised several important points.

Professor Witzel was formally invited to make a presentation of his research but did not oblige with acceptance. He nevertheless came and participated in the Conference. He was offered to make a formal presentation he wished. He considered it but refused to make a formal presentation. His participation was in the form of questions and answers.

The atmosphere of the Conference was tense, as many terse comments were made, mostly by and at Professor Witzel. I myself coming from science background had never seen such a level of scholarly hostility at conferences. The exercise was nevertheless useful. Scholars from varied fields, and many times differing with each other, were exposed to perspective from other fields. There were some genuine differences of opinion, but most of the good discussion was lost in semantics or accusations about who was not qualified or trained in appropriate fields to be taken seriously. Major clashes occurred between Witzel and Rajaram, formally trained in linguistics and mathematical sciences, respectively, on archaeological evidences. Fortunately, a well-respected archaeologist, Dr. B.B. Lal, participated in the Conference to comment on some of the contentious issues.

Prof. Witzel and Dr Eltsov agreed that the so-called Haṛappan and Vedic civilization were coterminous. This was an important convergence for scholars from different schools of thought. Dr N.S. Rajaram and Dr B.B. Lal have been long arguing in their research that the Haṛappan and Vedic civilizations were one and the same.

While not in complete agreement, yet for Witzel and Eltsov to acknowledge that the Haṛappan and Vedic civilizations were concurrent, is an important landmark in the debate on the Indic civilization. Prof. Witzel also stated for the first time to many in the audience that he and his colleagues no longer subscribe to the Aryan Invasion Theory (AIT). Prof. Witzel agreed with the scholars present that the Aryan invasion theory is a nineteenth-century concept and a spent force today. He said "Nobody in the right mind believes in something like Aryan Invasion Theory."

Comprehensive population genetics data along with archaeological and astronomical evidence presented overwhelmingly concluded that the Indian civilization and its human population are indigenous.

Leading evidence came from population genetics, presented by two leading researchers in the field, Dr V.K. Kashyap, National Institute of Biologicals, India, and Dr Peter Underhill of Stanford University. Their results generally contradicted the notion of Aryan invasion/migration theory for the origin of Indian civilization. In fact, the original people and culture within the Indian subcontinent may even have been a likely pool for the genetic, linguistic, and cultural origin of other parts of the world, particularly Europe and Asia.

Dr Underhill concluded, "the spatial frequency distributions of both L1 frequency and variance levels show a spreading pattern emanating from India," referring to a Y-chromosome marker. He, however, put several caveats before interpreting genetic data, including "Y-ancestry may not always reflect the ancestry of the rest of the genome." Dr Kashyap, on the other hand, with the most comprehensive set of genetic data asserted that there is "no clear genetic evidence for an intrusion of Indo-Aryan people into India, [and] gene flow."

To a question that the "genetic evidence may not provide the time resolution to explain ancient events," Dr Kashyap replied that even though the time resolution needs further work, the fact that there are clear and distinct differences in the gene pools of Indian population and those of Central Asian and European groups, the evidence negates any Aryan invasion or migration into Indian subcontinent.

Nineteenth-century European philologists had dated *Ṛgveda* to 1500 BCE, and claimed its origin from the Vedic Aryans coming out of Central Asia and Europe. Archaeologist Dr B.B. Lal and scientist-historian Dr N.S. Rajaram disagreed with the position of linguists, in particular with Prof. Witzel who claimed literary and linguistic evidence for the non-Indian origin of the Vedic civilization.

Dr Narahari Achar, a physicist from University of Memphis clearly showed with astronomical analysis that the Mahābhārata war took place in 3067 BCE, seriously challenging the outside "Aryan" origin of Vedic people.

Drs Bajpai, Kazanas, and Rosser have argued how differences in interpretation of the same historical, linguistic, and archaeological data tend to support opposite positions. There is at least a need for presenting both sides of an argument in any discussion or presentation.

A DVD of the proceedings of the symposium will be available for direct review of the discussions and questions and answers that took place.

Post-Conference Developments

A major publication in the form of book entitled *How Deep are the Roots of Indian Civilizations? Archaeology Answers* (B.B. Lal, 2009) has appeared after the Conference at UMass Dartmouth. In this book Dr B.B. Lal (one of the Conference participants) argues that at least 5000 year old Indian civilization, known variously as Indus, Indus-Sarasvatī, or Haṛappan Civilization, is basically indigenous as Haṛappan is same as the Vedic people. B.B. Lal further asserts that archaeological and literary evidences together suggest that some time in the second millennium BCE a section of Vedic people themselves emigrated westward, and thus refuting the AIT.

In addition, several population genetic studies have been published. According to a *Science News* article (Bauer, 2009) "India's initial settlers arrived around 60,000 years ago. Speakers of Draviḍian languages arrived roughly 5,000 years ago, followed by Indo-European speakers approximately 3,500 years ago. If the new analysis holds up, these early populations wouldn't have contributed to modern mainland India's genetic make-up. And founding populations of today's Indian groups wouldn't have reached South Asia until well after Indo-European speakers." Herein lies the paradox of the theory that Aryans came from outside and Draviḍians were the original inhabitants, the new findings published recently (Reich et al., 2009) asserts that none of these groups seem to be the founders of modern Indian population. This type of scientific analysis and conclusions is normal, except when it comes to historically and politically charged issues of human civilization there is a great deal of posturing, and even scientists get carried away.

For example, Reich et al. (2009) state,

> Many Indian and European groups speak Indo-European languages, whereas the Adygei [a Caucasian outgroup] speak a North-west Caucasian language. It is tempting to assume that the population ancestral to ANI [ancestral north Indian] and CEU [European] spoke "Proto-Indo-European," which has been reconstructed as ancestral to both Sanskrit and European languages, although we cannot be certain without a date for ANIASI [ancestral south Indian] mixture.

This obviously pre-supposes Proto-Indo-European origin of Sanskrit, an idea hotly contested, and is certainly traced to colonial scholarship. This was tacitly hinted by the News and Views article of Arvind Chakravarti (*Nature*, 261, 2009: 487-88) when he states, "without accounting for local ancestry, genetic association studies can suffer from numerous false positives arising from systematic differences in ancestry between cases and controls. Indeed, language and caste membership may not be adequate control factors."

Reich et al. (2009) carried out a statistical analysis of Europeans (CEU) and Chinese (CHB) along with 22 Indian groups (*fig*. 4) to understand their connections with each other. In this analysis it was found that CEU is quite distinguishable from CHB, and that the Indian ancestry is quite unique. The most remarkable feature of that was revealed in this analysis was a gradient of proximity to western Eurasians (an analogous analysis in Europeans did not produce a gradient of proximity to India). It was called as the "Indian Cline," and proposes to reflect the fact that different Indian groups had inherited different proportions of ancestry from the "Ancestral North Indians" (ANI) who are related to western Eurasians, and the "Ancestral South Indians" (ASI). Analysis of these groups along with Europeans (CEU) and Chinese (CHB) shows a gradient of relatedness to CEU that runs through most Indo-European and Draviḍian groups, with the Kaśmīrī paṇḍit most related to CEU (*fig*. 5). Both the Austro-Asiatic speaking groups (Kharia and Santhal) and the tribal Sahariya are off-cline, whereas the two Tibeto-Burman speaking groups cluster with CHB.

Another prominent genetic study by V.K. Kashyap group (Kashyap presented his results at the Conference and has contributed a chapter in these proceedings) had given clue to the relatedness between Indian and European populations by stating "European populations (without R2 and R* in most cases) is more parsimoniously explained by gene flow in the opposite direction, possibly with an early founder effect in South or West Asia." The authors further explained the origin of Indian civilization in following terms. "The Y-chromosomal data consistently suggest a largely South Asian origin for Indian caste communities and therefore argue against any major influx, from regions north and west of India, of people associated either with the development of agriculture or the spread of the Indo-Aryan language family."

Several other genetic studies have added substantial information on the diversity and lineage of Indian population, most pointing to indigenous origins going back to over 50,000 years (Danino, 2006).

fig. 4: Map of India showing 22 different groups included in genetic relationship (taken from Reich et al., 2009).

Future Prospects

Understanding all the civilizations, defined by any rubric, is critical for the advancement of the society through peace, harmony, and co-operation. The requirement is objective and unbiased examination and analysis. There are ample cases to suggest that scholarship, academic or otherwise, is biased, parochial, and sometimes outright political. Such a situation is neither appropriate for the twenty-first century world, nor is tenable in a globalized world. Walls of nation-state structure

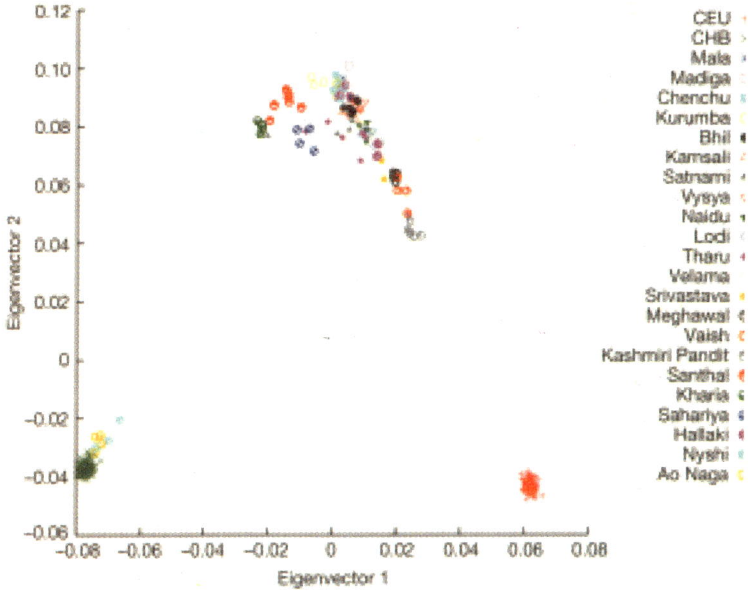

fig. 5: Statistical relatedness among 22 groups of Indian Subcontinent, European, and Chinese (taken from Reich et al., 2009).

are crumbling due to the interconnection of people in climate, business, science, technology, social bonds (inter-ethnic marriages and families), and common knowledge through internet. Current socio-political tension and impending climatic change is bringing people together globally, who are keen to understand each other better. There is more appreciation for indigenous cultures and their own perspective of themselves and their civilization. There is a need for indigenous view of not only Indian civilization but all the civilizations. This view can be realized by promoting indigenous studies. Fortunately, the Center for Indic Studies has accepted indigenous perspective of the Indian traditions as its niche area, and will foster collaborations in academia to promote the concept of indigenous studies.

Approaches to advance indigenous studies will require

more scientific and natural history by means of astronomy, genetics, archaeology, and computational modelling studies. Current crop of humanities and social studies scholars are ill-equipped for such a task independently, and thus is the need for interdisciplinary collaboration and debate. The Center plans to gather scholars from all relevant fields to continue this conversation, and hope this exercise will eventually prove to be fruitful.

References

Bauer, B. (2009), "DNA Points to India's Two-pronged Ancestry", *Science News*, 23 September 2009.

Chakravarti, A. (2009), "Human Genetics: Tracing India's Invisible Threads," *Nature* 461, 487-88.

Clark, S. (2000), "Sex Preference and Sex Composition of Children: Evidence from India", *Demography* 37, 95-108.

Dahl, G.B. and E. Moretti (2004), "The Demand for Sons: Evidence from Divorce, Fertility, and Shotgun Marriage", National Bureau of Economic Research Working Paper No. 10281, Issued in February 2004.

Danino, M. (2006), "Genetics and the Aryan debate", *Bulletin of the Indian Archaeological Society*, New Delhi, No. 36, pp. 146-54.

Jha P., R. Kumar, P. Vasa, N. Dhingra, D. Thiruchelvam, R. Moinuddin, "Low Male-to-Female Sex Ratio of Children Born in India: National Survey of 11 million Households", *Lancet* 367: 211-18.

Khanna, R., A. Kumar, J.F. Vaghela, V. Sreenivas, and J.M. Puliyel (2003) "Community based Retrospective Study of Sex in Infant Mortality in India", *Brit. Med. J.* 327, 126.

Reich, D., K. Thangaraj, N. Patterson, A.L. Price, and L. Singh (2009), "Reconstructing Indian Population History", *Nature* 461, 489-94.

Singh, B.R. and S. Roy (Forthcoming), "Indic Traditions and Social Evils — Facts and Fictions of Gender Favoritism", in: *"Vedic Heritage for Global Harmony and Peace of Next Generation"* Proceedings of the Sixth WAVES Conference Hall in 2006, ed. Surendra N. Dwivedi, New Delhi: D.K. Printworld (in press).

1

An Ostrich-like Attitude is Perpetuating the "Aryan Invasion" Myth

B.B. Lal

BEFORE we go into the details of the ostrich-like attitude adopted by certain scholars which prevents them from seeing the light so conspicuously shed by the new archaeological discoveries made during the past three-four decades, completely debunking the "Aryan Invasion" theory, it may be well worth while to briefly summarize the events that gave rise to the theory itself.

In the nineteenth century, Max Müller, a renowned German scholar, dated the Vedas to *c*. 1200 BCE. This he did on a very ad hoc basis. While accepting that the Sūtra literature was datable to the sixth century BCE, he assigned a duration of just 200 years to each of the preceding periods of the Vedic literature, namely those of the *Āraṇyaka*s, *Brāhmaṇa*s and Vedas. Thus, he arrived at the figure of 1200 (600 + 200 + 200 + 200) BCE. But when his contemporary scholars, like Goldstucker, Whitney and Wilson, raised a hue and cry on this kind of ad-hocism, he had to retreat by saying (in his Preface to the *Ṛgveda*):

> I have repeatedly dwelt on the merely hypothetical character of the dates, which I have ventured to assign to the first periods of Vedic literature. All I have claimed for them has

> been that they are minimum dates, and that the literary productions of each period which either still exist or which formerly existed could hardly be accounted for within shorter limits of time than those suggested.

But this kind of explanation did not satisfy the other scholars. Thus, in sheer desperation Max Müller had to surrender, with the following statement (Max Müller 1890, rpt. 1979):

> If now we ask how we can fix the dates of these periods, it is quite clear that we cannot hope to fix a *terminum a qua* [*sic*]. Whether the Vedic hymns were composed [in] 1000 or 1500 or 2000 or 3000 BC, no power on earth will ever determine.

However, in spite of such a candid confession by the savant himself, it remains a matter of great pity that most of his blind followers even now tenaciously stick to 1200 BCE as the date of the *Ṛgveda,* though of late a few of them have come down, vaguely accepting a date "somewhere around the middle of the second millennium BCE," but no more.

With the discovery, in the 1920s, of a unique civilization in the north-western part of the Indian subcontinent, an altogether new chapter was added to Indian history, taking the clock back to the third millennium BCE. Known variously as the Haṛappan, Indus or Indus-Sarasvatī civilization, it covered an area much larger than did the two other contemporary civilizations, viz. those of the Nile Valley and Euphrates-Tigris Valleys, put together. This Indian civilization is characterized by a grid-patterned layout of the towns, duly fortified and often subdivided into two parts, called the Citadel and the Lower Town. Another noteworthy feature of the town-planning was the provision of an underground drainage system. These features were not to be found in the other contemporary civilizations just mentioned. Likewise, unique are the steatite seals which, for their meticulous carvings, can be the envy of any artist, ancient or modern.

The authorship of this unique Indian civilization became at once a matter of debate. Since the Vedas had already been dated, though admittedly wrongly, to 1200 BCE, the Indus-Sarasvatī civilization was at once declared to be non-Vedic. And since the only other major language-group on the subcontinent was the Draviḍian, it was readily assumed that the Haṛappans were a Draviḍian-speaking people.

The year 1946 saw the climax of the "Aryan Invasion" thesis. In that year Mortimer Wheeler (later to be knighted) discovered a fortification-wall around one of the mounds (Mound AB) at Haṛappā. On learning that the Aryan god Indra was mentioned in the *Ṛgveda* as *puraṁdara,* i.e. "destroyer of forts," he lost no time in declaring that *Aryan Invaders destroyed Haṛappan Civilization* (*Ancient India,* no. 3, 1947: 82). Further, in order to support his "Invasion" theory, Wheeler cited the presence of some human skeletons at Moheṅjo-dāṛo, adding that these were the people who had been massacred in the invasion (ibid.).

That Wheeler's inference from these skeletal remains was wrong is clearly proved by the fact that the skeletons had been found at different stratigraphic levels of the site — some from the Intermediate levels, some from the late levels and yet some from the deposits that had accumulated at the site after its desertion. If these persons had died as a result of an invasion, one expects that the bodies would have been found in the uppermost level after which the site was abandoned. The skeletons, therefore, cannot be related to an invasion. George F. Dales (1964) has very rightly called it a "Mythical Massacre."

In this context it needs to be added that no evidence whatsoever of an invasion has been found at any of the hundreds of Haṛappan sites. On the other hand, at most of these sites there is ample proof of continuity of habitation, though as time passed a gradual devolution did take place in the material culture. An outside invasion also envisages the entry of a new people. But we have no such evidence. That no new people at all arrived between 4500-800 BCE, is duly established by a detailed study of human skeletal remains by Hemphill and his colleagues (1991). (The time of the supposed "Aryan Invasion" is assumed to be around 1500 BCE.)

Thus, if there is no evidence of warfare nor of an alien people and their material culture, where is the case for any "invasion," much less by Aryans?

According to the "Aryan Invasion" thesis, the invading Aryans drove away the Draviḍian-speaking Haṛappans to south India. If there is any truth in it, one would find settlements of Haṛappan refugees in south India, but there is not even a single Haṛappan or even Haṛappā-related settlement in any of the Draviḍian-speaking states, be it Tamil Nadu, Andhra Pradesh, Karnataka or Kerala.

Further, it is seen that even if new people arrive and occupy a land, the names of at least some places and rivers in that land, given by the earlier people do continue. For example, in USA names of rivers like Missouri and Mississippi or of places like Chicago and Massachusetts, given by earlier inhabitants, have continued even after the European occupation. But there is no Draviḍian river/place-name in the entire area once occupied by the Haṛappans, viz. from the Indus in the west to upper reaches of the Yamunā — in the east.

All told, therefore, there is no evidence whatsoever for holding that Haṛappans were a Draviḍian-speaking people.

Having failed to establish an "Aryan Invasion," Romila Thapar (1988-91: 259-60) invokes a mechanism of migration.

Says she:

> If invasion is discarded the mechanism of migration and occasional contacts come into sharper focus. The migrations appear to have been of pastoral cattle-herders who are prominent in the *Avestā* and *R̥gveda.*

Toeing her line and elaborating this newly-found thesis, R.S. Sharma (1999: 77) comes out with the following statement:

> . . . the pastoralists who moved to the Indian borderland came from Bactria-Margiana Archaeological Complex or the BMAC which saw the genesis of the culture of the *R̥gveda.*

But can Sharma cite even a single site in India, east of the Indus — which was the main scene of the activity of the R̥gvedic people as per *R̥gveda* (10.75.5-6) — where the supposed immigrants from the Bactria-Margiana Archaeological Complex got settled? He cannot, since there is none. A recent attempt to show that a few seals of the BMAC-type have been found east of the Indus, viz. at Gilund in the Banas Valley of south-eastern Rajasthan (Possehl 2004), hardly meets the requirements of an immigration of the BMAC people. In the first place, these few seals are not of the characteristic types on the basis of which Sarianidi regards the BMAC as associable with the Indo-Iranians. Secondly, must these few seals alone imply "Immigration," there being a total lack of other characteristic aspects of the BMAC — such as the settlement pattern, ritualistic components, pottery, typical bronze axes, burial practices, etc. Cannot these few simple seals be explained by a contact, a mechanism by which we have always been explaining the occurrence of a number of typical Haṛappan objects at Central Asian sites, such Namazga Depe, Altyn Depe, etc. (Lal 1997: 188-90). Indeed, if the evidence is so meagre and shaky, then why indulge in invoking a migration, and that too on such a scale as would set in "the genesis of the culture of the *R̥gveda'* (Sharma, op. cit.)?

But then there seems to be no end to speculations. And one more is like this. Possehl (1996: 65) holds:

> One thing seems certain; the speakers of Vedic Sanskrit are the earliest *well documented* (italics in the original) speakers of an Indo-European language in the subcontinent, and they came from elsewhere. This conclusion comes from . . . Indo-European words for trees which are species such as birch, Scotch pine, linden, alder and oak. These are plants from a temperate environment and the fact that their names are shared among the early languages of the family suggests a homeland in this environment.

Let it be categorically stated that the *Ṛgveda* does not mention any of the cold-climate trees referred to by Possehl. On the contrary, all trees mentioned in it, e.g. *aśvattha* (*Ficus religiosa* L.), *nyagrodha* (*Ficus benghalensis* L.), *kiṁśuka* (*Butea monosperma* L.), etc. belong to a tropical climate.

Indeed, the same is true in respect of the Ṛgvedic fauna as well. Mentioned most prominently in the *Ṛgveda* are animals like the lion (*Panthera leo*), elephant (*Elephas maximus*), buffalo (*Bubalus bubalis*) or birds like the peacock (*Pavo cristatus*) which are typical of a tropical region and not of cold. Thus, a "cold-climate-home" thesis is absolutely baseless (see Lal 2005).

In order to give a prop to the "Aryan Invasion" theory, Witzel (1995: 320-21) deliberately mis-translates a part of the *Baudhāyana Śrautasūtra* (18.44) as follows: . . . Āyu went eastwards. His people are the Kuru-Pañcāla and Kāśī-Videha. This is the Āyava (migration). (His other people) stayed at home in the west. His people are the Gāndhārī, Parśu and Araṭṭa. This is the Amāvasu (group).

According to the rules of grammar, the correct translation would be: Āyu migrated eastwards. His people are the Kuru-Pañcālas and Kāśī-Videhas. Amāvasu *migrated* westwards (and not stayed back, as Witzel says). His people are Gāndhārī,

Parśu and Araṭṭa. In other words, the parting took place from an intermediary region, between Gandhāra on the west and Kurukṣetra on the east (cf. *fig.* 1). There is no question of any kind of migration eastwards into India from the west. (For finer details, see Lal 2003.)

If there was no "Aryan Invasion" nor were the Haṛappans

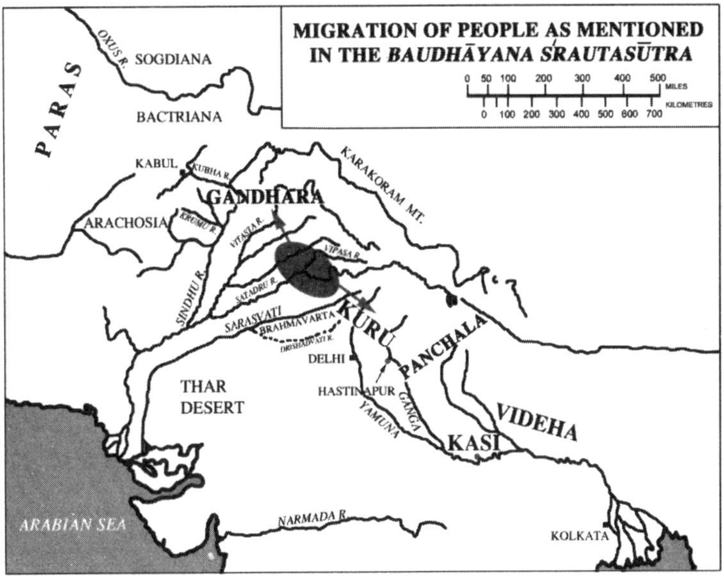

fig. 1: Migration of people as mentioned in the Baudhāyana Śrautasūtra

Dravidian-speaking people, could the Haṛappans themselves have been the Vedic Aryans?

Against such an equation four objections have been raised, namely:

(i) Whereas the Vedic people were nomads, the Haṛappans were urbanites;

(ii) The Vedic people knew the horse, while the Haṛappans did not;

(iii) Whereas the Vedic people used spoked wheels, the

Haṛappans did not; and finally,

(iv) Since according to Max Müller the Vedas were only as old as 1200 BCE and Haṛappan Civilization was of the third millennium BCE, how can the two be equated, chronologically?

All these objections are baseless. Very briefly, the counter-arguments are as follows (for a detailed discussion see Lal 2005: 76-82).

Nomads?

The Vedic people lived a settled life and constructed forts. In *R̥V* (10.101.8) the prayer is: "O gods, make strong forts as of metal." *R̥V* (4.30.20) mentions "hundred fortresses of stone."

Trade was carried on not only overland but even across the seas. *R̥V* (9.33.6) states: "O Soma, pour thou forth four seas filled with a thousand-fold riches." The ships had sometimes as many as "a hundred oars (*śatāritra* — *R̥V* 1.116.5)."

The Vedic people had *sabhā*s and *samiti*s and even a hierarchy of rulers: *samrāṭ*, *rājan* and *rājaka*s (*R̥V* 6.27.8 & 8.21.8). That these gradations were real is confirmed by the *Śatapatha Brāhmaṇa* (V.1.1.12-13): "By offering the *Rājasūya* he becomes a *rājā* and by the *Vājapeya*, a *samrāṭ*; the office of *rājā* is lower and that of *samrāṭ*, higher."

Can we still call the R̥gvedic people "Nomads"?

The Horse

In his Mohenjo-dāṛo report, Mackay states: "The most interesting of model animals is one that I personally take to represent the horse." Wheeler confirmed Mackay's view. Now a lot of new material has come to light: from Lothal, Surkoṭadā, Kālibaṅgan, etc. Lothal has yielded a terracotta figure (*fig.* 2)

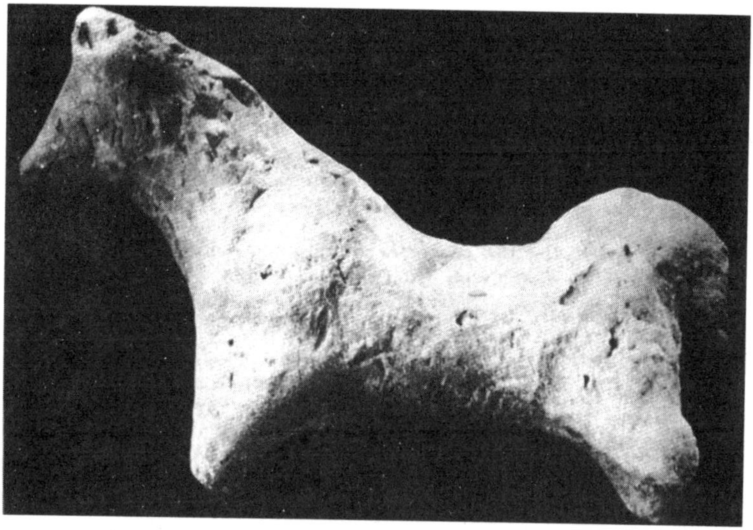

fig. 2: Lothal Terrocotta horse. Mature Haṛappan

as well as faunal remains of the horse.

Reporting on the faunal remains from Surkoṭadā, the renowned international authority on horse-bones, Sandor Bokonyi of Hungary, emphasized:

> The occurrence of true horse (*Equus caballus* L.) was evidenced by the enamel pattern of the upper and lower cheek and teeth and by the size and form of the incisors and phalanges (toe bones).

The Spoked Wheel

Though the hot and humid climate of India does not let wooden specimens survive, there are enough terracotta models from Kālibaṅgan, Rākhīgaṛhī, Banawālī, etc. which confirm the presence of spoked wheels (cf. *fig.* 3).

The Chronological Horizon

It is crucial to ascertain the exact chronological horizon of the

fig. 3: Rākhīgaṛhī: Terrocotta wheel. The painted lines represents the spokes. Mature Haṛappan.

Vedas, since the 1200 BCE fatwa of Max Müller is at the root of the "Aryan Invasion" theory.

The mention of a shift of vernal equinox from Mṛgaśiras to Rohiṇī in the *Aitareya Brāhmaṇa* has led many astronomers to assign this text to *c*. 3500 BCE and thus the Vedas to the fourth millennium BCE. I am not competent to offer any comments on the astronomical data, but would suggest that an international seminar be held on this topic to thrash it out.

However, of immense help is the combined evidence of archaeology, geology, hydrology and radiocarbon-dating. In this context, the role of the Ṛgvedic Sarasvatī is vital. According to *ṚV* (10.75.5), it lay between Yamunā and Sutlej; and flowed from mountains to the sea (*ṚV* 7.95.2). It is identifiable with the Ghaggar–Sarasvatī combine which is now dry downstream from Sirsā.

On the left bank of the Sarasvatī there stands an important site of the Haṛappan Civilization, called Kālibaṅgan. Hydrological investigations (Raikes 1968) have revealed that the site had to be abandoned because of the drying up of the Sarasvatī — an event that took place because of rise of Bata-Markanda Terrace in the Himalayas (Puri and Verma 1998). It is interesting to note that the *Pañcaviṁśa Brāhmaṇa* (XXV.10.16) also refers to the drying up of the Sarasvatī.

Radiocarbon dates show that Kālibaṅgan was abandoned

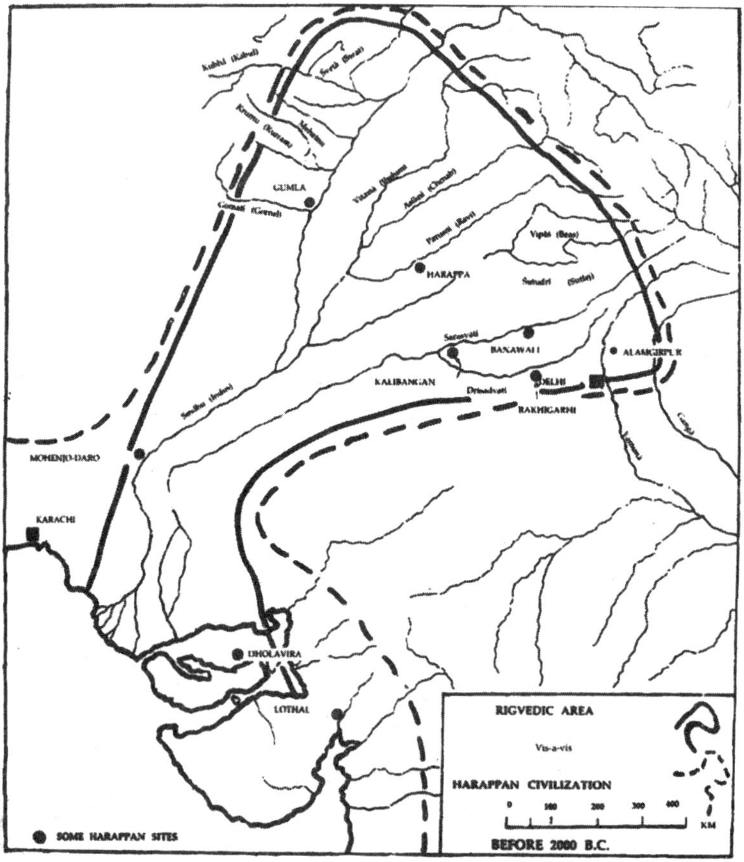

fig. 4: Map showing a correlation between the Ṛgvedic area and spread of the Haṛappan Civilization, before 2000 BC.

around 2000 BCE (Lal 1997: 245-46). Since the Sarasvatī was a mighty flowing river during the Ṛgvedic times and it dried up around 2000 BCE, the *Ṛgveda* has got to be dated to a period prior to 2000 BCE. Now, since the *Ṛgveda* must be dated prior to 2000 BCE and, according to *ṚV* (10.75.5-6), the Ṛgvedic people occupied the area from the Gaṅgā in the east to the Indus in the west, a question may straightaway be asked: "Archaeologically, which civilization flourished in this very area prior to 2000 BCE?" The inescapable answer will have to be: "the Haṛappan." Hence a Vedic–Haṛappan equation, which, however, awaits a further reinforcement by a satisfactory decipherment of the Haṛappan script itself.

Now, even if the Vedic people and Haṛappans were the same, were they **indigenous?** The answer is "Yes." There is ample archaeological evidence to demonstrate that the Haṛappan Civilization, which attained maturity in the third millennium BCE, had its roots back in the fifth millennium BCE, if not earlier. Some of the Carbon-14 dates from the recent excavations at the Haṛappā-Culture site of Bhirrana in the Sarasvatī Valley in Haryana are as follows:

> Sample No. BS 2314. Calibrated age: 1 Sigma 4770 (4536, 4506, 4504 BCE) 4353 BCE
>
> Sample No. BS 2318. Calibrated age: 1 Sigma 5336 (5041 BCE) 4721 BCE
>
> Sample No. BS 2333. Calibrated age: 1 Sigma 6647 (6439 BCE) 6221 BCE

Even if we temporarily ignore Sample No. BS 2333, the other two samples clearly show that the ancestry of the Haṛappan Civilization in the Sarasvatī Valley goes back to the beginning of the fifth millennium BCE. In other words, the Haṛappans were the "sons of the soil." Thus, the Vedic people, whose material manifestation is the Haṛappan Civilization, were "indigenous."

In recent years a great deal of genetic research has been carried out which throws light on this issue and I quote here Sanghamitra Sahoo et al. (2006: 843-48):

> The sharing of some Y-chromosomal haplogroups between Indian and Central Asian populations is most parsimoniously explained by a deep, common ancestry between the two regions, with the diffusion of some Indian-specific lineages northward. . . .
>
> . . . The Y-chromosomal data consistently suggest a largely South Asian origin for Indian caste communities and therefore argue against any major influx, from regions north and west of India, of people associated either with the development of agriculture or the spread of the Indo-Aryan language family.

In conclusion, thus, one can only say: Seeing thou seeth not; knowing thou ignoreth. How long wouldst thou continue with this ostrich-like attitude? Shouldn't thou re-think and give the "Aryan Invasion" theory a ceremonial burial?

References

Dales, G.F. (1964), "The Mythical Massacre at Mohenjo-daro," *Expedition*, 6(3):36-43.

Hemphill, B.E., J.R. Lukacs and K.A.R. Kennedy (1991), "Biological Adaptations and Affinities of Bronze Age Haṛappans" in R.H. Meadow, ed., *Harappa Excavations 1986-1990*, pp. 137-82, Madison. Wisconsin: Prehistory Press.

Lal, B.B. (1997), *The Earliest Civilization of South Asia*. New Delhi: Aryan Books International.

——— (2003), "Should One Give up All Ethics for Promoting One's Theory," *East and West*, vol. 53, nos. 1-4: 285-88.

——— (2005), *The Homeland of the Aryans: Evidence of Ṛgvedic Flora and Fauna and Archaeology*, New Delhi: Aryan Books International.

Müller, F. Max (1890), rpt. 1979, *Physical Religion*, New Delhi: Asian Educational Services.

Possehl, Gregory L. (1996), *Indus Age: The Writing System*, New Delhi: Oxford & IBH Publishing Co. Pvt. Ltd.

——— et al. (2004), "The Ahar-Banas Complex and the BMAC", *Man and Environment*, vol. XXIX, no. 2: 18-29.

Puri, V.M.K. and B.C. Verma (1998), "Glaciological and Geological Source of Vedic Sarasvati in the Himalayas", *Itihas Darpan*, vol. IV, no. 2: 7-36.

Raikes, Robert (1968), "Kalibangan: Death from Natural Causes", *Antiquity*, XLII:268-91.

Sahoo, Sanghamitra et al. (2006), "A Prehistory of Indian Y chromosomes: Evaluating demic diffusion scenarios, *PNAS*, 24 January, vol. 103, no. 4, 843-48.

Sharma, R.S. (1999), *Advent of the Aryans in India*, New Delhi: Manohar.

Thapar, Romila (1988-91), In *Journal of the Asiatic Society of Bombay*, vol. 64-66, pp. 259-60.

Wheeler, R.E.M. (1947), "Harappa 1946: The Defences and Cemetery R 37", *Ancient India*, 3: 58-130.

Witzel, Michael (1995), "Rigvedic History: Poets, Chieftains and Polities. In George Erdosy, ed., *The Indo-Aryans of Ancient South Asia*, pp. 307-52, Berlin: Walter de Gruyter.

2

The Ṛgveda Date and Indigenism

Nicholas Kazanas

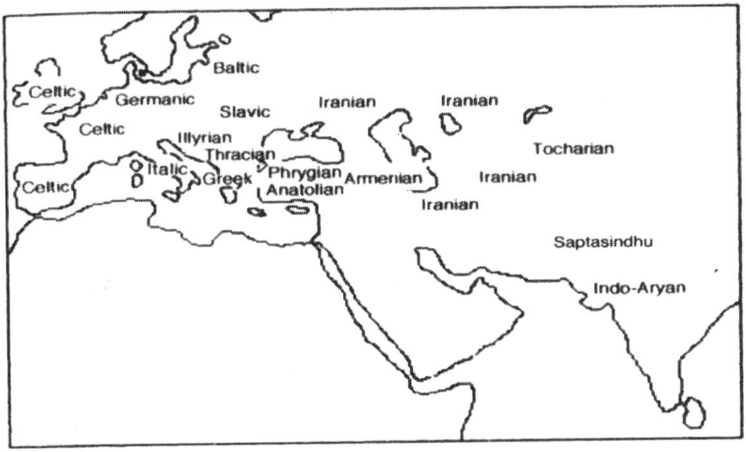

Argument

THIS article presents the evidences and arguments for *Ṛgveda* (*ṚV*) composed in its bulk in the fourth millennium BCE. A basic consideration (but not the only one) is that the *ṚV* has no knowledge at all of many features that characterize the Haṛappan culture which began to emerge solidly *c.* 3000. Since the bulk of the *ṚV* must be assigned to a period before 3000 and since this is by general consensus stated to have been composed in Saptasindhu, i.e. the land of the seven rivers in what is today north-west India and Pakistan, then the Indo-Aryans or Vedic people were present in that location before

3000 and must therefore be regarded as indigenous by 1500, when, they are alleged to move in by the Aryan Invasion/ Immigration Theory.

Horses and Chariots

1. Horses and Chariots arriving *c.* 1500 BCE in Saptasindhu, the land of the seven rivers in what is today north-west India and Pakistan, constitute the main argument/evidence whereby many scholars hold the AIT (=Aryan Invasion/Immigration/ Ingress Theory).[1] The AIT has been the mainstream doctrine regarding Indian proto-history since the latter part of the nineteenth century. It teaches that the IAs (=Indo-Aryans) came to Saptasindhu from the Pontic Steppes or the Urals (*c.* 1700–1500) and, although non-literate, they composed the *ṚV* (*c.* 1200–1000), the other Saṁhitās down to 800, the Brāhmaṇas and (early) Upaniṣads (*c.* 800–600), then the Sūtra literature (after 600) and then *c.* 300 BCE – CE 300 the two Epics, *Rāmāyaṇa* and *Mahābhārata*: all dates are approximate. The map shows the location of languages broadly, not peoples or races.

Several linguistic arguments have been adduced to prop up this fanciful scenario one of them being the (loan-)words in the *ṚV* language which were allegedly borrowed from other languages met by the IAs on their way to and at Saptasindhu. A closely related argument is the alleged common Indo–Iranian period during this journey to Saptasindhu.[2] Good examples of a combination of these two arguments are found in M. Witzel 2005 and F. Kuiper 1991. However, no amount of

1. I take the name Saptasindhu simply as a *bahuvrīhi* adjective. The 7 rivers are frequently mentioned in the *ṚV* — 1.32.12; 34.8; 35.8; etc. etc.

2. A common Indo–Iranian period there definitely was but this is to be found in Saptasindhu whence later the Iranians left (see n6 and §13).

arguing along these lines gives of itself any actual dates even approximately and the direction of movement can more reasonably be the reverse. There is B. Sergent who, although not at all an indigenist, argued in favour of a movement from Central Asia north-westward (1997). Also, Johanna Nichols, an eminent Indo–European linguist, found on purely linguistic grounds that "the locus of the IE spread was . . . somewhere in the vicinity of ancient Bactria" (1997: 113) which is only a stone's throw away from Saptasindhu. Linguists will continue to disagree violently among themselves about the original locus, about the direction of the movement and about the date: some give a late period somewhere *c.* 3000, others an early one, in the seventh millennium (Misra 1992). I ignore all such arguments and conclusions since they are so contradictory. The situation is in no way improved by claims that "I am right" and allegations that "the others are wrong." We must bear in mind also that all such arguments involve "reconstructed" protolanguages which are sheer conjectural affairs and therefore inadmissible in any impartial court of law. (See further §16, start).

2. One of the best known comparative linguists of our times, Hans Hock, pointed out (1999) that several dialects spoken in north-west India travelled north-westward at different times in the Common Era, the most notable one being that of the Gypsies in the early centuries CE (see also Fraser 1995). Hock stated that Indo–Aryan indigenism and even the Out of India Theory could theoretically be possible, provided the distribution of the IE isoglosses was accepted and the Vedic language was seen to be a devolved form of Proto-Indo–European. But he opted for the mainstream doctrine (=the AIT out of the Pontic Steppe) because of the archaeological evidence of horses and chariots arriving in Saptasidhu in bulk after 1700 BCE (1999: 13).

Hock was misinformed, I like to think. The evidence of horses and chariots proves the very opposite if examined with a modicum of attention. As one authority put it, "the horse was widely domesticated and used in India during the third millennium BCE over most of the areas covered by the Indus-Sarasvatī [or Haṛappan] Civilization" (Pande 1999: 344; the square brackets original). I myself collected much evidence for horse-finds in different ISC (=Indus–Sarasvatī Civilization/ Culture) sites in two papers in 2003, §10 (pp. 196-97) and 2002 (p. 305): thus one may further consult Kochhar 2000 (pp. 186, 192), Chakrabarti 1999, Lal 1997, Sharma 1996 (p. 17), Thomas et al. 1995, Dhavalikar 1995 (pp. 116-17), Allchin & Joshi 1995 (p. 95), Rao 1991 and, necessarily, Sharma 1980 (pp. 110ff). These publications show abundantly that the true horse, *Equus ferus* and *Equus cabalus*, was present in its wild state in India from *c*. 17000 and there is much evidence now for the domesticated horse in the Mature Haṛappan period. Moreover there are several terracotta figurines of this animal from different ISC sites as reported by Lal 2002 and Tharpar & Mughal 1994.

As for the chariot, S. Piggott established the presence of a sophisticated type of vehicle with "one or two pairs of wheels with their axles . . . from the Rhine to the Indus by around 3000" (1992: 18).

Archaeological evidence does not consist only of the actual remains of buildings, weapons, tools, chariots, etc. Pictures, reliefs, toys and figurines of these things are also evidence. Many years ago H.K. Sankalia had pointed out that the six-spoked wheel appears on seals and signs of the alphabet (1974: 363). S.R. Rao found at Lothal "terracotta wheels . . . with diagonal lines suggesting spokes" (1973: 124). This representational practice seems to have been widespread, for S. Piggott mentions similarly marked wheels found in the

Karpathian Basin from the Earlier Bronze Age (1983: 91-92). In his recent study, Lal presents four terracotta wheels (from Mature Haṛappan sites Banawālī, Kalibaṅgan, Rākhīgaṛhī) with spokes painted on (2002: 74, Figs. 3.28ff). The Haṛappans had the technology for making spoke-wheels (Kazanas 1999: 33; Basham 1954: 21).

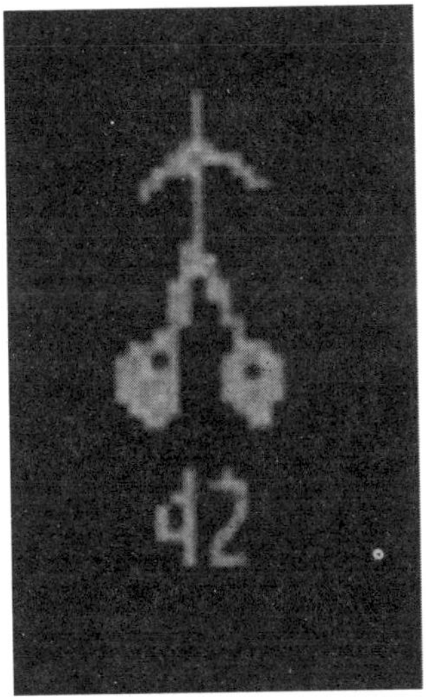

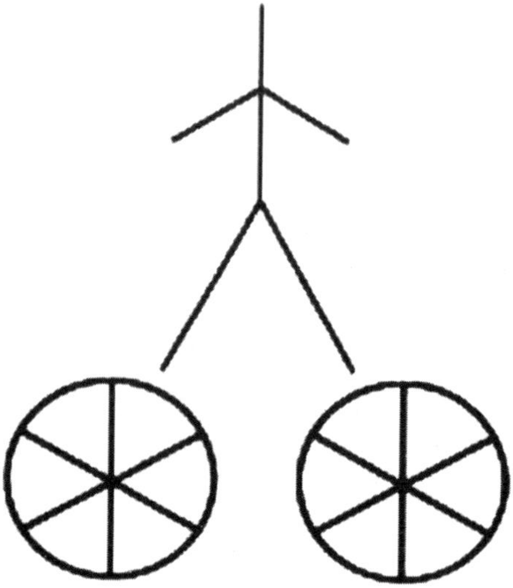

Finally, it was A. Parpola, an inveterate adherent of the AIT, who identified the figure on Haṛappan seal No. 3357 as representing simplistically a man with outstretched arms standing on two six-spoked wheels (of a chariot) realizing that this was "a later invention of the Aryans" (1969: 24). The later notion that it is a potter on two wheels is obviously far-fetched and, in any case, the wheel is spoked (Sethna 1992)!

3. The question of course is whether there were spoked wheels before 3000 since the *ṚV* uses the word *ara* which is usually translated as "spoke" (1.32.15; 5.58.5, etc). We don't know. Some Indian scholars approach the issue strategically and say that Ṛgvedic hymns with *ara*s are later intrusions from the second millennium when the spoked wheel was quite common. This is possible of course, since we know that some hymns are later interpolations. There could have been spoked wheels as we know them even at *c.* 3200 and before. But then again, *ara* need not mean "spoke." It could mean a section of the (solid) wheel. After all, different IE branches have a

different stem for spoke (Gk *aktis, knēmē*; L *radius*; Gmc *speca/ speihha*, etc.) which suggests that spokes were developed after the dispersal (in the sixth or eighth millennium, or whichever). So *ara* would have meant something other than spoke and only later acquired the meaning of "spoke," as we know it now. The spoked wheel poses, in fact, no problem for dating the *ṚV*. There are other more clearcut types of evidence.

The usual objection is that there are no chariot remains from that period. Here, there is the double assumption that *ṚV* chariots are necessarily like near-eastern ones of, say, 1500 and that there should be remains. But why assume that the *ṚV* chariots are like the near-eastern ones? The only real-life vehicle in a race that we know is in 10.102 and this is pulled by oxen not horses (Kazanas 2002) while 1.131.1 alludes to a "broad chariot" *pṛthū rathaḥ*! Then again, there are no remains of chariots in India from 1500 or 1000 or 700. So we shall say no chariots were brought in by the alleged IE entrants either.

Haṛappan Features Absent in the *ṚV*

4. The Haṛappan or Indus–Sarasvatī Culture has certain characteristics which help to define its uniqueness. A number of these features are absent from the *ṚV* and this absence indicates that the *ṚV* is pre-Haṛappan. Arguments *e silentio* are not decisive since absence of evidence is not always evidence of real absence. But in this case the features are far too many.

(a) *Iṣṭakā* "brick." The *ṚV* mentions as building materials metal, stone, mud and wood but not "brick," which was the basic material in Haṛappan constructions. This is found in post-Ṛgvedic texts.

(b) Urbanization is wholly absent in the *ṚV*. There certainly was "nomad pastoralism" as mainstreamers emphasize repeatedly but there were also agricultural settlements (a fact which mainstreamers underplay or do not mention). The hymn to Kṣetrapati "Lord of the Field/Soil" (4.57) alone should suffice but also the girl Apālā refers to her father's *urvarā* "fertile field" (8.91.5); then there are many cultivation implements *khanitra* "shovel," *lāṅgala/sīra* "plough," *sṛṇī* "sickle," etc. Moreover, there is weaving with loom, shuttle, warp and woof (*ṚV* 1.134.4; 1.3.6; etc., etc.) and metallurgy with smithies of sorts (4.2.17; 5.9.5; etc.). Such activities imply settlement.

Some writers think the Ṛgvedic and Haṛappan cultures converge (Gupta 2005, Bisht 1999, Lal 1998, Singh 1995). As evidence is cited the word *pur-* which denotes "city, citadel, fort, town" as its Greek and Baltic cognates "*polis*" and "*pil(i)s*" do. This is a very general misconception. In the *ṚV pur* never means anything other than an occult, magical, esoteric defence or stronghold which is not created nor ever destroyed by humans (Kazanas 2003: 224-25 and 2002 passim).[3] The ISC cities

3. Bisht, for example, cites the numerous occurrences of *pur* as evidence that the *ṚV* knew of towns and fortifications (p 410ff). So does D. Frawley (2002: 13). This is wrong, of course: *pur* in the *ṚV* never means "fort" or "town" but a magical, esoteric defence. Merely citing verses in the *ṚV* but not analysing and exploring their meaning is not very sound scholarship. Here are some examples merely cited by both writers. In II, 35 the Offsring-of-Waters *Apāṁ Nápāt* is protected in *āmā́su pūrṣú* (usually translated as "forts of unbaked bricks" even though bricks are nowhere mentioned!); the phrase means "non-artificial natural defences" (in this case obviously "divine"). In I 166, 8 Agastya prays to the Maruts to protect (*rakṣ-*) from evil *agha* and injury *abhihruti* the man they favour (*av-*) "hundredfold defences" *śatábhujibhiḥ pūrbhīḥ*: no such many-walled structure existed allowing for the hyperbole) and, moreover, it is difficult to see how people can be protected from evil by 100fold fort/towns! VI 48, 8 is a similar prayer to Agni to protect (*pā-*) from anxiety *aṁhas* the fire-kindler with "100 purs": clearly one cannot be protected from anxiety →

had regulars blocks, large buildings, also domestic and urban water supply (McIntosh 2001: 100-101): the *R̥V* knows nothing of all these.

The words for "council" *sabhā* and *samiti* are also cited but, surely, any community can have a council of elders without urbanization. Allusions in the *R̥V* to chiefs/kings *rājā* and overlords/emperors *samrāṭ* also do not show urbanization since such offices can just as easily exist in rural communities.

(c) Fixed altars or hearths are unknown in the *R̥V* but common in the ISC cities. The R̥gvedic altar is a shallow bed dug in the ground and covered with grass (e.g. *R̥V* 5.11.2, 7.43.2-3; Parpola 1988: 225). Fixed brick-altars are very common in post-R̥gvedic texts.

(d) Many cities were abandoned and fell to ruination after 1900 BCE when the Haṛappans began to move eastward because of the drying up of the Sarasvatī and of the more general desiccation due to tectonic disturbances and climatic changes. The *R̥V* knows nothing of such ruins even though, according to the AIT, the IAs moved through these regions *c.* 1700-1500 (in small waves, settled there, in the midst of deserts, and wrote the hymns which praise the mighty Sarasvatī!). Some attempts have been made to read hymn 1.133 with its *arma-ka* (= of unknown meaning, really) as a description of a ruined city (e.g. Burrow 1963, Rao 1991: 32) but, in fact, the hymn

---

→ with 100 forts/cities (again allowing for a hyperbole) but only with internal occult defences. A final example: X 101, 8 is a prayer to Viśvedevās "to fashion inviolable metal purs" to protect the rite of soma-pouring; obviously no forts or towns are meant to be built around the sacrificial locus but magical other-wordly defences against demons. Not one *pur* is built and not one is destroyed by human beings! See Kazanas 2003: 224-25 and no. 12; also <http://www.omilosmeleton.gr/english/en_index.html>'*R̥gvedic pur*'.

mentions no ruined buildings, no fallen walls and no materials such as wood, stone or bricks! It is a ghostly scene of frightful desolation, peopled only with unfriendly she-fiends and demons (*yātumati, piśācī* and *rākṣasa*). In sharp contrast the Old English poem *The Ruin* contains such persuasive details of the ancient remains (from Roman Times?) that some scholars think it refers to the town of Bath (Mitchell & Robinson 1996: 252-5).

(e) No cotton (*karpāsa*) appears in the *ṚV* although this plant was extensively cultivated in the ISC and the fabric was exported as far as Egypt in the middle of the third millennium while the Mesopotamians adopted the name as *kapazum* (? from Prākṛta *kapāsa*). The *ṚV* has "skin" *eta* (1.166.10; *ajina* in *AV* 5.21.7[4] etc.), "wool" *avi* (*ṚV* 9.78.1) and *śāmulya* (10.85.29) and numerous terms for clothing and weaving but no mention of cotton. Be it noted that *karpāsa* is the only word for cotton in Sanskrit.

(f) Silver (*rajata*) also makes no appearance in the *ṚV* though gold and copper are well attested and silver is plentiful in the ISC. The word *rajata* occurs in *ṚV* 8.25.22 and it denotes a steed or a chariot "shining white." Only in later texts is it used singly (*AV* 5.28.1) or with *hiraṇya* to denote "silver" or "white gold" = "silver" (see *Vedic Index* 2: 196-7 and Lubotsky 2: 1169).

(g) Rice (*vrīhi*) too is absent from the *ṚV* although it appears in various sites of the ISC from at least 2300 (and in the Ganges Valley from the sixth millennium).[5] The *ṚV* knows only *yava* "barley." Rice becomes important in post-Ṛgvedic ritual and the more general diet.

---

4. *AV* = *Atharvaveda*

5. Private communication from S.P. Gupta, Chairman of Indian Archaeological Society (June 2006). See also Sharma 1980 for rice in the Ganges basin.

(h) Literacy is not known in the *ṚV*. D. Frawley thought that a passage in *AV* 19.72 may refer to writing: "From whichever receptacle *kośāt* we have taken the Veda, into that we put it down." Books in ancient India consisted in collections of palm-leaves or strips of birch-bark and were kept in boxes (1991: 249). Whether this is enough to establish knowledge of writing is doubtful. But in any event, writing was known in the ISC but not in the *ṚV*.

(i) The *ṚV* has no allusions to artistic iconography — paintings, relief representations, statue(-tte)s or seals, all so common in the ISC. (The *ṚV* 4.24.10 asks "Who will buy this my Indra" and this is thought by some to refer to a statuette, but this could be a transfer of favour and it is the only reference in the whole *ṚV* without the use of any word for statue or icon.)

5. Now all the fore-mentioned features are found in post Ṛgvedic texts — the Saṁhitās, the Brāhmaṇas and fully in the Sūtra literature. For instance, brick altars are mentioned in *Śatapatha Brāhmaṇa* 7.1.1.37, or 10.2.3.1 etc. Rice *vrīhi* is found in *AV* 6.140.2; 7.1.20, etc. Cotton (*karpāsa*) appears first in Gautama's (1.18) and in Baudhāyana's (14.13.10) *Dharmasūtra*. The fact of the convergence of the post-Ṛgvedic texts and the Haṛappan culture was noted long ago by archaeologists. B. and R. Allchin stated unequivocally that these features are of the kind "described in detail in the later Vedic literature" (1982: 203).

If we had a case of two or three items we could bypass them saying indeed that absence of evidence is no evidence of absence; but the items are many and the absence of the building material *iṣṭakā* in the *ṚV* (against the presence of wood, stone, mud and metal) seems to me quite decisive.

We must also take into account that many iconographic motifs, Haṛappan artefacts, decorations or seals, show affinity with elements found in post-Ṛgvedic texts. Thus P.K. Agrawala (2005) draws attention to round-bottomed perforated pots from Haṛappan sites and a vessel (*kuṁbha*) with nine (*navavitṛṇṇa*) or 100 holes (*śatavitṛṇṇa*) mentioned in *Śatapatha Br* 5.5.4.27 and *śatatṛṇṇā kumbhī*, a pitcher with 100 perforations. of 12.7.2.13. These and other similar descriptions echo the *White Yajurveda* (*Vājasaneyī Saṁhitā*) verse 19: 87 "a pitcher with 100 streams." Such vessels were used for ritual sprinkling. A second parallel is furnished by the two-horned bovine-like animal, duplicated and facing itself, on a Moheṅjo-dāṛo seal with long necks and the pipal tree growing out of their juncture. This corresponds (writes Agrawala) to the two-headed cattle *dvāyā* in *AV* 5.19.7. Agrawala mentions other parallels of a two-headed tiger and a two-headed bird (2005: 10-13). Thus it is indeed the later Vedic texts that have parallels with the Haṛappan arts and crafts, not the *ṚV*.

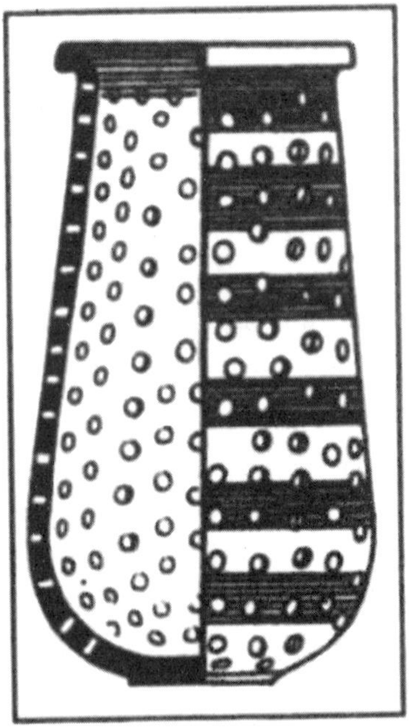

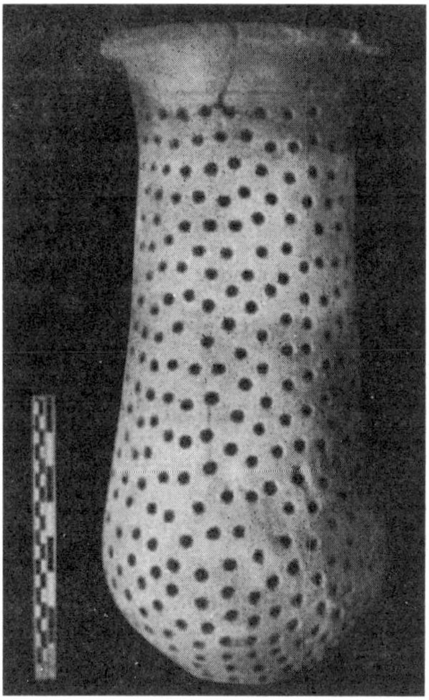

Pot with 100 perforations : *Śatapatha Br* 12.7.2.13.

Dvāyā in *Atharvaveda* 5.19.7; symbol for *OṀ*?

N. Rajaram follows a similar line of investigation (2005) and adduces iconographic motifs from Haṛappan seals but does not distinguish between Ṛgvedic (or early Vedic) and post-Ṛgvedic (or late Vedic) periods and cultures. Thus he cites the *aśvattha*-tree foliage and the horse and links them to the *ṚV* disregarding the fact that these are not exclusively Ṛgvedic and therefore could be simply from a post-Ṛgvedic period. Moreover he cites the *svastika* and the sign of sound *OṀ*, both of which are, as he states, from post-Ṛgvedic texts. It is also doubtful that the seal-sign which is horizontal, depicts the symbol for *OṀ*, which should be upright, anyway.

On this score, then, the bulk of the *ṚV*, is pre-Haṛappan, or 3000+.

6. Some Brāhmaṇas comment on or give explanations of incidents in the Ṛgvedic hymns. For example, the *Aitareya Br*

7.13.33 narrates extensively the story of Śunaḥśepa, alluded to briefly in *ṚV* 1.24.12-13 and 5.2.7, while the *Śatapatha Br* 11.5.1 comments on the the Pururavas and Urvaśī love story given elliptically in dialogue form in *ṚV* 10.95. Another point to note. Some legends in the *ṚV* remain unexplained. For instance, who was Bhujyu whom the Aśvins saved from a tempest (1.116.3-4, etc.) and how did he find himself in that predicament? The later texts say nothing more. Or, take the birth of Indra; was he an unwelcome child to Aditi and did he commit parricide (4.18.1ff, etc.)? Again, the Brāhmaṇas tell us nothing. Obviously such exegetical texts would not be composed until the understanding regarding the older texts has lapsed: this implies many centuries.

What is the date of the Brāhmaṇas? Well, S. Kak ascribes the *Śatapatha* to the early third millennium (1997, 1994) saying that the Pleiades/Kṛttikās not swerving from the east, as is stated in this *Brāhmaṇa* (2.1.2.3), could only occur *c.* 2950 BCE. Narahari Achar (Prof. Astrophysics, Memphis, USA) using computer and planetarium apparatus arrived at a date *c.* 3000 pointing out that S.B. Dikshit had arrived at similar conclusions 100 years earlier but was ignored by Western scholars (1999): these scholars really had no knowledge of astronomy. B.B. Lal too thought that "astronomical calculations (re *Aitareya Br*) would place the *ṚV* in the fourth millennium" but did not then adopt such a date only because he could not judge the evidence (1997: 286). So we could again place the *ṚV* easily before 3000.

7. The *Bṛhadāraṇyaka Upaniṣad* has three *vaṁśas*, i.e. list of teachers, each comprising 65-70 names. The first four or five are names of gods in the normal Indic way which ascribes the beginning of every human activity to some deity. Let us take the mainstream date of early sixth century for this text (say 550) according to the AIT premises and let us take 60 teachers giving to each one an average of 15 years, though 20 and 30 would be more realistic. These calculations (60 × 15 = 900 plus 550) give us a date *c.* 1450 for the inception of the doctrines in this Upaniṣad. The chief doctrine is that the self of man (*ātman*) is the same in all beings and is the same as the Self of the universe (*Brahman* "Mystic Spirit" or "Absolute"). We should also bear in mind that the teachers' names are quite different from those of the seers of the *ṚV* hymns as given by the native tradition. Following others M. Witzel thinks these lists "rest on typically weak foundations" (2001, §19) but this is a typically weak subterfuge because the results of calculating the number of years prove how unrealistic the AIT chronologies are! Let us see, then.

The Upaniṣadic doctrine of the identity of the individual self and the universal self should be known, then, *c.* 1500 or 1300 or 1200, when, according to the AIT, the *ṚV* was composed (§1). Yet, for unknown reasons, quite surprisingly, this doctrine is totally unknown in the *ṚV* and begins hesitantly to appear in the *AV* (e.g. 10.2.32-3, 11.4.23, etc.). Consequently, the *AV* should be placed at least *c.* 1600 and the *ṚV* *c.* 1800, always following the AIT assumptions. But the *ṚV* is composed, even according to Witzel (2005: 90), in Saptasindhu, yet the IAs do not appear in this area before, at the very earliest, 1700, and the *ṚV* gets composed after several centuries!

This is one of the comical paradoxes that the mainstream chronology refuses obdurately to resolve. Yet, on the grounds given in §§4-6 above, we saw that the *ṚV* should be assigned to the fourth millennium, say around 3500. Now subtracting 900 or 1000 years (for the teachers) we should place the early Upaniṣads at the start of the period of the Mature Haṛappan, i.e. 2600-2500 and the Sūtra texts immediately after. These dates satisfy yet another requirement. The word for cotton (*karpāsa*) is first used in the Sūtra texts as we saw in §5 above and the cultivation of the plant (although seeds of it were found in much earlier periods) gets well established *c.* 2500.

8. Astrophysicist Achar pursued his palaeoastronomical research into the *Mahābhārata* epic also, examining astronomical references in Books 3, 5 and 18. His sky map showed that all these converge in the year 3067. (For full details see Kazanas 2002: V, 3: pp. 295-97). Achar acknowledged that some 30 years earlier, in 1969, S. Raghavan had arrived at the same date. Now, it is obvious that the *Mbh* had acquired many accretions over many centuries and that it was streamlined stylistically at about the start of the Common Era. It is obvious that it contains much late material like 2.28.48-9, which mentions Rome and Antiochia (*romā* and *antakhī*): this could not be earlier than 300 BCE since Antioch was founded in 301. On the other hand, the frequent use of the bow, while the sword is virtually unknown and, more so, the use by Bhīma of a (tree trunk as a) club show much more primitive conditions.

Thus the war took place in 3067 and the core of the *Mbh* in poems and songs was laid down in that year. This and the native traditional view that the *Kali-Yuga* came at 3102 are both correct, according to Achar. He pointed out that the *Kali-Yuga* had no full force until the death of Kr̥ṣṇa which occurred 35 years after 3067, at 3032 (private communication June 2006), but immorality had set in already, as is shown by the unjust behaviour of the Kauravas and some reprehensible acts during the war itself. Surely no bards (compilers or redactors) in the third century CE or the third century BCE could possibly know the star and planet positions relative to the *nakṣatras* or the zodiac signs of the year 3067. The astronomical references examined by Achar (and Raghavan) are so numerous that chance coincidence has to be discarded.

9. The Sarasvatī River furnishes useful literary and archaeological evidence for dating the *R̥V*. It is a mighty river extolled in all Books of the *Ṛ*V except the fourth. It is *nadītamā, ambitamā, devītamā* "best river, best mother, best goddess" (2.41.16); it is swollen and fed by three or more rivers *pinvamānā sindhubhiḥ* (6.52.6); it is endless, swift moving, roaring, most dear among her sister rivers; together with her divine aspect, it nourishes the Indo-Aryan tribes (6.61.8-13). In 7.95.2 the river is said to flow pure in her course "from the mountains to the ocean" *giribhyaḥ ā samudrāt*. Then 7.96.2 and 10.177 pray to the river goddess for sustenance and good fortune while 10.64.9 calls upon her (and Sarayū and Indus) as "great" and "nourishing." Clearly then, we have here, even in the late Bk 10, a great river flowing from the Himalayas to the ocean in the south, fed and swollen by other rivers and sustaining the tribes of the IAs on its banks — not a river known in the past or in some other region, or a river now considerably shrunk (Witzel 2001).[6]

Some scholars claim that here *samudra* does not mean "ocean" but confluence and especially the place where a tributary flowed into the Indus. The last point can be discarded since there is not the slightest hint elsewhere that the Sarasvatī flowed into the Indus — in which case the Indus and not Sarasvatī would have been lauded as the best river (2.41.16). The meaning "terminal lake(s)" adopted by Witzel is entirely fanciful. In his Dictionary M. Mayrhofer gives for *samudra* only "confluence" and "ocean/sea" (1996 *EWA*). And the Vedic poet would certainly have used (not *ā samudrāt* but) *ā sarobhyaḥ* "to the terminal lakes" maintaining his - ∪ - - cadence. This phrase would then have indicated clearly the alleged fanciful

6. The mainstream view (Witzel's really) that the Vedic river is merely a memory of the Iranian Haraxvaiti which belongs to the common Indo-Iranian period, when the Irano–Aryans lived together in Iran before the IAs moved further south-east (according to the AIT), is no more than modern myth-making.

etymological connection of the name *Saras-vatī* "she who has (terminal) lakes." The name means rather "she who has swirls and currents," since the primary sense of √*sṛ* (>*saras*) is "movement" (*gatau*) or "flowing, leaping, rushing."

The river is thought to have dried up almost completely by 1900 (Allchins 1997: 117; Rao 1991: 77-79). In previous years it had lost tributaries to the Indus in the West and the Ganges in the East. Is there any evidence that it flowed down to the Indian (or Arabian) ocean at any earlier period?

G. Possehl examined (1998) all the palaeoenvironmental and geological data relevant to the Sarasvatī River and concluded that the river could have flowed down to the ocean only before 3200 at the very latest and, more probably, before 3800! He restated his finds in his study of 2002 (pp. 8-9). P-H. Francfort has been just as certain of a date 3600-3800 in his survey of 1992.

All this helps us place the passages ascribing the grandure of river Sarasvatī at a date before 3200 at least. (For a detailed examination of this entire issue see Kazanas 2005 and 2004a).

10. In a recent publication Dr S. Levitt (of New York), who is by no means an indigenist, examined the development of the "early Indic tradition" and the development of religion in ancient Mesopotamia.

After comparing several elements in the Vedic and Mesopotamian religions, Levitt concluded:

> We can date the early Indic tradition on the basis of comparable points in ancient Mesopotamia. By this, the *Ṛgveda* would date back to the beginning of the third millennium BCE, with some of the earliest hymns perhaps even dating to the end of the fourth millennium BCE.
>
> — 2003: 356).

However, unaware of Levitt's paper, I myself made at about that time a very detailed comparative study of Vedic and Mesopotamian religious (mythological) motifs, published in *Migration and Diffusion* vol. 24, 2005.[7] In this I showed that since more than 20 motifs in the Vedic texts had close parallels in other IE branches (e.g. the horse mythology, the skyboat of the Sungod, the Flood, the elixir from heaven, the creation of cosmic parts from the dismemberment of a divine being, etc.) and were therefore of Proto-Indo-European provenance, they could not have been borrowed by the Vedics from the Mesopotamians as is usually alleged (McEvilley 2002; Dalley 1998) but must be inherited and therefore older than the Near-eastern parallels. Since the Mesopotamian culture (starting with old Sumerian) surfaces *c.* 3000, the Vedic motifs must be earlier.

Thus again we arrive at a date before 3000 for the bulk of the *R̥V.*

11. Since, according to the preceding discussion we must now assign the (bulk of the) *R̥V* to *c.* 3200 at the latest and since the *R̥V* by general consent was composed in Saptasindhu, then it follows that the IAs were ensconced in Saptasindhu by 3200 and that the ISC was a material manifestation of the early oral Vedic tradition expressed in the *R̥V.*

Having held and taught for more than 18 years, but without investigating, the received doctrine that the IE branches dispersed from the South Russian or Pontic Steppe (as per Mallory 1997, 1989; Gimbutas 1985, 1970; and others), and that the IAs had entered Saptasindhu *c.* 1500, I began to examine these mainstream notions thoroughly and *c.* 1997

7. This was badly printed and the Sanskrit transliterations are unreadable! A revised version will be published in *Adyar Library Bulletin* 2006, See also <http://www.omilosmeleton.gr/english/en_index.html>

abandoned them. I decided that no evidence of any kind supported them; on the contrary, the evidence showed that by 1500 the IAs were wholly indigenous and that the elusive IE homeland was very probably Saptasindhu and the adjacent area — the Land of Seven Rivers in what is today north-west India and Pakistan; this area could well have extended as far north-west as the Steppe back in the eighth millennium.

Apart from the (recent) genetic studies, which at that time were not so well-known nor so secure (see §17, below) the decisive evidence for me now is the antiquity of Sanskrit indicated by its inner coherence and its preservation of apparently original PIE linguistic features (like the *dhātu*, five families of phonemes, etc.) and cultural elements. The Vedic language as seen in the *ṚV* alone, despite much obvious attrition and several innovations, has preserved many more features from the putative PIE language and wider culture. This was due to its well attested and incomparable system of oral tradition (Kazanas 2002, 2003, 2004, 2005, 2006) which preserved the ancient texts fairly intact (*ṚV*, *AV*, etc.) and continued even into the twentieth century. An oral tradition of this kind cannot be maintained by a people on the move for decades if not centuries over many thousands of miles, as the AIT proposes. Such a tradition could be preserved only by a sedentary people where the older generation would have the necessary leisure to pass the communal lore to the younger one.[8]

---

8. In a private communication, November 2004, Mallory mentioned the Jews who wandered much and long and preserved their traditions of the *Old Testament*. If we take the Hebrew traditional orthodox view (which is by no means accepted generally), the Judaic people had literacy certainly since the time of Moses (*c.* 1300-1100?) and most probably since their stay in Ur of the Chaldees *c.* 1700-1600 (*Genesis* 11), since the Mesopotamians had →

12. I was not of course the first to come up with such a view. On the strength of Sanskrit many European scholars in the early nineteenth century thought India was the original homeland (Mallory 1973: 26-9). Even after scholars rejected India in the later nineteenth century and began to adduce different urheimats from the Baltic to the Balkans rewriting Indian (proto-)history, there was a succession of Indian scholars, mainly, who maintained the indigenist view in one or other form: Rao 1880; Shri Aurobindo 1914; Dhar 1930 et al. Indeed, in recent years also many publications advocated indigenism: Sethna 1992; Elst 1993, 1999; Frawley 1994 and with Rajaram 1997; Feuerstein et al. 1995; and others.[9] In fact, more and more scholars in the West have re-examined the issue and rejected the mainstream view advocating a movement Out of India into Europe: Schildmann 1998; Klostermaier 1998, 2000; Friedrich 2004. Thus the mainstream strident cries of warning about "fundamentalists, nationalists, revisionists" in India and their colleagues in the West (Witzel 2003; Huld 2002; Kuzmina 2002) are seen to be either hollow

---

→ literacy for more than a millennium earlier. So we can't say that the Jews maintained an oral tradition during their long travels. Then, the Jews mention constantly the (*mis-*)adventures they had and the different people they met on their travels. If we assume that the IAs had their oral tradition even as (according to the AIT) they travelled from the Steppe to Saptasindhu, what was it they were transmitting? The Vedic texts were composed (it is universally agreed) in India. So what were they transmitting before?... Why is there not one mention in the Vedic texts of dangers, mishaps and alien people met on the way — as we find in the Judaic texts? There is no such mention for the simple reason that, unlike the Jews, the IAs did not migrate.

9. S. Talageri should perhaps be included but despite having some very good ideas, this author knows no Sanskrit and has no training in Archaeology or other related disciplines and so goes astray constantly.

slogans or unthinking echoes of those slogans; for neither the indigenist scholars mentioned above nor the archaeologists specializing in the ISC and insisting on its unbroken continuity down to the sixth century belong to this (non-existent) band of bogies. I benefited from all of them. Roughly the main evidence and arguments are as follows:

13. Since the 1980s, there has been full consensus among archaeologist specialists in the area that the ISC has unbroken continuity (Jarrige & Meadow 1980; Lal & Gupta 1984; Allchin 1997; Kenoyer 1999; Shaffer & Lichtenstein 1999; Possehl 2002; McIntosh 2002).

The early Vedic texts mention no migration at all (see n7 and n10). Both these facts are quite different with other branches. There is ample evidence of entry in Greece, Italy and the rest of Europe and Anatolia. Moreover, most of these branches have texts that mention a migration — Greek, Roman, Irish, Scandinavian and Iranian (Mallory 1989; Kazanas 2002, 2003). In the Vedic texts we read also that the IAs take it for granted that they have been "here" for a long time without any hint that they have recently arrived "here" from elsewhere (e.g. the Aṅgiras family in *ṚV* 4.1.3 or the Vasiṣṭhas in 7.76.4).

Some scholars, Witzel 1995 (p. 321), R. Thapar 1999, Sharma 1999, have claimed that Baudhāyana's *Śrautasūtra* 18.44 indicates that some IAs moved eastward while others stayed behind in the west. However, many Sanskritists have shown Witzel's translation of the passage with this "immigration" to be utterly wrong (Lal 2005; Elst 1999). What is astonishing here is that all these non-indigenists ignore the fact that neither the *ṚV*, which is so immediately close to this alleged ingress, nor the later Saṁhitās and Brāhmaṇas allude to any immigration and prior trekking; instead they resort to a text which by their own theory is almost 1000 years after the event (entry *c.* 1500)! It is, alas, with such serious scholarship that mainstreamers scrape not only the bottom but even the outside of the barrel to collect evidence for their theory (see full discussion of this whole issue in Agarwal 2006).

On the other hand the Iranians have quite a different tale to tell. Early on the *Avesta* names 16 regions through which the Iranians wandered before settling down (Darmesteter 1965, vol. 1: 4 10). One of them is *Haptahəndu* which transliterates the Vedic *Saptasindhu* "region of seven rivers" (see n1). Now, it is hardly likely that in that larger area there was another location with seven rivers. So we must take it that the Iranians recall having lived in the land of the Seven Rivers (= today's Punjab and environs). In addition they took with them the memory of the river Sarasvatī and gave the name to another river in their new habitat *Hara*^{x}*vaiti*. Here it should be noted that the Vedic *saras* has a root and many related words, e.g. √*sṛ* >*sar-* >*si-sar-ti* "flows/moves on", *sarit* "stream", etc.; moreover it has cognations in Tocharian *salate*, Latin *salire* and Greek *hiallo* "leap, move, rush" (Rix *Lexikon* . . . 527). The Iranian word for "lake" is *vairi-*. Avestan *hara-* (from *hara*^{x}*vaiti*) has no other cognates in Iranian. Now, no reasonable scholar would claim that the IAs left Iran taking with them the name Hara^{x}vaiti, came to Saptasindhu and gave the name Sarasvatī to a shrunken river (as it was by 1500 BCE) and then concocted all the related words (*sara, sarit,* etc.) and so, by an extraordinary coincidence, formed cognations with words in other IE branches! Yet this is precisely what mainstreamers tacitly claim as they propound the AIT.

Mainstreamers don't ignore only these simple linguistic data. They also ignore some other literary aspects. G. Gnoli studied in detail the early movements of the Iranians as recorded in the *Avesta* and concluded that all movements are from east to west and south to north, in other words a north-west expansion and not a south-eastward movement as per the AIT (1980). Gnoli is far from indigenist but no references to his study are found in recent mainstream indological publications.

All the preceding discussion indicates that the IAs did not come from a north-west direction but, rather, that the Iranians left Saptasindhu and moved north-westward. Thus the so-called "common Indo-Iranian" period was one in Saptasindhu (see nn 2, 6).

14. D. Frawley first pointed out in the 1990s that here in Saptasindhu in the ISC we have an extraordinary paradox regarding the AIT. On the one hand there is the third millennium — a technologically advanced civilization with large buildings, arts and crafts, trade that reached Mesopotamia and other distant regions, and literacy; yet, unlike Egypt and Mesopotamia, it has no literature at all! Then, even as this culture begins to collapse and the inhabitants move eastward, enter, as per the AIT, the IAs who are non-literate barbarians with highly developed poetics (Watkins 2001), and very swiftly produce the hymns of the *ṚV* and *AV*. It is "an astonishing coincidence of space, time and people" (Kazanas 2002: 292). But we have more paradoxes.

15. Yet another paradox is the "Aryanization of Saptasindhu." In the early 1990s the AIT adherents stopped writing about "invasion" and introduced the term "immigration," and in peaceful wave(s), at that. But how could two or ten peaceful waves of illiterate nomads (albeit with great poetic talents that had not yet flourished[10]) accomplish the "almost complete

---

10. Now this was so, as per M. Witzel (2003). If it was not so and the incoming IAs had already composed hymns and whatever else, then, surely, some passages would reflect their recent journey(s), the (mis-)adventures they went through and the various people(s) they met on the way. But there is not a hint of such things in the *ṚV* (See n 8.)

Indo-Aryanization in northern India"? The quotation is from M. Witzel (1995: 107). In the same passage Witzel, this most fervent and vociferous proponent of the AIT, expresses his bafflement at this: "The Indo-Aryan influence . . . was powerful enough from early on to replace local names in spite of the well-known conservatism of river-names. This is especially surprising in the area once occupied by the Indus Civilization, where one would have expected the survival of earlier names." But why be surprised? Such a change does not come about through peaceful means: only conquest can impose it and often not at all thoroughly. Consequently the claim for "immigration" is just as unrealistic and inapt as "invasion": both are contradicted by reason and the facts. There was neither invasion nor immigration.

16. The "Preservation Principle" is yet another aspect supporting the antiquity of the *R̥V* and IA indigenism. The vocabulary of the R̥gvedic language or Old Indo-Aryan is alleged to have four per cent foreign loans, as per Witzel 2005, Kuiper 1991. This, I and others doubt seriously (Kazanas 2002: IX, 2, pp. 316-17; Das 1995 passim). On the other hand, it is quite probable that Vedic does have some foreign loans since it did not exist in a vacuum; but there are no foolproof methods for determining these loans since *no other languages of the same antiquity (i.e. fourth millennium) are attested in that area.* Draviḍian and other languages that are supposed to furnish these loan-words are not attested until about the Common Era and after. However, even if the four per cent or six per cent could be established, the R̥gvedic language alone, in fact, has clearly discernible roots (*dhātu*s) and well-defined mechanisms generating verbal and nominal forms (Kazanas 2004b) and has preserved many more stems from the Proto-Indo-European mother tongue than any other IE branch (e.g. Hittite, Greek, Italic, Germanic, etc.).

For example, as we saw earlier (§13), root √*sr̥* "moving" gives verb *sisarti* "flows, moves," *sārayati* "causes to flow" and *sara* "motion" (noun), "fluid" (adjective) and *sarma* "flowing," *sr̥ti* "flow general," etc.; similarly √*bhr̥* "bearing" gives verb *bibharti* "bears, carries," *bhārayati* "causes to bear" and *bhara* "act of bearing, weight" (noun), "bearing" (adjective) and *bharma* "support," *bhr̥ti* "carrying," etc. Consider also √*vac* "speaking" > *vakti* "speaks," *vācayati* "makes someone speak," *vā̆cas* "speech," *vaktra* "instrument for speaking, mouth," etc.; and √*vas* "dressing" > *vasti* "dresses," *vāsayati* "makes someone dress," *vasas* "garment," *vastra* "instrument for dressing, cloth," etc. The table shows a limited but typical variety.

dhātu generating verbs and nouns					
	Verbal		**Nominal**		
√*sr̥* >	*sisarti*	*sārayati*	*sā̆ra*	*sarman*	*sr̥ti*
√*bhr̥* >	*bibharti*	*bhārayati*	*bhā̆ra*	*bharman*	*bhr̥ti*
√*vac* >	*vakti*	*vācayati*	*vā̆cas*	*vakman*	*vaktra*
√*vas* >	*vasti*	*vāsayati*	*vāsas*	*vasman*	*vastra*
And with prepositions like *upa(+bhr̥)*, *pra(+vac)*, etc.					

Furthermore, the *R̥V*, despite the repetitions in the hymns, has more theonyms of IE deities and more religious/mythological motifs than the other IE branches (Kazanas 2001, 2005, 2006). When I presented this PP evidence in the *Journal of IE Studies* (2002), J. Mallory criticized it as unscientific saying (2002) that in the Index of Gamkrelidze & Ivanov (1995) he counted 2441 Greek lexical retentions, Baltic 2376 and Indo–Iranian 2139: thus Old Indo–Aryan came third. But Mallory failed to notice that these numbers contain the very same stems present in declension and conjugation often more than five times and are therefore misleading and worthless. When I pointed this in a private communication in 2004, he replied (November 2004) repeating the objection that this was "unscientific," and produced M. Swadesh's 100 words where the Indic branch held 82, the Italic 82, Greek 80, Irarian 76, Germanic 75, Baltic 71, Celtic 64 and the other branches less than 50 per cent. I was surprised then because those lists are quite wrong and the work of Swadesh (glottochronology 1953, 1955) has now been thoroughly discredited: so, we can forget him.

I then examined more than 450 IE stems present in three or more IE branches. Of 402 significant stems Vedic lacks 55, Germanic 145, Greek 149, Baltic 185, Italic 205, Celtic 210 and Slavic 215. I left out Hittite as it has enormous losses and Iranian because it is so close to Vedic. This study is being published in the *Research Bulletin* of the Vishveshvaranand Vedic Research Institute in December 2006.

Mallory objected also saying that the greatest retentiveness will be found in languages "that are earlier attested and have the largest vocabularies, i.e. Vedic, Greek and Latin." This is manifestly untrue. Hittite is well attested in *c.* 1600 yet has meagre retentions and none of the closest personal relations (brother, daughter, father, husband, mother, sister, son, wife) which are found in almost all IE branches. Then, Germanic is attested in writing seriously only after 300 BCE while Greek is found in epigraphies in the seventh century BCE and Italic in the fifth. The *R̥V* is not attested in writing before late medieval times; it was transmitted orally even as late as the seventh century BCE (Winterwitz 1981: 31) and the early twentieth century.

The early Indic writing is Aśoka's Prākr̥ta (not Vedic or Sanskrit) Rock inscriptions after 300 BCE. So the R̥gvedic language appears in a written form many centuries later than the Hittite, Greek, Italic and even Germanic! These facts were spelt out in my paper published in 2003 in the *Journal of IE Studies*, of which Mallory is the editor.

The answer to this apparent problem is the unrivalled Vedic oral tradition whereby the Vedic sacred lore was passed on from one generation to the next. This and nothing else ensured the safe and accurate transmission of the ancient Vedic texts from the mists of prehistory (§11, above).

Now it is a well-known fact of history that a people on the move for a long period tend to lose elements of their original culture while their language will suffer many changes (like the Gypsies), as they meet with other cultures and/or have little leisure to pass their lore to the new generation(s) — much more than a people remaining sedentary. This was voiced many years ago by several comparativists (Hock 1991: 467-69; Burrow 1973:10; Lockwood 1969: 43).

Clearly then, the IAs preserved so many more of the IE linguistic and religious elements because they moved, as a people, very little or not at all. Thus they are by 1700 BCE fully indigenous in Saptasindhu. Corroboration comes from the fields of physical anthropology and genetics.

17. Recent genetic studies using more secure methods agree now that there was no Aryan immigration/invasion into India. K. Elst (1999) cited two geneticists (Hamphill and Christensen 1994) who had refuted the view that the IAs moved from Bactria into NW India: "[A.] Parpola's suggestion of movement of Proto-Ṛgvedic Aryan speakers into the Indus Valley by 1800 is not supported by our data. Gene flow from Bactria occurs much later and does not impact Indus Valley gene pools until the dawn of the Christian Era" (Elst 1999: 232; also Bryant p. 231). K. Kennedy (1995) confirmed this view: "There is no evidence of demographic disruption in the north-western sector of [India] . . . during and immediately after the decline of the Haṛappan culture" (again in Elst, p. 233, and Bryant p. 231). The Haṛappan decline is placed *c.* 1900-1600. However, Kennedy found a break in the continuity of the skeletal record in the region *c.* 6000-4500 — which could indicate some unspecified entry.

More recent genetic studies show that this break is not indicative of an influx of new people, the IAs, and even suggest that, on the contrary, the European peoples descended from the inhabitants of South-East Asia. Cavalli-Sforza and his team state that "Indian tribal and caste populations derive largely from the same genetic heritage of Pleistocene [=10000 to 3 mya] southern and western Asians and *have received limited gene flow from external regions since the Holocene* [=*c.* 10000 to present]. The phylogeography [=neighbouring branches] of the primal mtDNA and Y-chromosome founders suggest that these southern Asian Pleistocene coastal settlers from Africa would have provided the inocula for the subsequent differentiation of the distinctive eastern and western Eurasian gene pools" (emphasis and square brackets added; Cavalli-Sforza 2003).

Another geneticist, S. Oppenheimer, offers independent confirmation (2003) that there was no Aryan entry, either male or female; he focuses on the M17, or so-called "Caucasoid" (=Aryan!), genetic marker: "South Asia is logically the ultimate origin of M17 and his ancestors; and sure enough we find highest rates and greatest diversity of the M17 line in Pakistan, India and eastern Iran, and low rates in the Caucasus. M17 is not only more diverse in South Asia than in Central Asia but diversity *characterizes* its presence in isolated tribal groups in the south, thus undermining any theory of M17 as a marker of a "male Aryan invasion" of India" (2003: 152: emphasis mine). He adds that this M17 marker travelled from India or

Pakistan (= our Saptasindhu) through Kashmir, Central Asia, Russia and then Europe after 40000 BP (p. 154). Thus migration is from east westward.

A more recent study (Sahoo . . . Endicot, Kivisild . . . Kashayp 2006) concludes: "The Y-chromosomal data consistently suggest a largely South Asian origin of Indian caste communities and therefore argue against any major influx, from regions north and west of India" (p. 843); then again: "It is not necessary, based on the current evidence, to look beyond South Asia for the origins of the paternal heritage of the majority of Indians at the time of the onset of settled agriculture. . . . our findings do support a local origin of haplogroups F* and H" (p. 847).[11]

However, all these finds are by no means final and we need to be cautious; but the indications now are that there will be no reversal. If there was a migration, this was most probably out of Saptasindhu and the adjacent region.

Conclusion

18. All linguistic evidence is either false or ambivalent (Kazanas 2003a, 2002; Bryant 2001; Hock 1999) since the few reliable data can be interpreted as showing a movement out of India far more reasonably than the invasion/immigration into Saptasindhu.

All other types of evidence show no ingress at all between 4500 and 600 BCE. The literary evidence in the early and late Vedic texts betrays not one hint of immigration or long

11. In 2002 when the *JIES* debate took place, I was right to doubt the insecure finds of other researchers which were methodologically wrong. See Kazanas 2002, §IV, 1 and n 9, p. 287-88 and 2003, §14, p. 200). I am indebted here to Dr N. Rajaram of Bangalore (India) and Prof. S. Kak of Louisiana who notified me about these two 2003 publications.

trekking. On the contrary, this evidence whichever way it is examined asserts confidently that the IAs have been in Saptasindhu for several millennia BCE. Archaeologists agree unanimously that no intruding Aryans disturbed the ISC culture *c.* 1700-1500. Even archaeologists who favour an ingress like D.P. Agrawal make various conjectures (despite the hard evidence) and in the end admit that these immigrant Aryans are "elusive" (2002)! Archaeoastronomy also indicates indigenism and a *ṚV* date before 3000, as does the evidence for the Sarasvatī River. Finally genetic studies show now that the movement is out of Saptasindhu, thus agreeing with Nichol's linguistic evidence (§1) which has the IE locus of dispersal in ancient Bactria and adjacent areas.

Why mainstreamers insist on the AIT is a mystery. Lord C. Renfrew wrote of the AIT (1989: 182): "this comes rather from a *historical assumption* about the "coming" of the Indo-Europeans" (my emphasis). Then Edmund Leach wrote (1990): "Because of their commitment to a unilateral segmented history of language development that needed to be mapped onto the ground, the philologists took it for granted that proto-Indo-Iranian was a language that has originated outside India or Iran. . . . From this we derived the myth of the "Aryan invasion."" These are the two legs of clay upon which stands the AIT and its variants.

Leach went further saying that after the discovery of the Indus–Sarasvatī Civilization "Indo-European scholars should have scrapped all their historical reconstructions and started again from scratch. But this is not what happened. Vested interests and academic posts were involved" (1990). This is still true. But the new genetic evidence will soon force linguists to reconsider their theories.

References

Achar, B.N., 2001, "Planetarium Software and the date of the Mahābhārata War" paper read in Montreal, sent to N. Kazanas privately. 1999 "On exploring the Vedic sky . . ." *Electronic Journal of Vedic studies* 5-2 (3-9).

Agarwal, V., 2006, "Is there Evidence for the Indo-Aryan Immigration to India?" talk at WAVES Conference August. See <http://www.omilosmeleton.gr/english en_index.html>.

Agrawal, A., 2005, *In search of Vedic Haṛappan Relationship*, New Delhi: Aryan Books International.

Agrawal, D.P., 2002, "Comments on 'Indigenous IndoAryans", in *Journal of IE Studies*, vol. 30 (129-35).

Agrawala, P.K., 2005, "Two Haṛappan Motifs & their Vedic Affinity' in A. Agrawal ed. (10-13).

Allchin, B. & R., 1997, *Origins of Civilization*, Delhi: Viking/Penguins.

———, 1982, *The Rise of Civilization in India and Pakistan*, Cambridge: CUP.

Allchin, F., & J. Joshi (eds.), *Excavations at Malvan*, Delhi: Archaeological Survey of India (Memoir No. 92).

Aurobindo, Sri, 1914-1920, "On the Veda and The Secret of the Veda" articles in *Arya*, India (1956 rpt. in book form, Pondicherry).

Bisht, R.S., 1999, "Haṛappan and Ṛgveda: Points of Convergence" in G. Pande, ed. (393-442).

Bryant, E., 2001, *The Quest of the Origins of Vedic Culture*, Oxford: OUP.

Burrow, T., 1963, "On the Significance of the Terms *arma-, armaka-*", *Journal of Indian History*, vol. 41 (159-68).

Cavalli-Sforza et al. 2003, "The Genetic Heritage of the Earliest Settlers . . .", *American Journal of Human Genetics* 72 (313-32).

Chakrabarti, D.K., 1999, *India: An Archaeological History*, Cambridge: CUP.

Dalley, S., 1998, ed., *The Legacy of Mesopotamia*, Oxford: OUP.

Darmesteter, J., 1965, *The Zend-Avesta* (1883), Sacred Books of the East 4, 23, Delhi: Motilal Banarsidass.

Das P., 1995, "Hunt for Foreign Words in *ṚV*", *Indo-Iranian Journal* 38 (207-38).

Dhavalikar, M.K., 1995, *Cultural Imperialism . . .*, Delhi: Books & Books.

Dhar, L., 1930, *The Home of the Aryas*, Delhi: Delhi University Press.

Elst, K., 1999, *Update on the Aryan Invasion Debate*, Delhi: Aditya Prakashan.

———, 1993, *Indigenous Indians*, Delhi: Voice of India.

Erdosy, G. (ed.), 1995, *The Indo-Aryans of Ancient South Asia*, Berlin/NY, Guyter.

Feuerstein, Frawley D., S. Kak, 1995, *In search of the Cradle of Civilization*, Wheaton/Madras: Quest Books.

Francfort, P-H., 1992, "Evidence for Haṛappan Irrigation System", in *Eastern Anthropologist*, vol. 45 (87-103).

Frawley, D., 2002, "Witzel's vanishing ocean", http://www.bharatvani.org/davidfrawley/ReplytoWitzel.html

———, 1994, *The Myth of the Aryan Invasion*, Delhi: Voice of India (rep. 2000).

———, 1991, *Gods Sages & Kings*, Salt Lake City: Passage Press.

Frawley, D., and N. Rajaram, 1997, *Vedic Aryans & Origins of Civilization*, Delhi: Voice of India.

Frazer, 1995, *The Gypsies*, Oxford: Blackwell.

Friedrich, H., 2004, "A Diffusionist's View on the Concept of 'Language Families' ", *Migration and Diffusion*, vol. 5, no. 19, July-September (6-14).

Gnoli, G., 1980, *Zoroaster's Time and Homeland*, Naples: Instituto Universitario Orientale (Series Minor VII).

Gupta, S.P., 2006, "The Saraswatī and the Homeland of Early Ṛgvedic Ṛṣis" in A. Agrawal, ed. (55-73).

Hock, H.H., 1999, "Out of India? The Linguistic Evidence", in J. Bronkhorst and M. Deshpande (eds.), *Aryan and Non-Aryan in South Asia*, Camb, Mass.: HOS (1-18).

———, 1991, *Principles of Historical Linguistics*, (2nd edn.), Berlin/NY: de Gruyter.

Huld, M.E., 2002, "Linguistic Science, Truth and the Indocentric Hypothesis", *Journal of IE Studies* 30 (149-60).

Jarrige, J.F., R. Meadow, 1980, "Antecedents of Civilization in the Indus Valley", in *Scientific American*, August issue.

Kak, S., 1997, "Archaeoastronomy & Literature", October issue of *Current Science*.

———, 1994, *The Astronomical Code of the Rigveda* (rev. edn. 2000), Delhi: Munshiram Manoharlal Publisher Pvt. Ltd.

Kazanas, N., 2006, "Diffusion of IE Theonyms", in *Quarterly Journal of the Mythic Society* (Bangalore, India), vol. 97, no 1 (1-29).

———, 2005, "Vedic and Mesopotamian Cross-influences", in *Migration and Diffusion* (Vienna), vol. 24 (96-129).

———, 2004a, "Samudra and Sarasvatī in the *ṚV*", in *QJMS*, vol. 95 (90-104).

———, 2004b, "Sanskrit & Proto-Indo-European", *Indian Linguistics*, vol. 65 (75-100).

———, 2003, "Final Reply", *Journal of IE Studies*, vol. 31, 1&2 (187-240).

———, 2002a, "Indigenous Indoaryans & the Ṛgveda", *Journal of IE Studies*, vol. 30 (275-334).

———, 2002b, "Ṛgvedic *Pur*", in *Brahmavidyā: Adyar Library Bulletin*, 66 (1-14).

———, 1999, "The *Ṛgveda* and Indoeuropeans", *ABORI*, 80 (15-42).

Kenoyer, J.M., 1998, *Ancient Cities of the Indus Valley Civilization*, Karachi Oxford: OUP.

Klostermaier, K., 2000, *Hinduism*, Oxford: Oneworld Books.

———, 1998, "Questioning the Aryan Invasion Theory . . ." *Iskcon Communications Journal* 6:1 (5-16), Republished in *International Quarterly of Indian Philosophy*, June 2001 (63-78).

Kochhar, R., 2000, *The Vedic People*, Hyderabad: Orient Longman.

Kuiper, F., 1991, *Aryans in the Ṛgveda*, Amsterdam/Atlanta: Rodopi.

Kuzmina, 2002, "Comments on Kazanas", *Journal of IE Studies* 30 (161-69).

Lal, B.B., 2005, *The Homeland of the Aryans*, New Delhi: Aryan Books International.

———, 2002, *The Sarasvatī Flows On*, New Delhi: Aryan Books International.

———, 1998, *India 1947-1997: New Light on the Indus Civilization*, Delhi: Aryan Books International.

———, 1997, *The Earliest Civilization*, Delhi: Aryan Books.

Lal, B.B., and S.P. Gupta (eds.), 1984, *Frontiers of the Indus Civilization*, Delhi: Indian Archaeological Society.

Leach, E., 1990, "Aryan Invasions over four millennia", in E. Ohnuki-Tierney (ed.), *Culture Through Time,* Stanford: Stanford University Press (227-45).

Levitt, S., 2003, "The Dating of the Indian Tradition", *Anthropos,* vol. 98 (341-59).

Lockwood, 1969, *Indo-European Philology,* London: Hutchinson University Press.

Lubotsky, A., 1997, *A Ṛgvedic Word Concordance,* New Haven: American Oriental Society.

Mayrhofer, M., 1996, *Etymologisches Wörterbuch des Altindischen,* Heidelberg: Carl Winter.

———, 1956 *KEWA* (Kurtzgefasstes . . .), Heidelberg: Carl Winter.

McEvilley, Th., 2002, *The Shape of Ancient Thought,* New York: Allworth Press.

McIntosh, J.R., 2001, *A Peaceful Realm,* Boulder (Colorado): Westview.

Misra, S.S., 1992, *The Aryan Problem: A Linguistic Approach,* Delhi: Munshiram Manoharlal.

Mitchel, B., and F. Robinson, 1996, *A Guide to Old English,* Oxford: Blackwell.

Nichols, J., 1997-98, "The Epicentre of the IE linguistic spread" and "The Eurasian spread zone . . .", in R. Blench and M. Spriggs (eds.), *Archaeolology & Language,* NY/London: Routledge, vol. 1, 122-48 and 2, 220-66.

Oppenheimer, S., 2003, *The Real Eve: Modern Man's Journey out of Africa,* NY, Carroll & Graf.

Pande, G.C. (ed.), *The Dawn of Indian Civilization up to 600 BC,* New Delhi: PHISPC, Centre for Studies in Civilization.

Parpola, A. et al., 1969, *Decipherment of Proto-Dravidian Inscriptions . . .* Copenhagen: Scandinavian Institute of Asian Studies.

———, 1988, *The Coming of the Aryans to Iran and India,* Helsinki: Studia Orientalia.

Piggott, S., 1992, *Wagon, Chariot and Carriage,* London: Thames & Hudson.

———, 1983, *The Earliest Wheeled Transport,* London: Thames & Hudson.

Possehl, G.L., 2002, *The Indus Civilization,* Roman & Littlefield (Non-NBN).

———, 1998, "Did the Sarasvatī ever flow to the Sea?", G.S. Phillips et al.

(eds.), *Arabia & its Neighbours* (in *Honour of Beatrice de Cardi*), Turnhout, Brepols (339-54).

Rao, R., 1880, "Puzzles for the Philologists", *Theosophist* 1 (305-08).

Rao, S.R., 1991, *Dawn & Devolution of the Indus Civilization*, Delhi: Aditya Prakashan.

———, 1973, *Lothal & the Indus Civilization*, Bombay: Asia Publications.

Rajaram, N., 2005, "Connections between Haṛappan Seals and the Vedic Literature", in Agrawal A. 2005 (135-41).

Renfrew, C., 1989, *Archaeology & Language*, Hammondsworth: Penguins.

Rix, H., 1998, *Lexicon der indogermanischen verben . . .*, Wiesbaden: Reichert.

Sahoo, S., A. Singh, T. Kivisild et al., 2006, "A Prehistory of Indian Y-chromosomes", *Proceedings of the National Academy of Sciences* (USA) vol. 103, no. 4, 843-48.

Sankalia, H.D., 1974, *Prehistory & Protohistory of India & Pakistan*, Poona: Deccan College.

Schildmann, K., 1998, *Indus/Burrows Cave USA-Deciphering* Bonn: Studia Orientalia et Indo-Attentica, Fascicle 1.

Sergent, B., 1997, *La Genèse de l' Inde*, Paris: Payot & Rivages.

Sethna, D.K., 1992, *The Problem of Aryan Origins*, 2nd edn., Delhi: Aditya Prakashan.

Shaffer, J., 1984, "The Indo-Aryan Invasion . . . ", in Lucaks J.R. (ed.), *The People of South Asia: the Biological Anthropology, of India, Pakistan & Nepal*, New York: Plenum.

Shaffer J., D. Lichtenstein, 1999, "Migration, Philology & South Asian Archaeology" in J. Bronktorst, and M. Deshpande (eds.), *Aryans and Non-Aryan in South Asia*, Camb Mass.: HOS.

Sharma, G.R., 1980, *History to Protohistory: Archaeology of the Vindhyas and the Ganga Valley*, Allahabad: Allahabad University.

Sharma, R.S., 1999, *Advent of the Aryans in India*, New Delhi: Orient Longman.

———, 1996, *Looking for the Aryans*, Hyderabad: Orient Longman.

Singh, Bh., 1995, *The Vedic Haṛappans*, Delhi: Aditya Prakashan.

Swadesh, M., 1955, "Towards Greater Accuracy in Lexico Statistical Dating", *International Journal of American Linguists*, vol. 21 (121-37).

——, 1953, "Archaeological and Linguistic Chronology . . .", *American Anthropologist*, vol. 55 (349-52).

Talageri, S., 2000, *The Rigveda*, New Delhi: Aditya Prakashan.

Thapar, B., R. Mungal, 1994, "The Indus Valley (3000-1500 BCE)", in A Dani and J.P. Mohen (eds.), *History of Humanity*, vol. 2, London: Unesco/ Routledge (246-65).

Thapar, R., 1999, *The Aryan Question Revisited* <http://members.tripod.com/ascjnu/aryan.html>.

Thomas, P. et al., 1995, "Haṛappan Subsistence Patterns . . .", *Man and Environment* (India) 20, 2 (33-41).

Vedic Index 1995 (1912) by A. MacDonnell and A. Keith, Delhi: Motilal Banarsidass.

Watkins, C., 2001, *How to kill a Dragon . . .*, Oxford: OUP (1995).

Winternitz, M., 1981, *History of Indian Literature* (tr. by V.S. Sarma) 3 vols, Delhi: Motilal Banarsidass.

Witzel, M., 2005, "Central Asian Roots and Acculturation in South Asia", in Osada Tosiki (ed.), *Linguistics, Archaeology and the Human Past*, Kyoto: Indus Project, Research Institute for Humanity and Nature.

——, 2001, "Autochthonous Aryans", *Electronic Journal of Vedic Studies* 7-3, 1-93.

——, 1995, "Early Indian History" and "Ṛgvedic History" in G. Erdosy (ed). *Nepal*, New York: Plenum.

3

The Idea of the Ancient South Asian City

Piotr A. Eltsov

IT is a truism today to say that the study of the past is inseparable from the present. This volume is a good example of how heavily politicized and emotionally charged the study of the past can be. With senior academics reversing their interpretations, and archaeological and historical data being unapologetically applied to politics, one cannot understate the importance of the responsible writing of ancient history.

This chapter diverts attention from the politically charged controversies of South Asian protohistory and early history to an aspect of the ancient Indian literature, which has received the least attention of archaeologists. As an ancient historian, archaeologist, and philologist, I treat ancient Indian texts not as sources of factual information (for which they have very little to offer), but as sources of sociocultural ideas, which can be used in the analysis of material cultures and the conceptual rethinking of the lounge durée. Unusual for the study of ancient South Asia, this conjunctive approach is based on the simple yet salient assumption that the ideas of the historical agents present a plausible alternative to Western epiphenomenal theories in the writing of history. This is not to say that the ongoing debates on the identity of the Haṛappans and Vedic Aryans are unimportant, or that other ideas and theories — whether modern or ancient — are inappropriate. All that I intend to do is to show that it is possible to speak of continuity and Great Tradition in the context of South Asia without falling into the ideology of "one people, one nation, one culture" and without having the Haṛappans be Aryans, speak Sanskrit, and worship Śiva.

More specifically, the object of this chapter is the idea of the city in the two most ancient South Asian civilizations: the Haṛappan civilization of the third millennium BCE and the Ganges civilization of the first millennium BCE. Needless to say, the phenomenon of the city was one of the most remarkable achievements of the ancient South Asian civilization. Whether Moheṅjo-Dāṛo or Lothal, Śṛṅgaverapura or Rājgīr, the ancient cities of South Asia have fascinated the lay and attracted the attention of scholars since the pioneering research by Alexander Cunningham (1871). As far as the up to date state of research in the archaeology, philology and history of ancient South Asia is concerned, one must nevertheless admit that aside from numerous case studies dealing with the remains of separate cities or with the descriptions of cities found in Sanskrit and Pāli texts, there has been a clear lack of cross-disciplinary, conceptual, and holistic analyses of the earliest South Asian city, either as an idea or a historical phenomenon. This chapter is an attempt at filling this gap.

Torn Between the Two Cities

The idea of the city has produced an immense amount of literature in several fields of knowledge. On one hand, thinkers like Spengler (1918), Weber (1922), Christaller (1933), Mumford (1961), and Doxiades (1968) have brought about generic definitions highlighting morphological or functional traits that are allegedly shared by all cities. On the other hand, anthropologists, historians and ethnographers have produced a myriad of case studies pointing to the uniqueness of each individual case. To reconcile generic definitions with case studies is difficult and unnecessary. Both as an idea and a historical phenomenon, the city is so multifarious that it can accommodate almost any approach, whether it is the Central Place Theory, Ekistics or a murky historical poeticism in the style of Oswald Spengler.

What unites most generic theoreticians is that they assume the existence of one true definition. Indeed, despite all the differences between their teachings, Spengler, Christaller, Weber, Mumford, and Doxiadis, in one way or another, believed that the city was an organic and intelligible whole. Not denying a certain value of this premise for broad cross-cultural and philosophical studies, one must however admit that it has very little use for specific historical cases. The fact is that, despite all the developments in positivistic scholarship, the city has equally remained an object of humanistic studies. Moreover, its humanistic side cannot be adequately conceptualized by scientistic methods. Whether in the writings of a great nineteenth-century historian, Fustel de Coulange (1864), or in a recent ethnography of the Nepalese city by the anthropologist, Robert Levy (1984), the city continues to be perceived by scholars in humanistic terms, as a thing in itself, an entity consisting of autonomous units, an aesthetic object, or, as Levy (1984: 616) vividly puts it, as "a powerful device for turning accident and history into structure, for trying to escape the contingencies and consequences of history, for trying to capture change, to make change seem illusory within an enduring order." In other words, it is still vigorously debated whether the city is an objective historical phenomenon or an idea in the minds of historical agents, a sociopolitical and cultural whole or a myriad of sporadic elements, an object of scientific enquiry or a product of poetic imagination, a part of complex systems or a thing in itself, a static entity or a live organism.

Clearly, none of these dichotomies will ever have an unambiguous solution. Since its invention, the idea of the city has been innately dual. In the fifth century CE, Saint Augustine conceptualized this duality in theological terms, as an opposition between the City of God and the Earthen City. Today we see it as an opposition between the city as a product of poetic imagination and the city as an intelligible and objective whole. Figuratively speaking, we are still torn between the two cities. Our scholarly ways of thinking have not moved us far from the theology of the medieval mystic.

Against this intellectual background, my own epistemological stance is humanistic, structural, and reflective. With regards to the intelligibility and phenomenology of the city, it can be summarized in the three following points:

1. *There cannot be a single and universally comprehensive definition of the city.* For generic concepts of the city, whether scientific or humanistic, are not able to reflect the city in its totality. Being valuable for broad cross-cultural studies, these concepts have little use for the anthropology and history of spatially and temporally restricted cases. Moreover, many generic urban theories are Eurocentric and, by definition, fail to explain the specificity of cases outside of the Western world (Mumford 1961, Weber 1922). Choosing to use these theories in the study of ancient civilizations, anthropologists end up concluding that these civilizations had no cities (Wilson 1951, Coe 1961). To give credit to generic theoreticians, at least some of them were well aware of the limitations of their theories (Christaller 1933, Doxiades 1968).

2. *The city as a complex sociopolitical and cultural phenomenon can be studied and conceptualized in a multitude of ways from the viewpoint of several academic disciplines.* One can investigate and classify cities based on size, layout, economy, political structure, social organization, artistic life, and so on. One can look at cities from a morphological, structural, or functional angle. One can approach the city internally as a system consisting of numerous elements, or one can approach the city externally as part of a large network of settlements. Importantly, most of these approaches are complementary to each other, not mutually exclusive. For example, showing that Central Place Theory (Christaller 1933) works in the context of a given ancient culture does not mean that other approaches cannot be used in the context of the same culture.
3. *The city as a historical phenomenon is inseparable from the idea of the city in the minds of historical agents.* In other words, what the populace thinks about their city is important for the understanding of the phenomenon of the city. In this, I follow the subjectivist and reflective vision of history by R.G. Collingwood (1946: 214), who believed that the object of a historical study was "not the mere event, but the thought expressed in it." I would add that Collingwood's ideas may apply not only to historical events, i.e. the actions by historical agents, but also to historical phenomena, i.e. the products of the actions by historical agents. The city is exactly this kind of phenomenon and is consequently incomprehensible without the thought expressed in it. The thought expressed in the phenomenon of the city is simply the perception of the city by the historical agents.

Archaeology and Texts in Ancient South Asia

The use of sociopolitical ideas from Sanskrit and Pāli texts in the analysis of material culture of the Ganges civilization is justified by the fact that many of these texts were compiled and recorded at the time when the cities of Ahicchatra, Bhītā, Kauśāmbī, Mathurā, Śrāvastī and Vaiśālī were flourishing. Although we cannot penetrate into the minds of people who lived in these cities, it is not unreasonable to assume that the descriptions of historical and mythical cities found in the Sanskrit and Pāli texts that date roughly to the late first millennium BCE and the early first millennium CE were at least in part inspired by actual historical examples.

The use of ideas from Sanskrit and Pāli texts in the archaeology of the Haṛappan civilization is a much more contentious issue. The compilers of the Tipiṭaka, Śāstras, Sūtras, the Epics, the Purāṇas, and other genres of Sanskrit and Pāli literature that contain descriptions of cities, are clearly not the historical agents of the Haṛappan civilization. Their analytical perspectives are as remote to the realities of the third millennium BC as our analytical perspectives to the birth of Christianity or the fall of the Roman Empire. In both anthropological archaeology and history, comparing distinct cultural entities is nonetheless a widely practised method. Moreover, the use of ancient and indigenous ideas in the creation of contemporary interpretations presents an interesting alternative to the epiphenomenal models of Western origin. Many ancient concepts were as complex and profound as contemporary social theories, and it is certainly worthwhile to determine whether any of these concepts can be used in the reconstruction of South Asian past.

In sum, ancient Indian literature provides great potential for the search of alternative analytical models. Importantly, if we use ancient texts as the sources for ideas rather than facts, meticulous text-historical methods do no longer matter. On this, I follow Giorgio Bonazzoli who has proposed that orality, ritualism and the rules of recitation of the ancient Indian texts question the usefulness of text-historical methods (Bonazzoli 1979, 1983a, 1983b). The primary focus of Bonazzolli's analysis was the Sanskrit Purāṇas, yet his observations are applicable to the other genres of Sanskrit literature as well. The Purāṇas, according to Bonazzolli (1983a: 256), have a "multi-authenticity, each text of each age being authoritative for that particular period," and "the latest, and probably the final stage of the Purāṇas . . . is what should be taken as the starting text for any critical edition or any research." What this means in the context of other genres of ancient Indian literature is that the sociopolitical concepts found in the texts can be used regardless of their precise date and textual history.

The City in Ancient Indian Literature

Cities are described in many Sanskrit and Pāli texts of the late first millennium BCE and early first millennium CE. The Buddhist Canon, Śāstras, Sūtras, the Epics, the Purāṇas, as well as other genres of Sanskrit and Pāli literature, contain numerous descriptions of historical, divine and ideal cities. One could distinguish three main types of these descriptions: abstract sociopolitical concepts of the city, conventional manuals on the layout of cities, and panegyrics on divine, mythical or historical cities. Scholars have previously analysed some of these descriptions yet usually concluded that since by style and context they are repetitive, standardized and hyperbolic there is no use of them in archaeology and ancient history. No one has so far suggested that within the unreal and repetitive details, these descriptions may contain concepts of the city as a social, political or cultural phenomenon. These concepts are expressed in the attributes and features of the ideal cities; and the hyperbole and repetition are the best proof of this. In other words, if every single panegyric or conventional manual depicts the city as having attributes "x," "y" and "z," this may simply mean that in the view of these texts and people who stand beyond their composition, the city was defined by having attributes "x," "y" and "z."

One of the earliest manifestations of the idea of the city in Sanskrit and Pāli literature is found in the Book of the Sevens (the Sattaka Nipāta) of the *Aṅguttara-Nikāya*. This book is called the Book of the Sevens because each of its *sutta*s expounds on various sets of seven; e.g., seven auspicious qualities (*AN* VII.6), seven obsessions (VII.12), seven suns (VII.62) and so forth. Sutta 63 of the Book of the Sevens presents a definition of the king's frontier city, *raññо paccantima nagara* (*AN* VII.63.1). In the beginning of this *sutta*, Buddha tells the monks that in order to be properly protected, the frontier city must have seven characteristics and four types of storage (*AN* VII.63.1). The seven characteristics are further defined as: the deep-seated, well dug in, immovable and unshakable pillar; the deep and wide moat; the wide encircling road; the great armoury of spear and sword; the large quantity of troops; a clever, intelligent and wise gate keeper; and the high, wide and plastered rampart (*AN* VII.63.2-8). The four types of storage include: the great stores of grass, wood and water; the great stores of rice and corn; the great stores of sesame, beans, vetches and cereal; and the great stores of medicines, such as ghee, fresh butter, oil, honey, sugar, and salt (*AN* VII.63.9-12) In the concluding segment of the *sutta*, the seven characteristics are matched with the seven auspicious qualities of the Aryan disciple, while the four types of storage are matched with the four meditations. Specifically, it is said that just like the city has a pillar, an Aryan disciple has faith; just like the city has a moat, an Aryan disciple has consciousness; just like the city has the encircling road, an Aryan disciple has fear of blame; just like the city has a great armoury, an Aryan disciple has learning; just like the city has troops, an Aryan disciple has great energy; just like the city has a gatekeeper, an Aryan disciple has concentration; just like the city has a rampart, an Aryan disciple has wisdom (*AN* VII.63.13-19). The four meditations equated with the four types of storage are the first meditation, the second meditation, the third meditation and the fourth meditation (*AN* VII: 63.20-23).

The frontier city thus is conceptualized with the help of a rigid numerical formula typical of the *Aṅguttara-Nikāya*. Although this makes the concept of the city somewhat dogmatic, I believe it is unlikely that the traits of the city were chosen randomly and thoughtlessly just to match the formula. As the contents of the other *sutta*s indicate, there is a large degree of mundane practicality in the analogies provided by the Buddha. Used as succinct illustrations for the norms of the Buddhist teaching, these analogies are usually rational, logical and realistic. The *sutta* discussed here is no exception and the definition of the frontier city represents this kind of analogy. In other words, the traits selected for the *sutta* VII.63 must have been seen by the Theravādins as truly characteristic of the ideal frontier city. From a morphological perspective, these traits represent five constituent elements: a pillar, fortifications, the encircling road, troops and storehouses. Spoken by the Buddha and correlated with the qualities of a virtuous devotee, these traits, in my view, may be tentatively seen as indicative of the conceptualization of the idea of the city in the early Buddhist literature.

A later version of this definition is found in one of the chapters of the *Milinda Pañha*. When the king Milinda enquires of the monk Nāgasena whether Nāgasena himself or any of his teachers have ever seen the Buddha, Nāgasena answers negatively. Milinda then concludes that the Buddha did not exist. In response, Nāgasena provides a scrupulous explanation for the existence of the Buddha. The essence of this explanation is in the juxtaposition of the two cities: the *nagara*, the ordinary city built by an architect, and the *dhammanagara*, the City of Righteousness built by the Buddha. As the City of Righteousness is the work of the Buddha, Nāgasena concludes that the Buddha did once exist. Prior to arriving at this conclusion, Nāgasena provides the colourful descriptions of the two cities.

The Ordinary City is described by Nāgasena as regularly planned; with moats and ramparts all around; with strong gateways, watchtowers and battlements; with wide squares, open places and junctions; with king's highways; with lines of shops; with parks, gardens, lakes, lotus ponds, and wells; with storehouses of food; with the four *varṇa*s; with troops and barracks; with numerous craftsmen and street performers; with actors and prostitutes; and with foreigners from different countries. The City of Righteousness is described somewhat similarly, yet with a stronger emphasis on its abundant bazaars and diverse inhabitants. The main difference between the two cities is that the City of Righteousness is given a rigid definition, whereas the Ordinary City is described in plain narrative prose. The City of Righteousness has eleven traits: a rampart, moat, upper battlement, watchtower, pillar, gatekeeper, upper terrace, market place, cross-ways, and a judgement hall. Just as in the *Aṅguttara-Nikāya*, each of these traits is paired with an auspicious quality, e.g. righteousness, fear of sin, knowledge, energy, faith, concentration, wisdom, *suttanta*s, *abhidhamma*, *vinaya*, and constant self-possession. Unlike the traits of the frontier city however, the traits of the City of Righteousness are directly equated rather than compared with auspicious qualities; the rampart in the City of Righteousness *is* righteousness, the moat *is* the fear of sin, the upper battlement *is* knowledge, and so forth.

Thus, by the time of the composition of the *Milinda Pañha*, the concept of the city had become more abstract and acquired two new morphological traits: a market place and a judgement hall. The main emphasis in the definition had nevertheless remained similar to that of the *Aṅguttara-Nikāya*; fortifications — a rampart, moat, watchtower and a gatekeeper — continued to play a paramount role in the view of the city.

In contrast to abstract definitions, the conventional manuals on city layout are found in a larger variety of texts. The most famous among these texts is the *Kauṭilīya Arthaśāstra*, a treatise on warfare, politics and statehood allegedly composed by one of the ministers of Candragupta Maurya. Two chapters of the *Arthaśāstra* deal solely with the construction and layout of the ideal fortified settlement (*durga*) (*KA* 4.3-4).

In the first chapter, we are introduced to the basic principles of the construction of fortified settlements. We are told that the fortified settlements must be built in the four corners on the borderlands of the country (*janapada*). *Sthānīyas*, the centres for tax-collection, must be built in the centre of the country. Three moats must be dug around the fortified settlement. An earthen rampart must be built next to the moat. On the rampart, a brick pavement must be erected for the movement of chariots. Towers, covered roads with hidden traps, gateways and stores for weapons must be built in various parts of the fortified settlement (*KA* 4.3.1-35). In the second chapter, we are given details on the internal layout of the fortified settlement (*KA* 2.4.1-31).

Scholars have previously discussed and analysed information provided in this excerpt (Kalianov 1959, Kangle 1965). Recently, Rangarajan (1992) has given another graphic and descriptive abridgement of all the data from the *Arthaśāstra*. Yet, no one seems to have looked at the description of the *durga* as an idiosyncratic definition of the city. If treated this way, the city in the view of the *Arthaśāstra* has the following attributes: royal residence; construction plan; the alignment of streets and houses according to the cardinal directions; a network of roads; an elaborate defence system; segregation of residential areas in accordance with occupation, origin and the *varṇāśrama* affiliation of residents; ritual places; storehouses; stables for animals; temples; cremation grounds; an army; boundaries between households; and agricultural fields (the last attribute is debatable and depends on the translation of *KA* 2.4.24. For alternative interpretations, see Kalianov 1959: 61, Kangle 1963: 81, Rangarajan 1992: 81).

Various versions of this definition are found in many Sanskrit Purāṇas. In the *Vāyu Purāṇa,* for example, the layout of *durga*s is discussed in the context of the innovations of the *Tretā yuga,* the third stage in the sequence of cosmic ages. The *Vāyu Purāṇa* describes *durga*s very briefly. One feels that the Paurāṇikas who compiled the *Vāyu* had a text of reference in mind. Possibly, such text was the *Arthaśāstra*. In the view of the *Vāyu Purāṇa,* fortified cities ought to have huge mansions, ramparts, gates and a moat (*VP* 1.8.103-05). The difference between the city and the village is purely a matter of scale. We are told that a hamlet must be two times smaller in diameter than a city, whereas a village is bigger than a hamlet (*VP* 1.8.111.2). Similar descriptions are found in other Mahāpurāṇas.

Like the conventional manuals, panegyrics are numerous and can be found in a large variety of Sanskrit and Pāli texts. The description of Hastināpura of the *Mahābhārata,* Ayodhyā of the *Vālmīki Rāmāyaṇa,* Sāgala of the *Milinda Pañha,* and the divine abode of Lalitā from the *Lalitāmāhātmya* of the

Brahmāṇḍa Purāṇa provide good examples of this type of city descriptions.

The description of Hastināpura in the *Mahābhārata* is extremely conventional. In one of the episodes of the Sabhā Parva, the second book of the *Mahābhārata,* we are told that Hastināpura was adorned with ponds and trees and its buildings were like the Kailāsa peaks all beautiful, attractive and perfectly furnished. It had gold lattices, the floors were laid with jewels, the stairs rose smoothly, and so on (Mbh II.31.20-25). In the *Vālmīki Rāmāyaṇa,* the description of Ayodhyā is not much more informative, though more reminiscent of the one in the *Arthaśāstra.* In the second book of the *Rāmāyaṇa,* the Bālā Kāṇḍa, Ayodhyā is portrayed as a great and majestic city, twelve leagues long and three wide, with well-ordered avenues, and adorned with a great royal road. It is also depicted as a fortress surrounded by a deep moat which cannot be crossed by enemies. King Daśaratha is said to have populated Ayodhyā with thousands of charioteers and brāhmaṇas (*Rām* II.5). Compared to Hastināpura and Ayodhyā, the description of Sāgala from the *Milinda Pañha* is a bit more informative. The city of Sāgala, according to the *Milinda Pañha,* has many attributes that can be assembled in seven groups. Group 1 includes parks, gardens, groves, lakes, and tanks. Group 2 is comprised of rivers, mountains, and woods. Group 3 is represented by various types of fortifications: towers, ramparts, gates, entrance archways, and moats. Group 4 is commercial: it consists of shops, merchandise and money. Group 5 includes architectural features, such as residential houses and the royal palace. Group 6 has different types of storage, that is a variety of warehouses full of goods and food. Group 7 includes a large variety of animals (*MiP* I.2). Finally, the description of the divine city found in the *Lalitāmāhātmya,* a devotional attachment to the *Brahmāṇḍa*

Purāṇa, follows a similar pattern. In the *Lalitāmāhātmya*, we are told that the city of the goddess Lalitā has towers, city walls, and gates, as well as numerous stables for elephants, horses and chariots. It also has a royal residence with numerous halls and decorated with doors and gates. In this residence, "there is a luminous and beautiful throne hall, decorated with nine precious stones. A divine throne, made of Cintāmaṇi, stands in the centre of it: self-shining, matchless, reminiscent of the rising sun . . ." (*LM* 14.9-13).

Taken together, these excerpts reveal an interesting pattern. In all of the quoted texts the city is conceptualized through a number of morphological traits (see Table 1). Yet most of these traits are not uniquely urban. Roads, construction in accordance with cardinal directions, stores, animals, temples, cremation grounds, boundaries between households, trade, and the system of *varṇa*s and *āśrama*s are characteristic of both rural and urban settlements. The only two traits that are unmistakably urban and feature prominently in most of the quoted excerpts are fortifications and authority.

Fortifications play an important role in every single description or definition of the city discussed above. In the *Aṅguttara-Nikāya*, of the seven traits that define the frontier city, two — a rampart and a moat — are parts of fortifications and the remaining five are directly related to fortifications. Of the eleven traits that define the City of Righteousness in the *Milinda Pañha*, four — a rampart, a moat, an upper battlement, and a watchtower — are parts of fortifications; several other directly relate to fortifications. In the *Arthaśāstra*, of the two chapters that describe the fortified settlements (*durga*s), the first chapter deals solely with an elaborate system of fortifications: three moats, an earthen rampart, a brick pavement on top of the rampart, towers, hidden traps, gateways, and so forth. The panegyrics on the legendary cities

Table 1: City Traits in Sanskrit and Pāli Texts

Traits	*Pn*	*Dn*	*Vn*	*Dg*	*Hs*	*Ay*	*Sg*	*Vp*	*Lm*
Agricultural fields	-	-	-	+	-	-	-	-	-
Animals	-	-	-	+	-	+	+	-	+
Army	+	+	+	+	-	+	-	-	-
Authority	+	+	+	+	+	+	+	-	+
Cardinal directions	-	-	-	+	-	-	-	+	-
Construction plan	-	+	+	+	-	+	+	+	-
Cremation grounds	-	-	-	+	-	-	-	-	-
Fortifications	+	+	+	+	+	+	+	+	+
Household boundaries	-	-	-	+	-	-	-	-	-
Judgement hall	-	+	-	-	-	-	-	-	-
Parks, gardens, etc.	-	+	+	-	-	-	+	-	-
Pillar	+	+	-	-	-	-	-	-	-
Roads	+	+	+	+	-	+	-	+	+
Storehouses	+	+	+	+	+	+	+	-	-
Temples	-	-	+	+	-	-	-	-	-
Trade and money	-	+	+	-	-	+	+	-	-
Social diversity	-	+	+	+	-	+	+	-	-

Pn The King's Frontier City, *pacantima nagara*, the *Aṅguttara-Nikāya* VII.63.

Dn The City of Virtuousness, *dhammanagara*, the *Milinda Pañha*.

Vn An Ordinary City, *nagara*, the *Milinda Pañha*.

Dg The Fortified Settlement, *durga*, the *Kauṭilīya Arthaśāstra* (2.3-4).

Hs Hastināpura, the *Mahābhārata* (II.31.20-25).

Ay Ayodhyā from the *Vālmīki Rāmāyaṇa* (II.5).

Sg Sāgala from the *Milinda Pañha*.

Vp An ideal city from the *Vāyu Purāṇa* 1.6.103-05.

Lm The abode of Lalitā, the *Lalitāmāhātmya*.

— Hastināpura, Ayodhyā, Sāgala, and the abode of the goddess Lalitā — always speak of deep moats, high walls, massive ramparts, towers, bastions and gates. Even in a very brief description of the *durga*s in the *Vāyu Purāṇa*, the Paurāṇikas refer to fortifications rather than any other trait of the *durga*s.

Similar to fortifications, authority is present in most of the discussed descriptions and definitions of the city. The *Arthaśāstra* unambiguously states that the place for the king's residence needs to be properly selected and planned. The *Mahābhārata* describes Hastināpura as the capital of the Kauravas. The *Vālmīki Rāmāyaṇa* depicts Ayodhyā as the capital of Kōśala and the place of residence of King Daśaratha. The Sāgala of the *Milinda Pañha* and the abode of Lalitā are portrayed as the seats of great power. Even the definitions of the Frontier City in the *Aṅguttara-Nikāya* and of the City of Virtuousness in the *Milinda Pañha* indicate the importance of authority. Although authority — whether divine or secular — is not mentioned in the list of traits, its presence is unambiguously clear: for the City of Virtuousness is built by the Buddha and the full name for the Frontier City is the King's Frontier City. The only example when authority is not mentioned is the description of the *durga* in the *Vāyu Purāṇa*. As I have noted above however, the Paurāṇikas who compiled the *Vāyu* must have had a text of reference in mind and more importantly the reference to *durga*s in the *Vāyu* is too fragmentary to be taken seriously.

Bridging the Gap: From Texts to Material Culture

The discussed texts cover more than a millennium of Sanskrit and Pāli literature and represent very different literary genres and ideological traditions. The *Aṅguttara-Nikāya* is a product of the early Buddhist thought, the Purāṇas reflect the mature

Brāhmaṇic world-view, the *Kauṭilīya Arthaśāstra* presents a unique political teaching, and the great epics of the *Mahābhārata* and *Rāmāyaṇa* can be seen as an encyclopaedia of ancient Indian thought and mythology. Such a great ideological and chronological diversity makes it more likely that the concepts of the city hidden within these texts stand for a wide spectrum of groups and individuals and makes it possible to treat the combination of fortifications and authority as a hypothetical model for the analysis of archaeological data. Evidently, this model is not meant to portray the city in its complexity. What it can do is to draw a link between agency and structure and to reveal the previously unknown aspects of the ancient South Asian city. Moreover, the archaeological data of both the Haṛappan and Ganges civilizations provide great potential for investigating the processes of the construction of fortifications and the formation of authoritative structures.

On the Gangetic sites, the number and magnitude of ramparts, moats, walls, gates, and bastions are striking. Moreover, fortifications are one of the few morphological elements that have been relatively well excavated. Compared to the data available on settlement patterns, domestic architecture and other aspects of material culture, the data on Gangetic fortifications are quite abundant. Scholars have previously analysed some of these data, yet the method of these analyses was predominantly descriptive and typological (Erdosy 1987, Mate 1969-70, T.N. Roy 1986, U.N. Roy 1954). In the Haṛappan civilization, fortifications are also one of the most evident traits. Free-standing walls, platforms, and gates are present on many of the excavated sites. Judging from the lack of evidence for warfare, the function of these fortifications is quite intriguing; particularly so as very little research has been undertaken with the purpose of determining the role of these fortifications in the process of Haṛappan urbanization.

The term "fortification," one must add, carries a functional connotation. Unfortunately, the English language does not have a good neutral term that would designate various types of dividing and circumvallating structures. The term "circumvallation" is not a much better option; because it implies the surrounding of a settlement from all the sides (several case studies show that some of the walls and ramparts did not surround sites entirely). Although I use the term "fortifications" for perimeter walls, bastions, ramparts, and even platforms, I do not imply at this point any certain function.

In contrast to fortifications, it is difficult to trace author in archaeological record. Fortifications are, in most cases, an objective structural feature while authority is a concept that needs to be shown theoretically through a combination of archaeological traits. Since the texts discussed above are the products of several distinct ideologies, their views on authority vary. What unites these views is that authority — whether an individual ruler, a deity, or a group of secular governing officials — is seen as a distinct institution of power. This institution of power, i.e. a group of full-time specialists whose sole business is to govern, is what can be shown archaeologically. Authority nonetheless takes different forms in different cultures. In some cultures, it is expressed in architecture and settlement layout. In other cultures, its presence is evident from burials or the objects of ritual paraphernalia. There are cultures, in which authority is barely distinguishable through material record. Overall, one must admit that there is no universal archaeological signature of authority and whether architecture, settlement pattern, burials or some other traits of material culture can be used as evidence of authority must be decided on a site-by-site and culture-by-culture basis.

Many archaeologists who worked in South Asia at the turn of the twentieth century carried with them preconceived notions of authority from West Asian and European archaeology. They were eager to find palaces, rich burials and assembly halls. For example, Bloch (1904: 94) and Spooner (1914: 99) saw the discovery of a palace as a major goal of their mission in Vaiśālī; the palace to them, apparently, was the sole and most important evidence of authority. In a similar way, some scholars envisioned the "pillared hall" at Kumrahār, Pāṭaliputra, as the Mauryan assembly hall; the power of the Mauryas in their view must have been expressed in imposing architecture. In the Haṛappan civilization, the lack of palaces and temples have for a long time perplexed researchers and led many to the conclusion about the uniqueness of its sociopolitical order; Piggott (1950) saw the Haṛappan culture as static and monotonous, Fairservis (1967, 1975, 1992) characterized its sociopolitical organization as chiefdom, and Possehl (1998, 2002) sees it as a unique and previously unknown sociopolitical structure.

In my view, in order to trace the emergence of authority on the Haṛappan and Gangetic sites, one needs to abandon any preconceived notions and to approach the existing data in totality. The emergence of authority then can be established by tracing drastic and simultaneous changes in the settlement size, layout and at least several aspects of material culture, such as architecture, sphragistics, numismatics (in the case of the Ganges civilization), figurines, pottery, weapons, agricultural tools, and the like. Archaeological records of both the Ganges and Haṛappan civilizations offer a broad range of traits to be tested for such changes. Of course, the number and nature of these traits will vary depending on the quality, quantity, availability and credibility of archaeological data on each specific site.

Finally, in order to determine whether the idea of the city — a combination of fortifications and authority — reflects any actual historical processes and presents a plausible model for the conceptualization of the ancient South Asian city, one must look into the relationship between the construction of fortifications and the formation of authority from site to site both in the Ganges and Haṛappan civilizations.

Of Walls and Rulers in the Ganges Civilization

The patterns of the emergence of authority and the structural history of fortifications on the archaeological sites of the Ganges civilization reveal some interesting regularities.

FORTIFICATIONS

Kauśāmbī, the capital of the *janapada* of the Vatsas, is one of the largest early historical sites in northern South Asia. Located near Allahabad, on the left bank of the Yamunā River, it is spread over eight square miles and is enclosed by a chain of well-preserved massive ramparts and walls (see *fig.* 1). Particularly massive are the walls, revetments and bastions in the south-western corner and on the eastern side of the site. Yet from the viewpoint of military defence, both the layout and size of the Kauśāmbī fortification system raise serious doubts.

On one hand, given the grandiose scale of fortifications warfare would be the easiest explanation; structural periods III.14, III.16, IV.19 and IV.24 allegedly indicate destruction and contain a significant amount of weapons, 370 arrowheads and 58 fragments of spears for periods III and IV (Sharma 1960: 45-48). On the other hand, the layout of fortifications has several very puzzling features. First, fortifications are truly massive in only two areas: around the so-called palace in the south-western corner of the site, and on the eastern side of

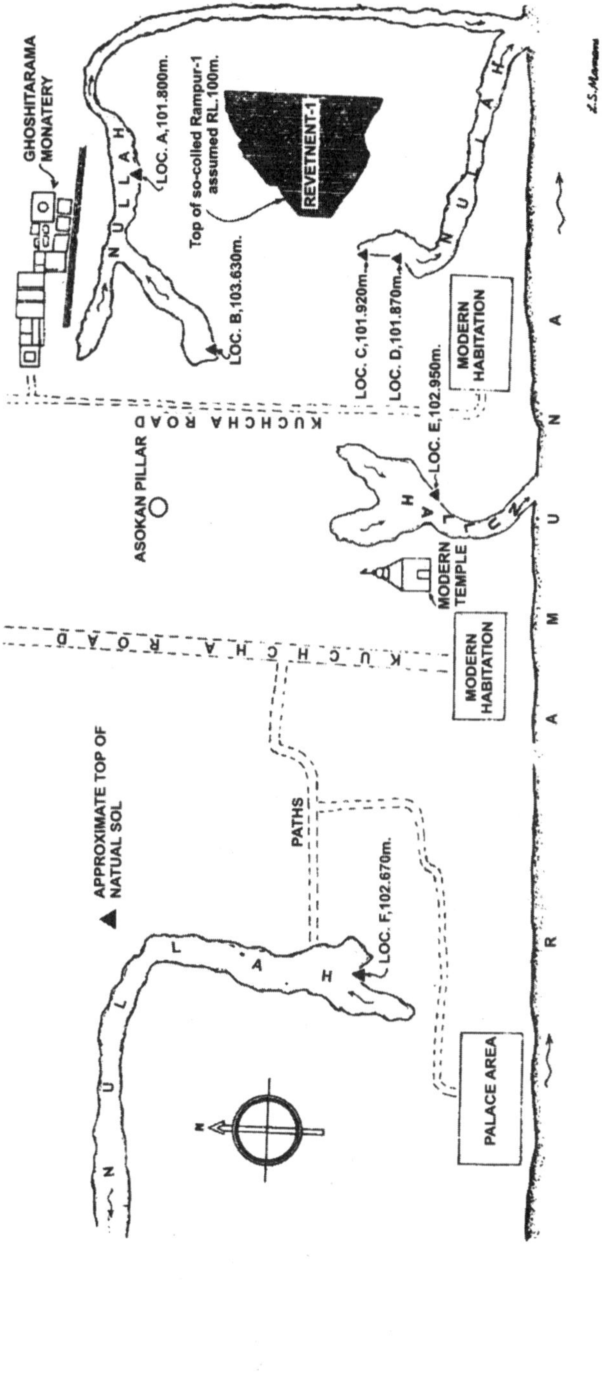

fig 1: Kauśāmbī (after Lal 1979-80)

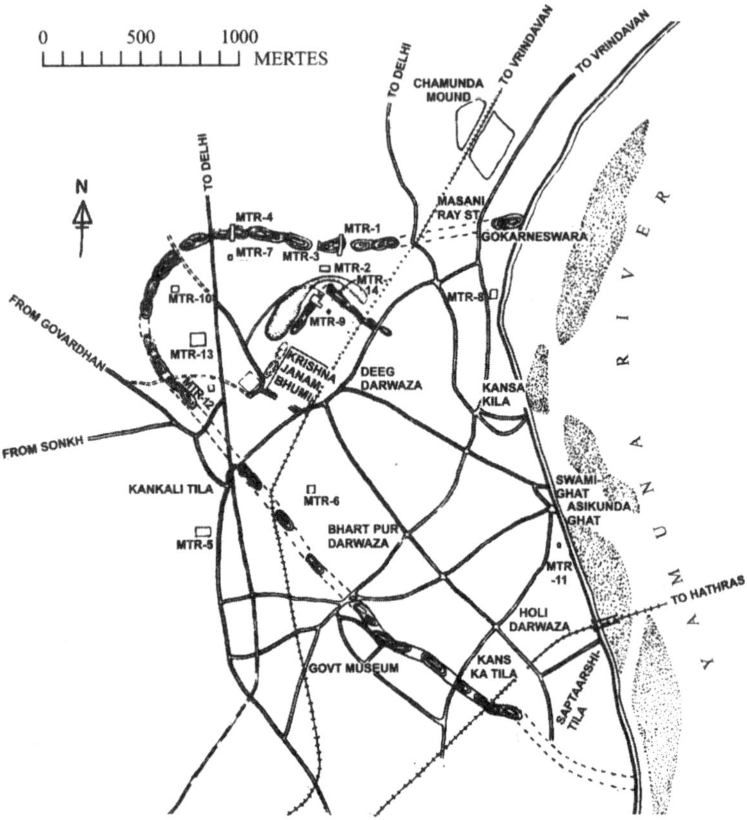

fig. 2: Mathurā (after Joshi 1989)

the site south of the Ghoṣitārāma Monastery. In other areas, ramparts, are much less imposing. Second, there are many wide openings between the ramparts and significant parts of the site are unprotected. For example, the rampart along the Yamunā River has long gaps, which make protection from floods impossible. Third, the chronology of the ramparts has never been properly determined. Yet differences in size, structural history and, most importantly, in the time of initial occupation of the adjacent areas indicate that different ramparts may have been built in different periods of time. If this was the case, Kauśāmbī was fortified not as a one-time event but during a long period of time. Finally, judging from Sharma's structural history, fortifications at Kauśāmbī underwent two main stages of development: the first one centred on ramparts, revetments and the moat; the second one centred on guardrooms, towers and flank walls. Transition from the first to the second stage marked a significant technological shift, which was likely to be caused by a shift in the function of fortifications as well.

Mathurā is another very important early historical site of northern South Asia. Located on the Yamunā River in the district that carries the same name, it is surrounded by ramparts from the west, north and south, and at the first sight, it is quite reasonable to suggest that military function played an important role in the construction of these ramparts; the dimensions of the walls and bastions at Mathurā are massive, the line of fortifications is solid, and in addition to the main fortification system there is a massive internal fort (see *fig.* 2). Nonetheless, other traits of the structural history and layout of the outer rampart challenge both military and ecological explanations. First, the rampart does not protect the site fully. Encircling the site from the west, north and south, it leaves the bank of the Yamunā River completely unprotected. The ecological function, under this scenario, can be completely excluded: even if the site had some protection from floods, the rampart clearly played no role in it. The military function is not certain either; the length of the Yamunā embankment in Mathurā was over 3 km, and it is difficult to imagine how without additional protection the river itself could defend the site militarily. If there had been a necessity to defend the site from military threat by building a high and massive rampart, the bank of the Yamunā River would not have been left unprotected. Second, Joshi notes that in Period III the

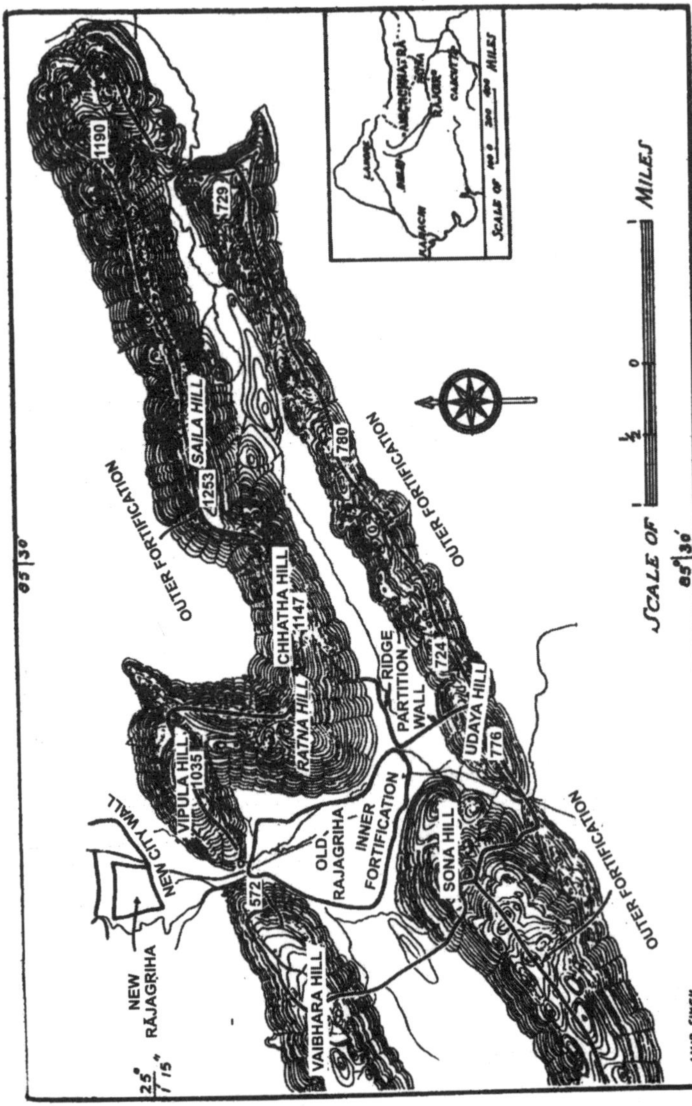

fig. 3: Rājgīr (after Ghosh 1958)

defence wall lost its original function "as a defensive or protective enclosure for the occupants" (M.C. Joshi 1989: 168). Joshi explains this by the presence of occupational deposits over portions of the wall. Yet during Period IV, he notes, the function of the wall was rejuvenated (M.C. Joshi 1989: 169). From the point of view of the history of military conflict in northern India, this structural history makes no sense. If the wall had indeed protected the site from the military threat during Period II, it would not have lost its function during Period III; for it is known that the second and first centuries BCE, to which Period III belongs, was a time of significant military conflict. Moreover, Mathurā was directly involved in this conflict; during the reign of Puṣyamitra Śuṅga the city was allegedly lost to the Greeks.

Rājgīr, or Rājagṛha, is located in Bihar in the district Nālandā, south-west of Biharsharif. Judging from the literary sources, it had been the capital of Magadha until the fifth century BCE when the capital was moved north to Pāṭaliputra. The remains of ancient Rājgīr are thought to consist of two parts: Old Rājgīr and New Rājagṛha (see *fig*. 3). Both parts have been sporadically explored and excavated since the middle of the nineteenth century and both are fortified. Yet, the function of these fortifications is not as clear as it may first seem. There are three sets of fortifications: the outer fortification, the inner Old Rājgīr fortification, and the New Rājgīr fortification. The scale of the outer fortifications is truly unique. No other early historical site in northern India has such a long system of walls. Built of massive and carefully trimmed stones on top of high hills, these walls must have required a very significant consumption of time and labour. Given the role that Rājgīr played in the political history of northern India according to the texts, it is reasonable to assume

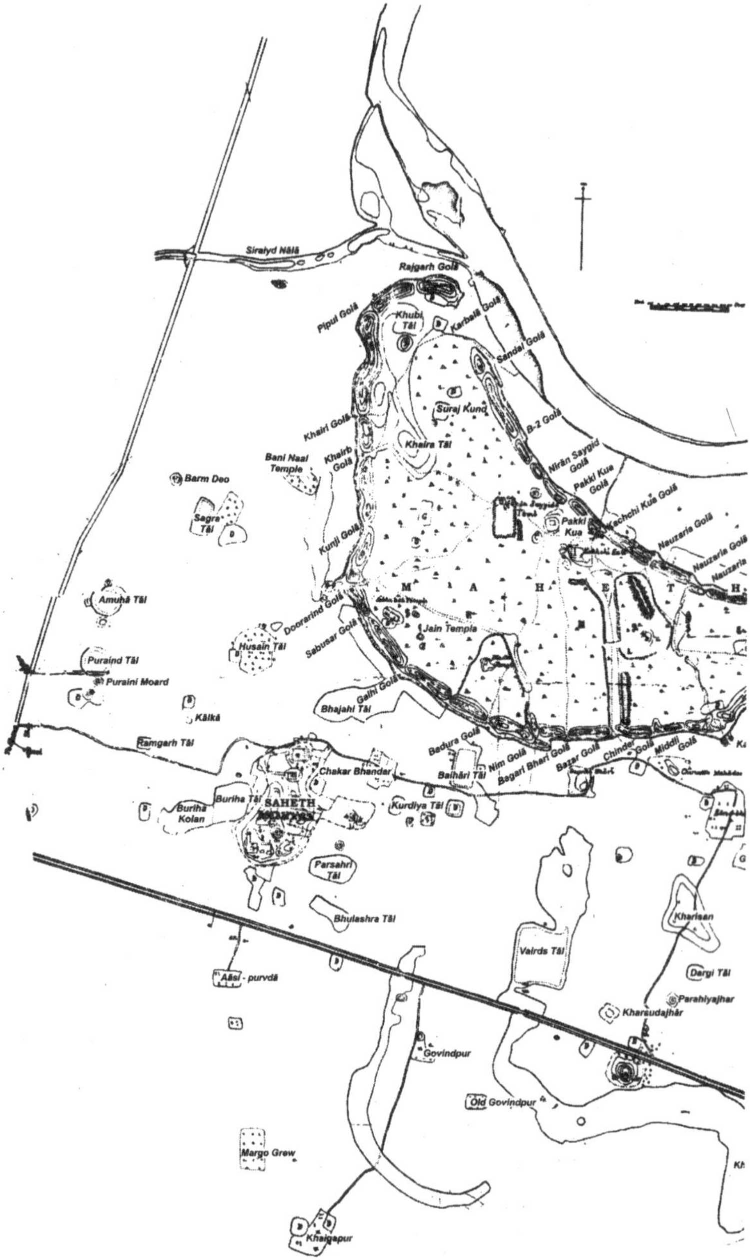
Siraiyd Nālā
Rajgarh Golā
Pipul Golā
Khubi Tāl
Karbalā Golā
Sandai Golā
Suraj Kund
Khairi Golā
Khaira Tāl
B-2 Golā
Bani Naal Temple
Khairb Golā
Barm Deo
Sagra Tāl
Pakki Kua Golā
Pakki Kua
Kachchi Kua Golā
Neuzaria Golā
Kunji Golā
Amuhā Tāl
M A H E T H
Doorarind Golā
Jain Templa
Sabusar Golā
Husain Tāl
Puraind Tāl
Puraini Moard
Galhi Golā
Bhajahi Tāl
Kālkā
Ramgarh Tāl
Badura Golā
Nim Golā
Bagari Bhari Golā
Bazar Golā
Chinder Golā
Middli Golā
Chakar Bhandar
Baihāri Tāl
Buriha Tāl
SAHETH
Buriha Kolan
Kurdiya Tāl
Parsahri Tāl
Bhulashra Tāl
Kharisan
Vairds Tāl
Aāsi - purvdā
Dargi Tāl
Parahiyajhar
Kharsudajhār
Govindpur
Old Govindpur
Margo Grew
Khaigapur

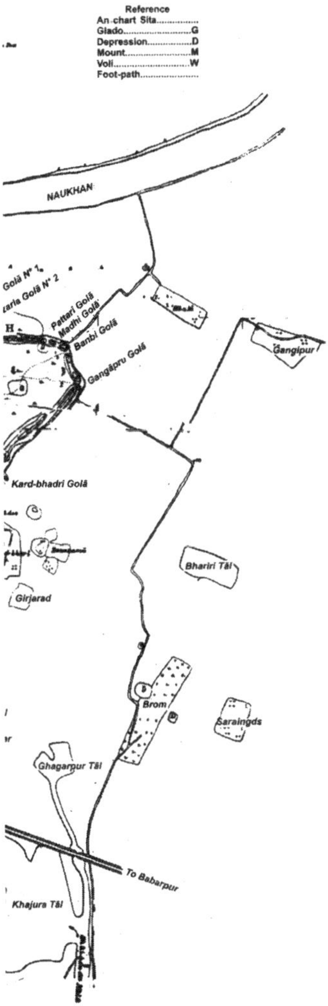

fig. 4: Śrāvastī (after Vogel 1908)

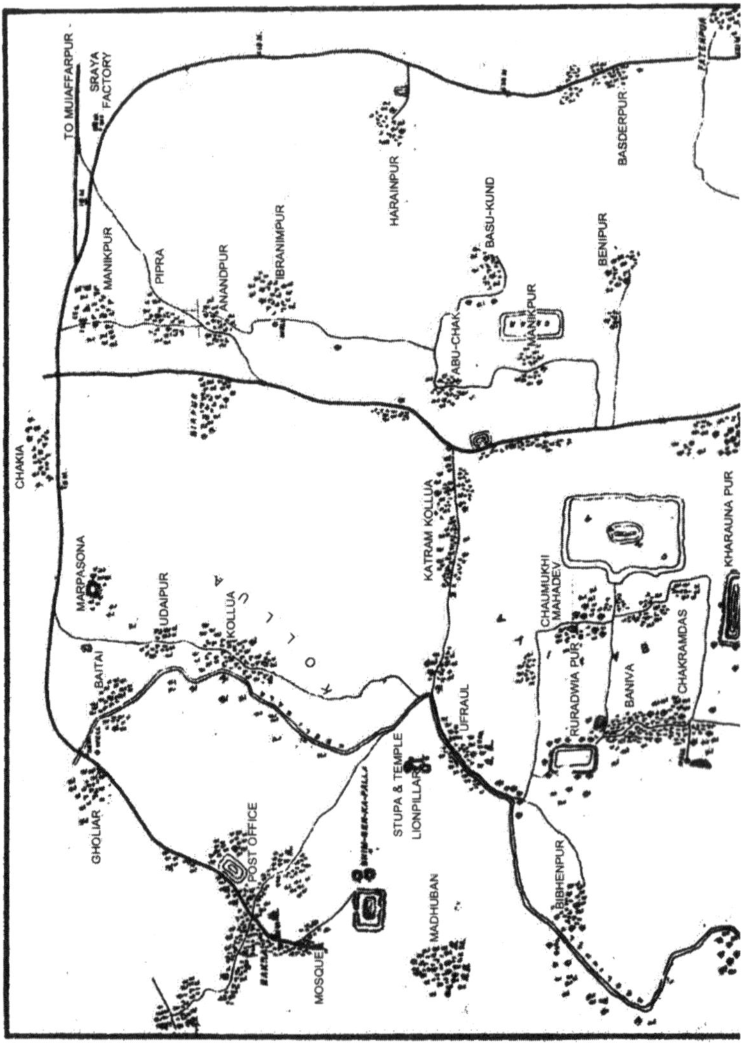
TO MUIAFFARPUR
SRAYA FACTORY
MANIKPUR
PIPRA
ANANDPUR
IBRANIMPUR
HARAINPUR
BASU-KUND
BENIPUR
BASDERPUR
ABU-CHAK
MANIKPUR
CHAKIA
KATRAM KOLLUA
KHARAUNA PUR
MARPASONA
UDAIPUR
KOLLUA
CHAUMUKHI MAHADEV
CHAKRAMDAS
BANIYA
RURADWIA PUR
UFRAUL
BAITAI
STUPA & TEMPLE
LIONPILLAR
GHOLIAR
POST OFFICE
MADHUBAN
BIBHENPUR
MOSQUE

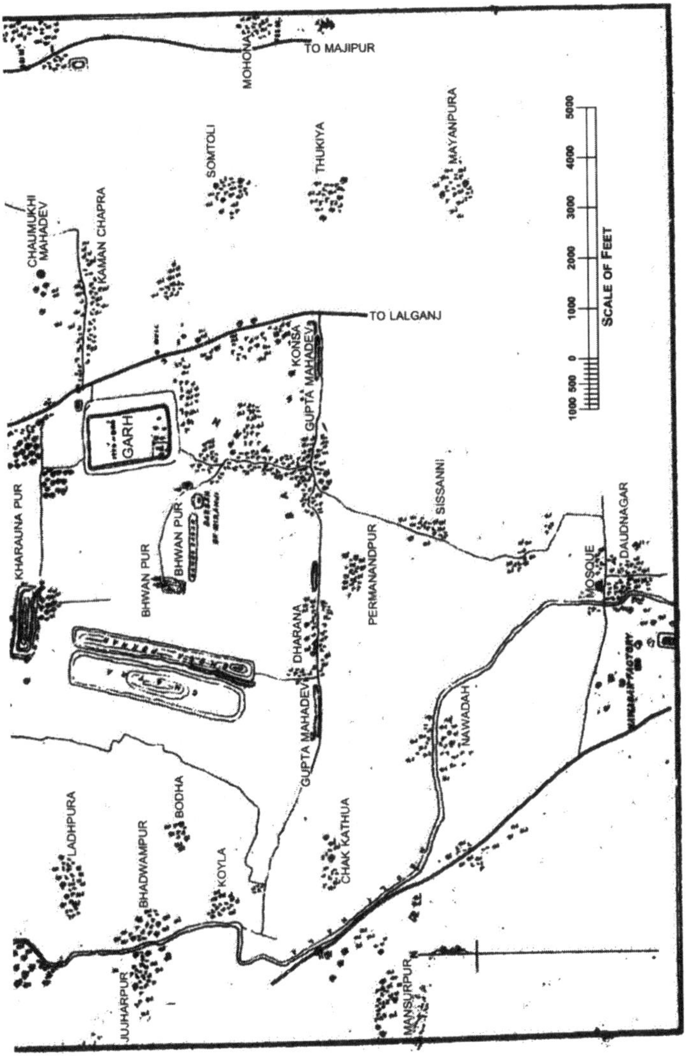

fig. 5: Vaiśālī (after Sinha and Roy 1969).

that the sole reason for the construction of such an elaborate network of fortifications was military conflict. Indeed, as the first capital of Magadha, Rājgīr was involved in several military conflicts during the sixth and fifth centuries BCE. Under Bimbisāra and his son Ajātaśatru, Magadha waged at least three important wars: with the kingdom of Aṅga, with the kingdom of Kosala, and with the confederacy of Vṛjji. Nevertheless, the complexity of the three-levelled fortification system of Rājgīr seems to exceed its military needs. The internal ramparts and parapet walls surrounded by high hills with narrow passes must have provided sufficient defence without long and massive outer fortifications. In fact, Rājgīr was the only early historical site in northern India which had such an advantageous location from the viewpoint of defence. Furthermore, if the outer fortification wall had been built prior to the transfer of the capital from Rājgīr to Pāṭaliputra, one would expect for the fortification system of Pāṭaliputra to have been at least as powerful as the fortification system at Rājgīr; for in the fifth century, military conflicts between the *janapada*s intensified yet the location chosen for Pāṭaliputra was more vulnerable than the location of Rājgīr. If the outer wall had been built after the transfer of the capital from Rājgīr to Pāṭaliputra, one would still expect for the fortification system of Pāṭaliputra to have been more powerful; for after the transfer of the capital the centre of power, trade and military defence would have certainly gravitated towards the capital. Texts and archaeology nevertheless show the opposite. Wooden palisades that surrounded Pāṭaliputra clearly did not match the strength and elaboration of the fortification system of Rājgīr.

The magnitude of the defence system of Rājgīr thus appears to have been militarily unjustified. In my opinion, it is likely that the construction of the outer fortifications was motivated by a combination of military and symbolic concerns. Considering that Rājgīr gave birth to a consecutive chain of dynasties, one of which eventually united northern South Asia under the imperial rule, it is not unreasonable to suggest that its fortification system played a certain role in the glorification and solidification of authority. Moreover, fortifications are currently the only archaeological proof of authority in Rājgīr during the pre-Mauryan and Mauryan periods.

Śrāvastī or Sahet-Mahet is located in the districts of Goṇḍā and Bahraich, near the modern border between India and Nepal. According to literary tradition, it was one of the two capitals of Kosala, a *janapada* that played a very important role in early Indian history. The archaeological remains of Śrāvastī are scattered on two sites, Sahet and Mahet that are separated from each other by a small strip of land (see *fig*. 4). Sahet is a Buddhist establishment; Mahet is a large city, surrounded by a rampart with a brick wall on top of it. Despite the massive size and technological sophistication of this rampart, there are many indicators of its symbolic use. First, the rampart had many wide openings located at similar intervals from each other. None of these openings revealed the remains of gates. Second, during the first two structural phases (*c*. third-second centuries BCE), the rampart was low, its slope was gradual and at some point it might have been used as a "dumping ground." Third, the site of Sahet is not well protected and there are numerous signs of occupation beyond the rampart of Mahet. Fourth, the current dating of the rampart places its initial construction in the third century BCE, i.e. after the struggle for power between the *janapada*s was over and a significant portion of northern South Asia was united under the rule of the Mauryas. Finally, fifth, the parapet wall was built either during the late Mauryan period or in the third century CE.

What unites all these traits is that, if one takes all of them into consideration, neither military defence nor protection from floods can sufficiently explain the function of the rampart. Wide openings and the gradual slope makes the rampart vulnerable. The use of the rampart as a dumping area makes no sense from a military perspective. The fact that the rampart was built well into the Mauryan period is odd given the history of the military conflict in northern India. Finally, if Aboshi et al. (1999: 135) are right in dating the wall on top of the rampart by the third century CE, this means that the major strengthening of the fortification system was carried out past many important military conflicts.

Vaiśālī or Basārh is located about 22 miles north of Patna, Bihar. According to literary tradition, it was the capital of the republic of Licchavis and was founded by King Viśāla of the Ikṣvāku lineage. The site comprises a number of localities scattered around a large area (see *fig*. 5). No trace of a fortification system that would enclose all of these localities has been discovered. The only locality that has a circumvallation is Rājā-Viśāla-kā-Gaṛh, a rectangular mound measuring approximately 500 by 240 m. This circumvallation was built around the second century BCE and consisted of a rampart, a moat and a brick wall. Three points are particularly important for the understanding of the function of this fortification system. First, it was built quite late, in the beginning of the Śuṅga period around the second century BCE. Second, the structural history of this fortification system is quite unusual; the construction of a brick wall precedes the construction of a rampart and moat, and not vice versa. Third, the relationship and the degree of integration between separate localities of Vaiśālī — Rājā-Viśāla-kā-Gaṛh, Kharauna tank, Buddhist stūpa, Bhīmsen-kā-Palla, Cakramdas, Baniyā, Lālpura and Virpur — are very unclear. Are all these localities parts of a single entity or are they separate sites? No one, so far, has properly addressed this question yet everyone treats these sites as innate parts of Vaiśālī. The nature of the relationship between these localities may however shed light to the function/s of fortifications on Rājā-Viśāla-kā-Gaṛh. If the mound of Rājā-Viśāla-kā-Gaṛh represented only one district of Vaiśālī the rampart evidently carried a segregative or symbolic function. Taking into consideration the proximity of localities to each other, the small size of Rājā-Viśāla-kā-Gaṛh, and the information about Vaiśālī found in Sanskrit and Pāli texts, I tend to believe that the localities of Vaiśālī were indeed parts of one entity, and the meaning of fortifications around the Gaṛh had to do with the symbolical demarcation of space. Interestingly, Sinha and Roy (1969: 118), who excavated at Vaiśālī on behalf of the Jayaswal Research Institute, suggested that Gaṛh was a market place. Based on the reading of several seals, they asserted that "it was wise to make a market place on a comparatively higher ground that the surrounding ground level, so that the place might not become damp and spoil the articles stored therein." Consequently, "the ramparts in different periods were nothing but strong revetments of this artificial elevated ground."

Such is a brief summary of archaeological data from the sites that provide the most convincing evidence for the non-utilitarian meaning of their fortifications systems. This evidence can be summarized in the six following traits:

1. The excessive monumentality of ramparts, bastions and revetments;
2. The layout impractical from the military or ecological point of view (wide gaps and large unprotected areas);
3. Inefficient military characteristics such as the low height and gradual slopes of ramparts and walls;

4. The disuse of ramparts in certain periods expressed in the creation of dumping areas and the construction of buildings on top of ramparts;
5. Chronological incongruity between the construction of fortifications and the history of military conflict in northern India, i.e. the construction of fortifications in the periods of a relative political stability and the absence or disuse of fortifications in the periods of active military conflict; and
6. The presence of important habitational areas beyond the line of fortifications.

In addition, Gangetic fortifications display significant similarities, i.e. the shape and layout of ramparts and parapet walls, the presence of wide openings, and certain patterns of structural history. Importantly, these similarities are characteristic of many sites, not just of those mentioned above. For example, Ahicchatra, Atrañjikherā, Bhītā, Pāṭaliputra, and Rājghāṭ are likely to follow similar patterns. The rampart at Ahicchatra is excessively monumental, displays military inefficiencies during its early structural phases, and is characterized by chronological incongruities with the history of military conflicts (see *IAR* 1963-64: 43-44; 1964-65: 39-42; Bajpai 1986, Ghosh and Panigrahi 1946, Law 1942, Paul 1986, Singh 1979). The rampart at Atrañjikherā is too small during the first two structural phases and the parapet wall is not built until the end of the Mauryan or even Śuṅga periods (see Gaur 1983: 6-10, 254-56). Bhītā is divided into two parts by a large segregative rampart (see *IAR* 95-96: 74, Marshall 1915: 40). The wooden palisades of Pāṭaliputra are too weak to provide an effective military defence of the site which was the capital of the first great South Asian empire and one of the biggest cities of the ancient world (see Altekar and Mishra

1959, Devi, Sahai, and Sinha 1980, Kumar 1987, McCrindle 1877: 66-68, Mukherji 1898, Patil 1963: 394-400, Sinha and Narain 1970, Spooner 1913, Waddel 1892, 1903). Rājghāṭ, although being an obscure case — Narain and Roy (1976: 21-35) never found a convincing evidence of circumvallation in the area that they excavated — reveals remains of massive freestanding structures which are unlikely to have carried a utilitarian function (see *IAR* 1957-1958: 50-51; 1960-1961: 35-39; 1961-1962: 57-59; 1962-1963: 41-42; 1963-1964: 58-59; 1964-1965: 44-45; 1965-1966: 54-55; 1966-1967: 44; 1968-1969: 41; Narain and Roy 1976).

By using the term "non-utilitarian" with regard to fortification systems on all of these sites I mean that their overall significance was ideational and symbolic, rather than military, ecological, or technical. Since the archaeology of the Ganges civilization does not provide much evidence for monumental architecture, fortifications remain the main symbol of conspicuous consumption and control of labour. By delineating space in a monumental manner, the walls, ramparts, and bastions must have marked some important sociopolitical changes and processes that took place in the Ganges civilization. Figuratively speaking, fortifications created the inner worlds or the mesocosms of the first urban centres. This is not to say that the military or ecological concerns played no role whatsoever; in one way or another, warfare and floods may have contributed to the construction of fortification systems. Yet the main meaning of these massive dividing structures must have been ideological rather than utilitarian. What kind of ideas they carried of course is a much more difficult question. Archaeological evidence for authority comes handy as an aid for addressing this question.

AUTHORITY

Tracing the emergence of authority from site to site in the

Ganges civilization, one comes across a number of important transformations in material culture. These include settlement expansion, intensification and sophistication of structural activities, the introduction of burnt-brick architecture, the beginning of regular planning, the minting of coins, the emergence of seals and sealings, the manufacture of human figurines, the transition to mass-produced and simplified pottery, the increase in the amount of weaponry, and the emergence of hierarchies in settlement patterns. In its own unique way, each of these changes is indicative of social transformations. Settlement expansion usually points to the increase in population density. Population density in turn implies a higher social complexity, and, potentially, the shaping of authority. The drastic sophistication and differentiation of architecture often indicates changes in kinship and sociopolitical organization that result in the emergence of elites and forming of authoritative structures. Coins and seals are indicative of authority, for their production, use, and circulation require the existence of complex trade mechanisms, ownership rights, control of minting, high-level political decision-making, the existence of steady sociopolitical or religious groups, and generally a high degree of economic complexity. One by one, these traits are not necessarily indicative of authority. Conjointly, they constitute a much more substantial proof of social transformations and the emergence of strong authoritative structures. In some cases, it is possible to trace concurrent change in all of these traits. In other cases, one can only find evidence of changes in architecture, settlement size, seals, and coins. The following examples provide a good sample of data currently available from the Ganges civilization.

In Ahicchatra changes indicative of major social transformations include the construction of fortifications, the emergence of brick structures, site expansion, the introduction of coinage, and planning in accordance with cardinal directions. All these changes are attributed to a relatively short period of time and appear in Strata 6 (first century BCE) of the periodization by Dikshit and Ghosh (see Ghosh and Panigrahi 1946) and in Period IV (Kuṣāṇa Period) in the periodization by Banerjee (see *IAR* 64-65: 39-42). In Atrañjikherā, evidence for authority is more substantial. It includes the construction of fortifications, the expansion of settlement, intensification of structural activities, the emergence of brick architecture, the introduction of coinage, increase in weaponry, the appearance of human terracotta figurines, and the manufacture of agricultural tools made of iron (*IAR* 1967-68: 45-46; 1968-1969: 37-38; Gaur 1983: 6-10). All these changes occur during Phases B and C of Period IV (500-200 BCE). Bhītā provides ample evidence for the presence of authority. Fortifications, architecture, regular planning, seals and coins point to the presence of authority roughly by the Mauryan period (Marshall 1915: 30-31, 35-36, 40-41, 44-61). It is however impossible at this point to reconstruct the precise chronological context for the emergence of authority at Bhītā; for the chronology and periodization of this site are basically non-existent. In Kauśāmbī, the main criteria for tracing authority are fortifications, architecture and coins. Since the chronologies of the fortifications and the alleged palace are poorly defined, archaeological evidence for the formation of authority is best traced in the areas of the Aśokan pillar and the Ghoṣitārāma monastery. Each area has its own periodization. In the area of the Aśokan pillar, major qualitative changes can be attributed to Sub-Period IA, dated to mid-fourth century BCE (Sharma 1969: 24-25, 37). In the area of the Ghoṣitārāma monastery, changes indicative of authority are associated with the construction of the *stūpa* and can be attributed to Phase II dated to around fifth century BCE (*IAR* 1955-56: 20). In Mathurā, evidence for authority includes the construction of fortifications, the expansion of the settlement, the emergence of brick architecture, the introduction of coins, the manufacture of human figurines, simplification and mass production of standardized pottery, and hierarchy in the settlement patterns of the adjacent region (Joshi 1989). All these changes are associated with the transition from Period I to Period II of Joshi's periodization (fourth century BCE). Pāṭaliputra provides no evidence for authority during the pre-Mauryan period. In the Mauryan period, the only possible indication of authority is the famous Pillared Hall of Kumrahār. The function, archaeological context and structural history of this hall are however poorly understood. In Rājghāṭ, the changes that are indicative of authority include the emergence of complex burnt brick architecture, seals, sealings, and coins. The changes become evident in the beginning of Period II (third-second centuries BCE) (Narain and Roy 1976: 21-35). In Rājgīr, the main evidence for a complex sociopolitical organization and authority in the pre-Mauryan and Mauryan periods is the system of fortifications. In Soṅkh, the formation of authority is associated with the emergence of baked brick architecture, regular planning of houses and residential units, inscribed coins, new weapons and iron tools. All these innovations are attributed to Layer 27 (second century BCE) according to the periodization by Hartel (1993: 33, 85). In Śrāvastī, evidence for authority includes fortifications, burnt-brick architecture, planning of houses and residential units, mass-produced, simple and utilitarian red ware, human figurines, inscribed seals and several workshops (K.K. Sinha 1967: 9, 19-20, 41-46, 52-57, 69-71, 73-77). All these innovations are the result of the transition from Period I to Period II in the periodization by K.K. Sinha (1967: 7-16) and from Period II to Period III in the periodization by Aboshi et al. (1999: 135). In both periodizations, this transition takes place around the third century BCE. Finally, in Vaiśālī the emergence of authority is associated with the construction of fortifications and burnt-brick house complexes on Rājā-Viśāla-kā-Gaṛh, with the expansion of the site and the establishment of new neighbourhoods, with the production of simplified and standardized Red and Buff Wares which gradually replace the NBPW, with the emergence of human figurines, and with the introduction of coinage, seals and sealings. In the periodization by Deva and Mishra (1961: 11-13), all these

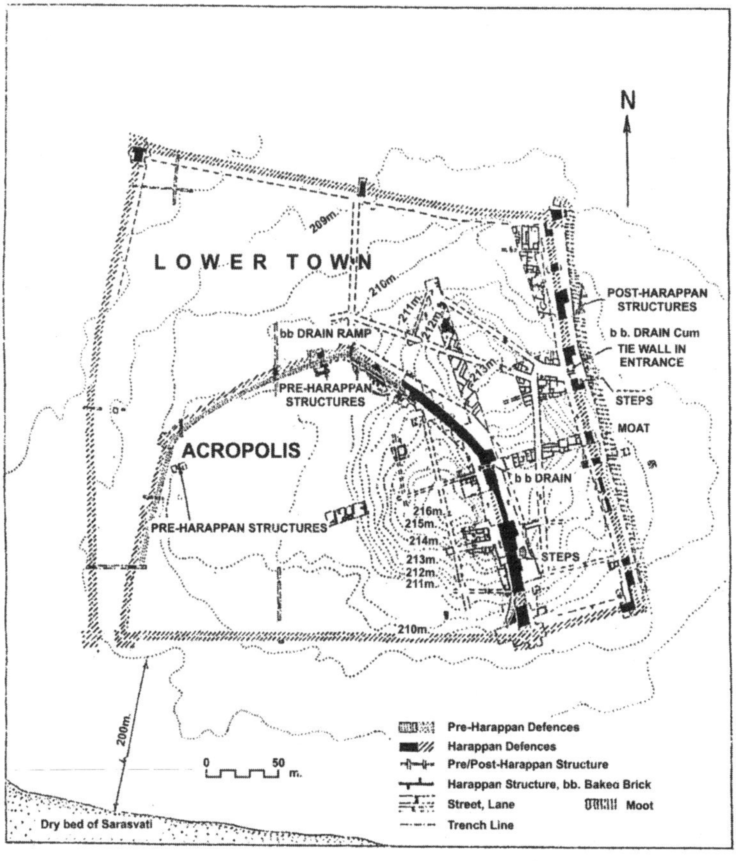

fig. 6: Banawālī (after *IAR* 1987-1988).

changes occur in Period II (150-100 BCE). In the periodization defined by Sinha and Roy (1969: 9-16, 26-28, 33-35, 118), these changes are attributed to the first part of Period III (second-first century BCE).

Thus, currently available data from Ahicchatra, Atrañjikherā, Kauśāmbī, Mathurā, Rājghāṭ, Śrāvastī, Soṅkh and Vaiśālī provide substantial evidence for the existence of strong authoritative structures. Importantly, the emergence of these structures can be placed in a chronological context. Data from Bhītā, Pāṭaliputra and Rājgīr provide enough evidence for showing the presence of authority, yet not for establishing the chronologies of its genesis.

Nevertheless, when placed in the context of cross-cultural and comparative studies, most of the traits indicative of

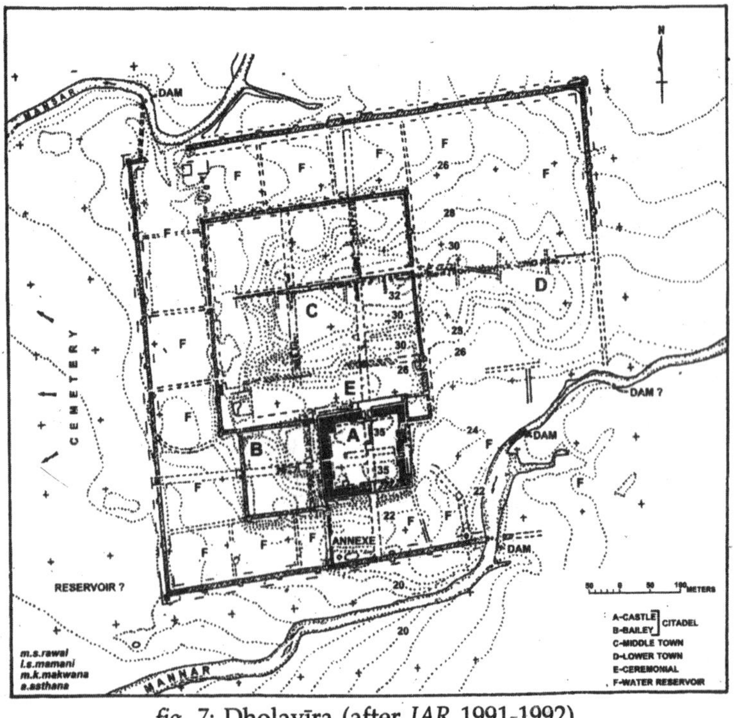

fig. 7: Dholavīra (after *IAR* 1991-1992).

authority on the sites of the Ganges civilization leave a sense of deficiency. For example, the changes in architecture being important in the local context are modest if compared to the changes that took place at the initial stages of urbanization in Mesopotamia, Egypt, or Mesoamerica. There are no pyramids, monumental palaces, and spacious assembly halls at the sites of the Ganges civilization; the pillared hall at Pāṭaliputra and the alleged palace at Kauśāmbī are neither properly identified, nor credibly dated. As far as the ritual or authoritative paraphernalia, monumental art, and inscribed seals are concerned, none of these traits are present on the sites of the Ganges civilization at least until the Mauryan period. The only archaeological feature which is unmistakably indicative of major social transformations and the emergence of strong authoritative institutions is an elaborate system of fortifications. In a sense, fortifications have become the epitome and symbol of complexity, social disparity, and power in the Ganges civilization. In Rājgīr, the stone wall, which runs for more than 40 km over several ranges of hills, is currently the only archaeological proof of sociopolitical complexity prior to the Gupta Period. In Kauśāmbī, colossal bastions, ramparts and revetments surpass in magnitude all other structural remains and constitute the main evidence for authority and control of labour. In a similar way, ramparts, bastions, parapet walls, and revetments are the most unambiguous evidence for the existence of authoritative structures in Ahicchatra, Atrañjikherā, Bhītā, Mathurā, Śrāvastī, Vaiśālī and possibly Rājghāṭ.

The archaeological signature of authority in the Ganges civilization thus is quite unique. In a number of ancient civilizations, authority is symbolized by lavish material expressions; monumental architecture, elite burials, luxurious objects of art, writing, seals, and the like. In the Ganges civilization, evidence for authority comes mostly from fortifications and, to a lesser degree, from the dynamics of settlement expansion, the sophistication of architecture, the introduction of regular planning, and the emergence of inscribed seals. For some reason, authorities of the Gangetic sites did not need palaces, temples, rich burials, and objects of luxury; their ethos was expressed in ramparts, walls, bastions and revetments.

This unusual expression of power evokes a number of possible scenarios for the genesis of sociopolitical complexity. In one way or another, each of these scenarios points, in my view, to the same sociocultural process: the formation of territorially bound identities. In other words, the crystallization of authority in the Ganges civilization must have been accompanied by the formation of new local identities, while the delineation of space by massive ramparts, walls and bastions was the material expression of the division between ours and theirs, internal and external, domestic and alien. This shaping of identity, i.e. the emergence of a sense of belonging to a certain place, group, sociocultural entity or any other imagined world, was an impetus and an essential part of the processes of the formation of authority. The emergence of authority and the formation of territorially bound identities thus were the two facets of the same process, which was materialized in the encircling of important sites by massive fortifications. In this respect, it is worth noting that many of the Gangetic fortifications had their own original shapes; the top plans of the fortifications at Bhītā, Mathurā, Śrāvastī, Vaiśālī, as well as at several other Gangetic sites presented unique and individual patterns. It is not impossible that these patterns were also part of the symbolic expression of local identity.

Many sites of the Ganges civilization match this model. Even Soṅkh, which has no fortifications, arguably falls in the same pattern. Located only 30 km away from Mathurā, Soṅkh was in the shade of Mathurā's political power. Before the rise of Mathurā there was an attempt to build a circumvallation at Soṅkh (Hartel 1993: 25). At that time, Soṅkh was equal to Mathurā and its population must have experienced similar processes of the formation of identity and authority. The further rise of Mathurā to political power overrode these processes. Soṅkh did not develop the form of authority that would need to define its identity through the construction of massive fortifications. It is no coincidence that qualitative changes that characterize Level 27 in the cultural sequence of Soṅkh were chronologically contemporaneous with the reign of Sūryamitra in Mathurā (Hartel 1993: 33).

This model also agrees with the information provided by literary sources. The rise of the *janapada*s could not be complete without the formation of *janapada* identities. Given that most of the reviewed sites were the capitals of *janapada*s, the notions of space, territory and of one's own sociocultural world must have played a key role in this process.

To conclude, one must say that it is difficult to reconstruct the precise form of authoritative structures of the Gangetic sites from the existing archaeological record. What the current state of data allows us to do instead is to understand some processes involved in the genesis of these structures. One of such processes was the formation of local identities expressed in the symbolic delineation of space by means of the construction of massive fortification systems.

Of Walls and Rulers in the Haṛappan Civilization

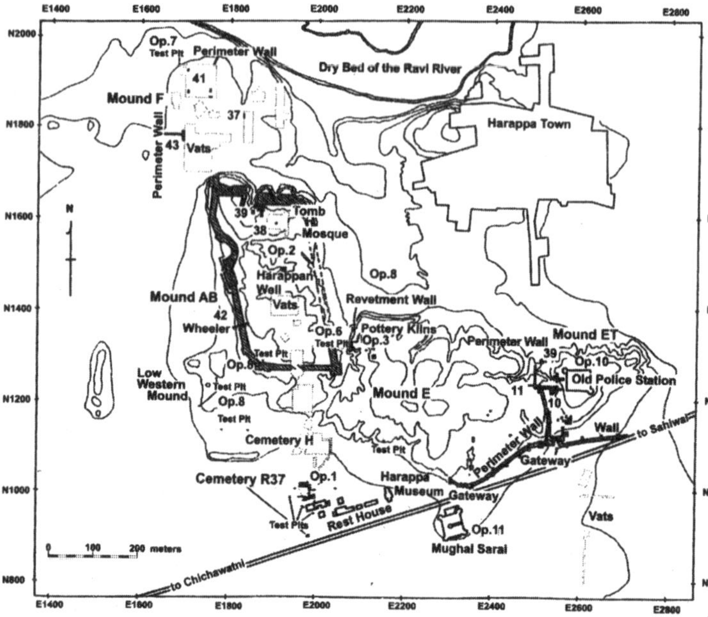

fig. 8: Haṛappā (after Meadow et al. 1999)

As in the case with the Ganges civilization, the reassessment of data on fortifications and authority from a representative sample of sites of the Haṛappan civilization reveals a number of intriguing regularities.

FORTIFICATIONS

Most Haṛappan sites are fortified and provide circumstantial evidence for the ideational meaning of their fortification systems. The archaeological remains of Banawālī, Dholavīra, Kālibaṅgan, Haṛappā, Lothal, Moheṅjo-Dāṛo, Nausharo, and Surkoṭaḍā are particularly revealing.

Banawālī is located on the banks of the lost Hakra River in the district Hissar in Haryana, and, despite being a relatively small site (400 × 400 m), has an elaborate and impressive system of fortifications. Besides being surrounded and divided by mud-brick walls, it has a moat and a channel on the eastern

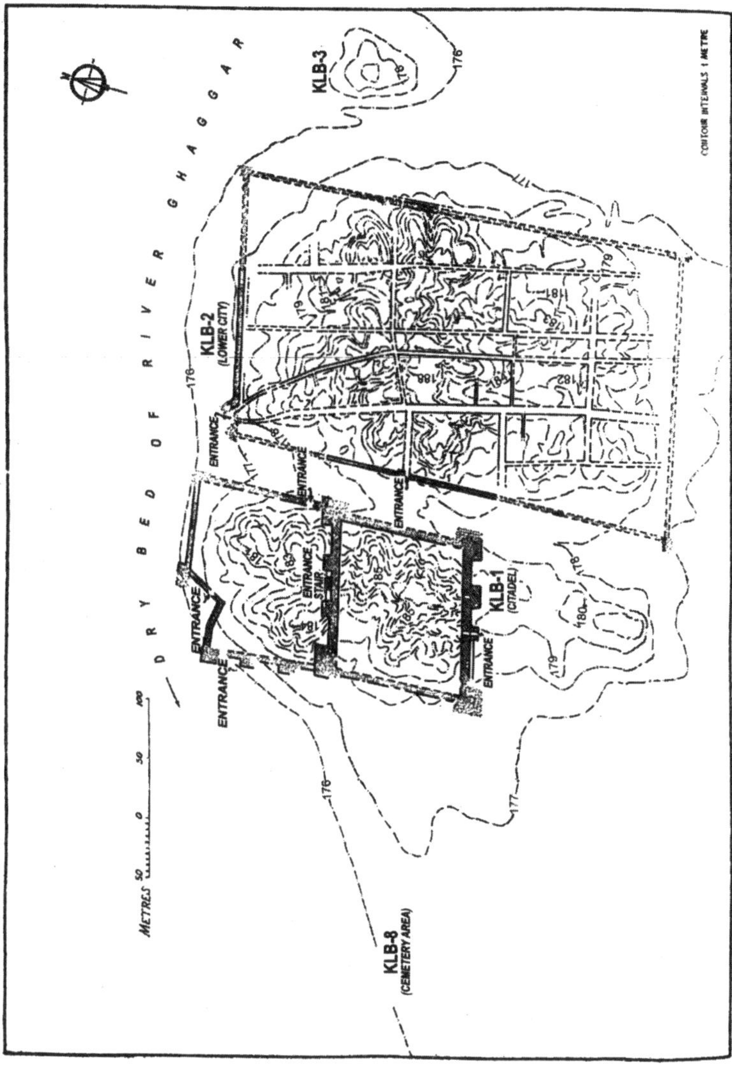

fig. 9: Kālibaṅgan (after *IAR* 1968-1969)

side, several bastions and gates, a ring road running on the outer side of the perimeter walls, an internal system of roads related to fortifications and gates, and at least one platform (see *fig*. 6). As far as the function of this fortification system is

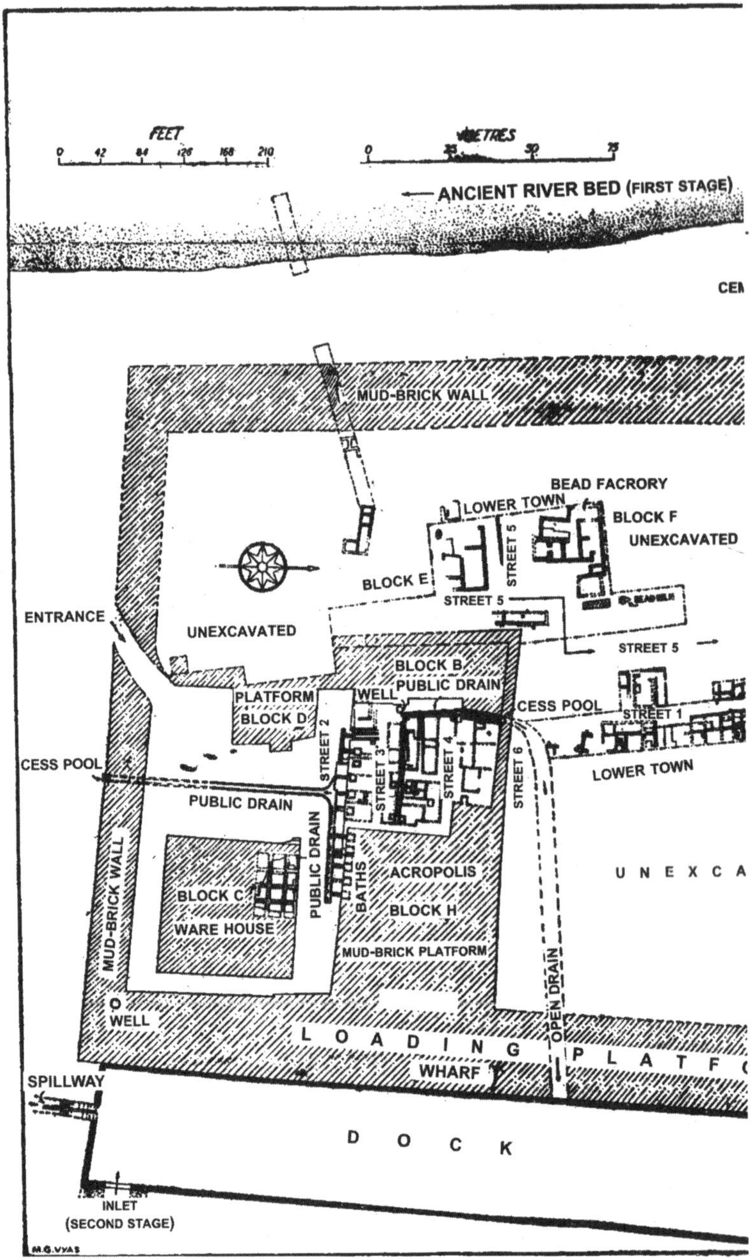
FEET
0 42 84 126 168 210
METRES
0 25 50 75
ANCIENT RIVER BED (FIRST STAGE)
MUD-BRICK WALL
BEAD FACRORY
LOWER TOWN
BLOCK F
UNEXCAVATED
STREET 5
BLOCK E
STREET 5
STREET 5
ENTRANCE
UNEXCAVATED
BLOCK B
PUBLIC DRAIN
PLATFORM
BLOCK D
WELL
CESS POOL
STREET 1
STREET 2
STREET 3
STREET 4
STREET 6
LOWER TOWN
CESS POOL
PUBLIC DRAIN
PUBLIC DRAIN
MUD-BRICK WALL
BLOCK C
WARE HOUSE
BATHS
ACROPOLIS
BLOCK H
MUD-BRICK PLATFORM
UNEXCA
OPEN DRAIN
WELL
LOADING
PLATF
WHARF
SPILLWAY
DOCK
INLET
(SECOND STAGE)
M.G.VYAS

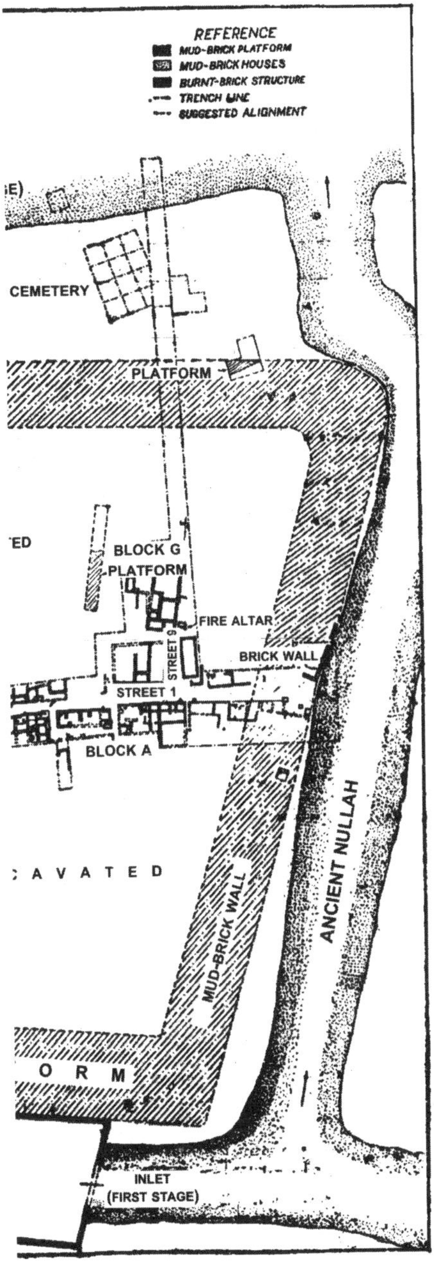

fig. 10: Lothal (after Rao 1973).

concerned, it appears that at least until the Mature Haṛappan period, it performed a symbolic role. First, the wall was too thin to carry a military function. Second, the first significant structural modification resulted in the segregation of space that must have had direct sociopolitical or religious implications. Third, only one platform was so far detected. Given the locations and size of this platform, it is unlikely that it was built as a measure against floods. More likely, similar to the platforms of Moheṅjo-Dāṛo and other Haṛappan

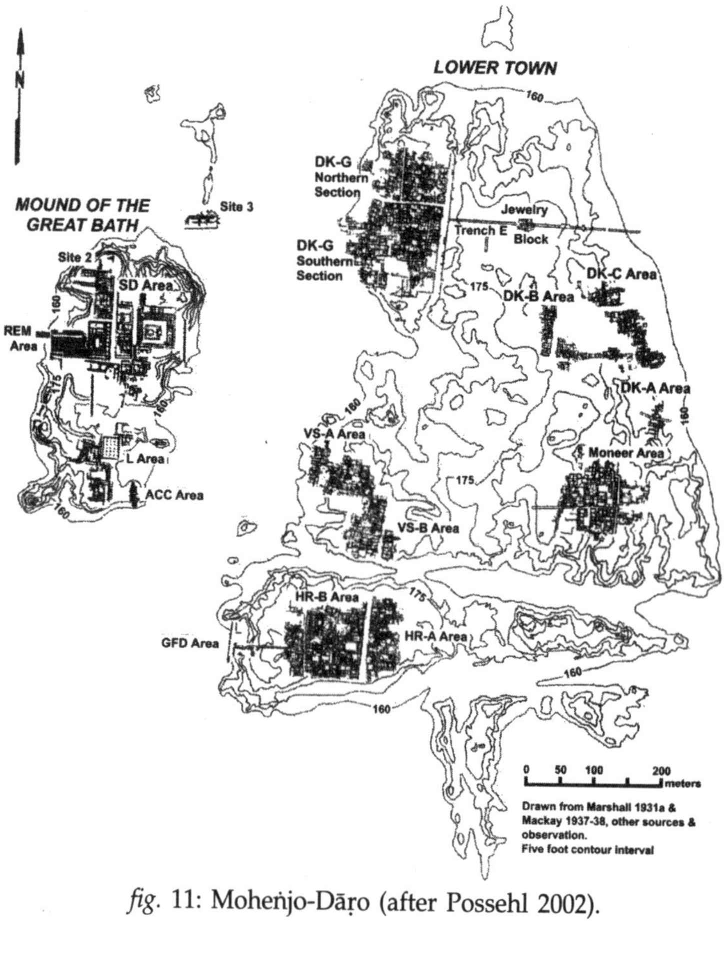

fig. 11: Moheṅjo-Dāṛo (after Possehl 2002).

sites, this platform elevated an important structure and by doing so carried a political or religious function (*IAR* 1987-88: 25). Fourth, there were structures outside the fortifications wall (Bisht 1998-99: 15-16). In fact, the earliest wall was built right on top of the structures constructed during Period IA (Bisht 1987: 142). Hence, even at the earliest stages, the wall did not mark the actual boundary of the settlement. Fifth, the shape of the pre-Haṛappan wall was smoothly incorporated in the natural landscape. According to the excavators, it was "designed like a large oval following the existing natural elevation" (*IAR* 1987-88: 23).

Dholavīra is located on Kadir Island off the Great Rann of Kutch in the district Kutch of Gujarat, India. Bisht believes that in its heyday, the site covered over 100 hectares; for the fortified area alone measures at 800 × 650 m, or 52 hectares (see *fig*. 7). The system of fortifications is one of the most striking and characteristic features of this remarkable site. Judging from the available data, it evolved gradually from the local pre-Haṛappan traditions and by stage III of the periodization by Bisht (1999: 403; *IAR* 1991-92: 26-31) transformed into a complex network of walls, gates, passages, bastions, and encircling roads. The immensity and complexity of the Dholavīra fortification system during the Mature Haṛappan Period is so amazing that many of its structural features have no parallels on other Haṛappan sites. Based on the currently available data, one can highlight five points, which, in my view, are the most characteristic of this unique architectural complex and, in one way or another, are indicative of its possible meanings.

1. From the time of its initial construction during Stage I, fortifications at Dholavīra were truly grandiose. For example, the earliest perimeter wall reached 11.1 m in

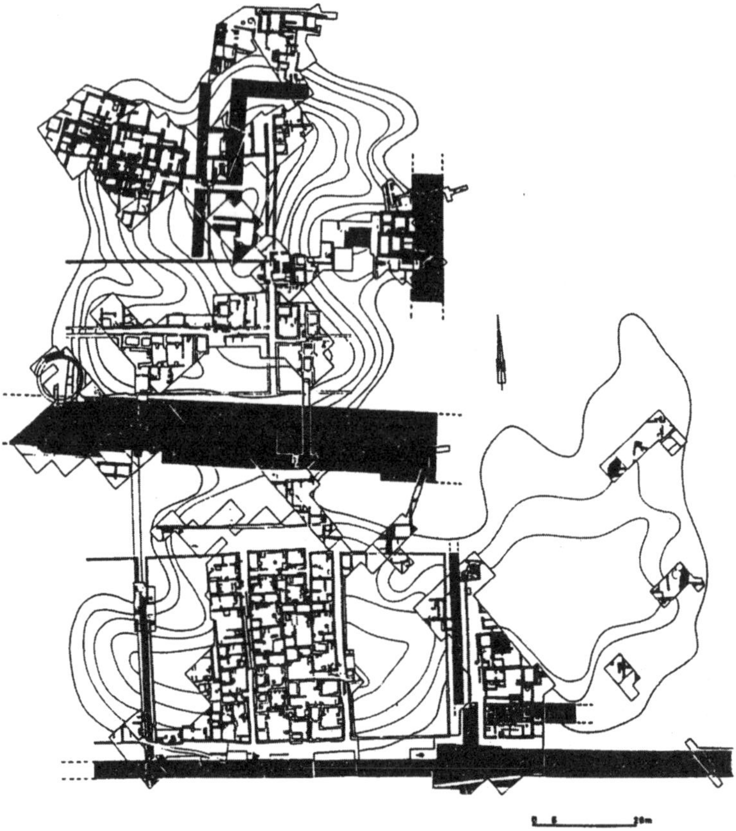

fig. 12: Nausharo (after Jarrige 1995-1996).

width and 4 m in height (*IAR* 1991-1992: 26). The castle, built by Stage IIIA as the most heavily fortified part of the settlement, was surrounded by double ramparts with stone walls and stood to a height of 16 m (*IAR* 1984-1985: 14)! Some of the fourteen city gates — particularly those surrounding the castle — were immensely high and wide, yet had narrow passages (Bisht 1998-99: 30).

2. Many architectural elements incorporated within the

fortification system at Dholavīra had conspicuous non-utilitarian or non-military significance. The following two examples illustrate this point:

(a) Of the two stadia detected between the citadel and the middle town, the smaller one was surrounded by massive walls on three sides, whereas the larger one did not have any circumvallation (Bisht 1999: 404); and

(b) The east gate of the castle had symmetrically arranged, neatly cut and highly polished limestone blocks and pillar bases incorporated in the design of its internal elevated chamber. Bisht (1998-99: 79) proposed that the arrangement of blocks and pillar bases was based on aesthetic principles. Other gates of the castle display similar structural elements.

3. During its heyday, Dholavīra was a highly segregated place and the scale of the internal fortifications was greater than the scale of the external fortifications. The three main fortified sections were the citadel, the middle town and the lower town. The citadel in turn was divided into two sections termed by Bisht "the castle" and "the bailey." North of the citadel, there was a walled passage. South of the citadel, there was a partly walled section. Finally, on the eastern side of the lower town there were a number of water reservoirs, all protected by massive walls with bastions and towers.

4. One of the most interesting features of Dholavīra layout is the presence of *empty spaces and open areas* encircled and accentuated by walls. Some of these spaces and areas reach 140 m in width (Bisht 1998-99: 72). The most obvious empty space is located between the northern side of the citadel and the southern side

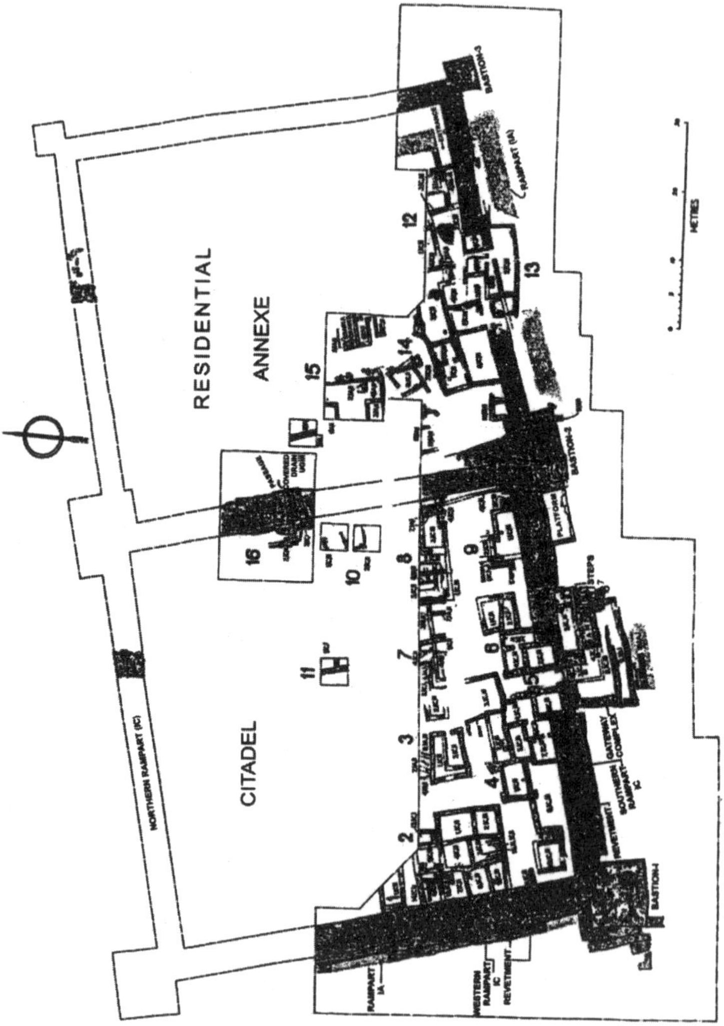

Figure 13: Surkoṭaḍā (after J.P. Joshi 1990)

of the middle town (*IAR* 1991-92: 31). Connecting the grandiose North Gate of the Castle with the main stadium of the Middle Town, it clearly had a strategic position. Bisht proposed that it performed a ceremonial function and served as the main entrance to the Castle.

5. Another unique feature of the urban landscape of Dholavīra is the large number of free-standing walls. Besides dividing the city into sectors, walls partially or fully surround one of the stadia, the southern annex of the castle, water reservoirs, empty spaces, and some residential units.

In terms of functionality, each of these traits is indicative of sociopolitical structures and deeper ideational meanings. For example, the grandiose scale of architectural elements is too overwhelming to be explained away by the military demands of the ruling elite. The conspicuous consumption of labour necessary for the construction of massive ramparts, walls, gates and bastions is certainly indicative of the desire to express power and authority by means of architecture. The presence of non-military and non-utilitarian elements shows that ritual, symbolic and aesthetic considerations were an integral part of the fortifications' meaning. The intricate urban segregation augmented by empty spaces and open areas points to the great role that social considerations played in the construction of Dholavīra fortification system. Finally, the large number of free-standing walls makes one wonder whether some kind of symbolism of space and border played a role in the creation of Dholavīra's urban landscape. Like the idea of water (wasserluxus) was a key element in the ideology of Moheṅjo-Dāṛo (Jansen 1993), the division of space by walls must have played an important role in the world-view of the Dholavirites.

Haṛappā, located in the district Sāhiwāl in Punjab, is the most excavated site of the Haṛappan civilization. The site consists of the four main mounds — Mound AB, Mound E, Mound ET, and Mound F — and each of these mounds is fortified (see *fig.* 8). As far as the meaning of fortifications at

Haṛappā is concerned, one may consider the following. First, beginning with the Koṭ-Dīji phase, segregation was one of the most distinctive characteristics of the layout at Haṛappā. Already during the Koṭ-Dīji phase, the site was divided into two distinct areas, Mound AB and Mound E (Dales and Kenoyer 1991, Meadow, Kenoyer, and Wright 1997: 14-15). During Period III, Haṛappā had at least four fortified areas: Mound AB, Mound E, Mound ET and Mound F. Second, access to the areas enclosed by perimeter walls as well as communication between these areas was restricted and controlled. For example, the passage in the gate located in the southwestern corner of Mound ET was only 2.6 m wide. Moreover during the later part of Period III, this passage was blocked (Meadow, Kenoyer, and Wright 1995: 4-5). Third, the layout of Haṛappā was explicitly three-dimensional; sectors, blocks and buildings stood on mud and mud-brick platforms of different heights.

Kālibaṅgan, located on the southern bank of the Ghaggar River in the district Hanumāngaṛh, northern Rajasthan, was fortified both during the pre-Haṛappan and Haṛappan periods (see *fig*. 9). As far as the meaning of its fortifications system is concerned, the following traits deserve particular attention. First, during the initial phase, the walls were too thin to protect the settlement from any significant threat (*IAR* 1965-1966: 40; Lal et al. 2003: 53). Second, despite the drastic nature of innovations that took place in the beginning of Period II, there was a significant degree of continuity between the pre-Haṛappan and Haṛappan fortifications. For example, the walls built on the Western Mound during the pre-Haṛappan Period were fully incorporated into the fortification system of the Haṛappan period (*IAR* 1965-66: 41; Lal 1979: 76, Lal et al. 2003: 41). Third, no evidence for flooding was established during the excavations. Fourth, south of the fortified area the excavators discovered the remains of an agricultural field (Lal et al. 2003: 95-98). If the identification and dating of this field is correct, it is not unreasonable to suggest that one of the functions of perimeter walls in Period I was to separate spaces between agricultural and domestic worlds. Fifth, beginning with Period II, the site consisted of four distinct areas; the southern part of the western section, the northern part of the western section, the eastern section, and the area south of the western section. Three of these areas were fortified. Sixth, the scale of the internal fortification was greater than the scale of the external fortification. For example, the southern part of the western section was fortified heavier than the northern one: it had thicker walls (up to 11 m), corner towers, salients, and several mud-brick platforms. Seventh, platforms were separated from the walls, had no traces of superstructures, and were concentrated in the southern part of the western section (Lal 1979: 76-77). It is not unlikely that their function was to elevate some ritually significant loci (Lal 1984).

The site of Lothal, located between the Bhogawo and Sabarmati Rivers, 80 km south-west of Ahmedabad, Gujarat, is surrounded by a mud-brick perimeter wall and is divided into two fortified sectors (see *fig*. 10). Access to the site is restricted; there is only one entrance to the enclosed space throughout Phases I and II. Interestingly, this entrance has no traces of a gate or blocking device. Located in the south of the site behind the so-called acropolis, it presents a narrow opening in a mud-brick wall and is not unlikely to have been a result of the intentional restriction of access due to some kind of sociocultural segregation.

Another intriguing aspect of the fortification system at Lothal is the explicit three-dimensionality created by platforms of different heights. For example, platforms underneath the acropolis rise to about 12 ft above the ground level (Rao 1979: 86), while platforms of the immediately adjacent Block A, named by Rao (1979: 88) "the bazaar part of the Lower Town," are on average only 2 to 4 ft in height. Evidently, it is very unlikely that the creation of this three-dimensional layout within a relatively small area was caused by practical rather than ideational considerations. Moreover, like at Kālibaṅgan some platforms of the acropolis have no traces of superstructures, yet the dimensions of these platforms are massive (Rao 1979: 111, 113, 115) For example, Block D has a platform measuring 96 by 80 ft in size and 9 ft in height (Rao 1979: 115). Located across from the "warehouse" and next to the alleged ruler's residence, this platform is clearly an important structural element of the acropolis and is not unlikely to have served public or ritual purposes.

Moheṅjo-Dāṛo, located in the Larkānā district, Sind, Pakistan is the best known site of the Haṛappan civilization (see *fig.* 11). For a long time, it has been thought to be unfortified. Recent investigations by the team of German, Italian and Pakistani archaeologists have altered this view. In particular, new light on the structural history and functions of platforms and revetments in the Lower City was shed by remote sensing, surface stripping and core drilling conducted in the HR East area by Leonardi (1988). Importantly, it was established that the entirety of the HR East area stood on a massive mud-brick platform encircled by a revetment wall. This platform was built in the beginning of urban phase and underwent at least five anthropic phases: the initial construction of the platform, the construction of a mud-brick wall on the edges of the platform, the filling of the gaps between the wall and the platform, the construction of a mud-brick structure next to the wall, and the construction of a baked-brick revetment (Leonardi 1988: 56). Given the extent of this platform, it is not unreasonable to suggest that similar patterns of structural development characterized other parts of the Lower City. In fact, it appears that all the excavated areas of Moheñjo-Dāṛo stood on artificial platforms surrounded by retaining walls and revetments. Moreover, as Jansen (1987: 13) has proposed, the city could have been encircled by a ditch resultant from the removal of dirt used in the construction of platforms. Taken together, these structures formed a truly unique fortification complex. The key element of this complex was the grandiose platform lying underneath the Stūpa Mound. Filled with alluvial sediments and encircled by a retaining wall, it alone contained more than 400,000 cubic m of clay (Jansen 1987: 13).

Evidently, there was no need to erect such an elaborate engineering complex if its sole purpose was to protect the city from floods. Neither could it be used for the purpose of military defence. Much more likely, the platforms, walls, and revetments at Moheñjo-Dāṛo carried ideational functions; i.e. they empowered urban segregation and elevated symbolically significant areas.

The site of Nausharo, located on the Kachi Plain at the foot of the Bolan Pass in Baluchistan, has one of the most intriguing fortification systems in the Haṛappan civilization (see *fig*. 12). The investigation of this fortification system has a long and complicated history; for J.F. Jarrige and his team have continuously revised and changed their interpretations (see C. Jarrige 1994, 2000, J.F. Jarrige 1974-1986, 1987-1988, 1989, 1990, 1993, 1995-1996, 1997, Quivron 1994, 2000).

The northern mound at Nausharo was fortified during Period ID (*c*. 2600-2500 BCE) shortly prior to the beginning of the Mature Indus phase. Massive compartmented platforms were built underneath the Northern Mound around the same time. Period II (*c.* 2500-2300 BCE), associated with the beginning of the Mature Indus phase, witnessed the strengthening of the existing fortifications on the Northern Mound and the construction of new fortifications around the Southern Mound. As far as the function of this fortification system is concerned, the most revealing trait is a massive wall dividing the northern and southern mounds. Standing on a large compartmented platform, this wall is significantly bigger than the two other excavated walls; the eastern wall of the northern mound and the southern wall of the Southern Mound. Moreover, having no gateway it complicates communication between the Southern and Northern Mounds. Evidently, this layout must have been caused by ideological or social needs that required restricted access to certain areas, control over communication, and demarcation of space.

The amount and layout of walls in Nausharo also point to non-utilitarian meanings. The fact of the matter is that besides free-standing perimeter walls Nausharo is laid out on a rigid rectangular grid, oriented in strict accordance with the cardinal points. Several blocks of the Southern Sector have been fully exposed and one can see that the mud-brick wall was a crucial element in conveying rectangular linearity as the main principle of settlement layout; long solid walls that surrounded each block served both as the backside of the houses and the markers of access and border for their respective sectors. Judging from the number of entrances to each block, access was restricted. It is difficult to imagine that such a rigid layout was created exclusively in response to practical needs. Aesthetic and symbolic considerations must have played a very important role as well. In fact, the symbolism of the wall as the divider of space based on sociopolitical, religious, professional or ethnic differences seems to have been an important principle in the construction of internal fortifications and block walls at Nausharo.

The site of Surkoṭaḍā, located on the bank of a lost river in Kutch, Gujarat, was encircled by a massive rampart. Pierced by gates and topped by bastions, this rampart not only protected the site all around, but also divided it, from the initial stage of occupation, into two parts: the eastern and western (see *fig.* 13). That such a small settlement was so heavily fortified and divided into two sections raises a number of intriguing questions. The five following points deserve particular attention:

1. If in Period IA, the rampart was only 1 m high (J.P. Joshi 1990: 33), it is very unlikely that it performed a military function. One can easily jump over such a rampart.
2. If the rampart carried a purely defensive function, one would expect it to increase rather than decrease in width. Nonetheless, the width of the rampart in the western section (the alleged "Citadel") significantly decreased from Period IA to Period IC (J.P. Joshi 1990: 33).
3. From a military perspective, there was no need to divide the settlement into equal parts by building a massive wall. Moreover, this wall was more imposing that the outer walls of the eastern sector.
4. The actual size of Surkoṭaḍā likely exceeded the size of the area encircled by fortifications. On the outer side of the revetted bastion, Joshi spotted traces of significant structural activities dated to Period IC (J.P. Joshi 1990: 51). Moreover, the fortified area covered

only one-third of the mound. With the cemetery on the northern end of the mound and the fortified area on the southern side, it is highly unlikely that the central part of the mound and other adjacent areas were unpopulated.

5. During all the three periods of the occupational sequence, there were openings in the walls of both sections that did not have gates, ramps, stairs or any other protections. In a similar way, in later periods there was an open passage connecting eastern and western sections (J.P. Joshi 1990: 47, 51-52, 57).

Such is a brief summary of archaeological traits indicative of the non-utilitarian meanings of the Haṛappan fortification systems. Taken together, these traits reveal a number of intriguing regularities which can be summarized under five broad topics: elevation, scale, access, segregation, and the accentuation of space.

Elevation: The landscapes of the Haṛappan sites were uneven, and the elevation of certain areas or structures by means of platforms was a key element of planning. I treated platforms as part of fortification complexes, for the platforms were either directly or indirectly related to other elements of fortification complexes. Functionally, platforms were incorporated into fortifications for three following reasons. First, in several cases, platforms were of different heights within the same site or even within the same area of the site (Mohenjo-Dāṛo, Lothal, and Nausharo). Second, some platforms had no structures on top of them (Kālibaṅgan and Lothal). Third, platforms did not necessarily cover the whole sites or even distinct sectors of the sites. For example, Banawālī had only a few platforms, while in Kālibaṅgan platforms covered only the southern part of the western sector.

Scale: Fortifications of many Haṛappan sites were monumental and their construction was extremely labour-consuming. This monumentality however characterized platforms (Moheñjo-Dāṛo, Haṛappā, Lothal, Kālibaṅgan, etc.) and internal fortifications (the castle of Dholavīra, the dividing wall at Nausharo and the southern part of the western sector at Kālibaṅgan). Most external fortifications (the outer walls) were not monumental.

Access: There are numerous indications that gates, entrances and connecting passages carried ideational functions. The south-west gate on Mound ET at Haṛappā was narrow in some periods and completely blocked in other periods. Lothal had very few entrances yet lacked massive gates, while Surkoṭaḍā had several wide unprotected entrances along with the massive gate. Some gates were monumental (Surkoṭaḍā, Haṛappā, northern gate at Dholavīra), while other gates were very simple and barely protected. Several gates had very narrow passages (Dholavīra, Haṛappā).

Segregation: One of the most obvious features of the Haṛappan fortification systems was segregation. Most of the reviewed fortified sites were divided into two or more sectors encircled by walls. Banawālī had two fortified sectors. Dholavīra had four fortified sectors. Haṛappā had four fortified sectors. Kālibaṅgan had three fortified sectors. Lothal had two fortified sectors. Moheñjo-Dāṛo is a controversial case, yet the recent research by the Italian team shows that some or possibly all of the mounds and areas of Moheñjo-Dāṛo were surrounded by perimeter walls. Nausharo had two fortified sectors. Surkoṭaḍā had two fortified sectors. In addition, most of these sites revealed occupational deposits beyond the city walls; in other words, besides fortified sectors, they had sectors not protected by walls yet separated from the rest of the site.

Accentuation of space: In addition to segregating sites into large distinct sectors, freestanding walls divided and accentuated important places. On some sites, they created empty spaces, long passages and open areas, some of which may have had ritual or political significance (Dholavīra). On other sites, they divided fortified areas into very small yet distinct sectors (Kālibaṅgan and Surkoṭaḍā). On many sites, walls delineated block borders and residential complexes (Nausharo).

Grouped this way, these traits clearly point to ideational meanings. Platforms must have accentuated the significance of certain buildings and areas by using elevations as means of ideological significance. Monumentality, being an important feature of platforms and internal fortifications, conveyed messages from one group to another, often within the same area of the site. Gates restricted access to the sites, making the passage of people and vehicles controlled. Free-standing walls that divided the sites into distinct sectors maintained the existing sociopolitical order. The creation of small sectors, passages and empty spaces must have served the needs of ritual or political ceremonialism; no military, ecological or any other practical reason would have justified the splitting of the western sector at Kālibaṅgan or the creation of a long passage in front of the north gate at Dholavīra. Finally, differences in the date of construction and the magnitude of some fortification systems — Haṛappā was surrounded by perimeter walls long before Nausharo, or Dholavīra had more elaborate fortifications than Banawālī and Lothal — must have been the result of the internal (sociopolitical or ritual) rather than external (military) functions.

Figuratively speaking, fortifications of Banawālī, Dholavīra, Haṛappā, Kālibaṅgan, Lothal, Moheñjo-Dāṛo, Nausharo, and Surkoṭaḍā created three-dimensional and segregated worlds with restricted access and hidden monumentality. The ethos of these worlds was predominantly ideological. To theorize on what kind of ideas these worlds conveyed and whether they were, in any manner, related to the formation of authoritative structures, we need to turn to the data indicative of the emergence of authority on the same archaeological sites.

Authority: In Banawālī, major social transformations took place in Phase IC, which marked a transition from the pre-Haṛappan to Mature Haṛappan Periods and was dated roughly to the middle of the third millennium BCE. During this phase, the whole settlement was rebuilt anew, fortification system was renovated, the division into two fortified sectors was established, architecture became more sophisticated, and the new street system oriented in accordance with cardinal directions was laid out (Bisht 1998-99: 16-17). In Dholavīra, the emergence of authoritative structures must have taken place either in Stage IIIA (*c*. 2500-2400 BCE) or in Stage II (*c*. 2550-2500 BCE). Based on three lines of evidence — monumentality, site expansion, and the principles of planning and architecture — one could argue that Stage II in fact had foreordained the efflorescence of Stage III and should be seen as the initial period of major social transformations (*IAR* 1991-1992: 26-28). In Haṛappā, authoritative structures must have been formed the latest by Period II, Koṭ-Dījī phase, which started around 2800 BCE. The innovations associated with this period and indicative of the emergence of authority included the construction of fortifications, the emergence of distinct fortified sectors, the expansion of the site, the intensification of structural activities, brick standardization, the emergence of seals and possibly standardized weights and measures, the sophistication of craft technology, and the intensive development of long-distance trade. In Kālibaṅgan, major social transformations took place in the beginning of Period II around 2600/2500 BCE. The innovations indicative of the emergence of authority included settlement expansion, the renovation of fortifications, the division into three fortified areas, orientation along the cardinal directions, and the construction of platforms in the southern part of the western sector (Lal 1979, Lal et al. 2003, Lal and Thapar 1967, Thapar 1973, Thapar 1975). In Lothal, archaeological evidence for authority could be associated with the transition from Phase I to Phase IIA. This transition witnessed settlement expansion, the construction of platforms, the renovation of fortifications, the division of the site into distinct fortified sectors, the construction of the "dock" and the "warehouse," a general intensification of structural activities, and the establishment of street layout in accordance with cardinal directions. Importantly, all these changes took place in a relatively short period of time; Phase IIA arguably lasted for less than a hundred years (Rao 1979: 24-36).

Moheṅjo-Dāṛo without doubt provides the strongest case for the presence of authoritative structures and the control of labour of all the known Haṛappan sites. The Stūpa Mound alone can be seen as an epitome of authority in the Haṛappan civilization. Platforms, public architecture, planning, and other characteristic features of Moheṅjo-Dāṛo would not have been possible without the existence of a rigid social system — whether hierarchical or heterarchical — and authoritative structures. The emergence of authority on this site is nonetheless obscure, as there are at least two possible scenarios for the early history of Moheṅjo-Dāṛo. According to the first scenario, Moheṅjo-Dāṛo was a founder's city. This means that it was built in a short period of time — as Jansen (1987: 15) believes it, in no longer than eighty years — by specialists who were well familiar with the environment and had prior technical experience. The key elements of architectural layout and building technology, according to this scenario, were planned well in advance and the city was built on an empty or abandoned spot (Jansen 1994: 271-72). This scenario assumes the arrival of population and specialists from some other place. According to the second scenario, Moheṅjo-Dāṛo had an Early Haṛappan settlement similar to those of some other Haṛappan sites. Around 2600-2500 BCE, this settlement expanded and underwent radical changes in settlement layout, architecture, and ideology. According to this scenario, it was the local population which was primarily responsible for the changes, and all the technological and ideological prerequisites necessary for the construction of Moheṅjo-Dāṛo had been acquired prior to the alleged transition from the Early to the Mature Haṛappan. Based on the analogy with other Haṛappan sites (particularly Haṛappā), I believe, the second scenario is more likely. The fact that an Early Haṛappan settlement has not been so far found at Moheṅjo-Dāṛo is not surprising. The remains of such a settlement must be well hidden under the platforms and thick layers of alluvium.

In Nausharo, the emergence of authority can be ascribed either to Period II dated to 2500-2300 BCE or to Period ID dated to 2600-2500 BCE. Period II is defined by fortifications, platforms, monumental architecture, grid planning in accordance with cardinal directions, and the division in sectors. Period ID witnessed the construction of the first fortifications, the beginning of the division into fortified sectors, and the building of a massive architectural complex on the northern mound. Following J.F. Jarrige (1993), it seems quite reasonable to accept that Period ID rather than Period II witnessed the most radical stage of social transformations. Finally, Surkoṭaḍā was a founder's settlement, the foundation of which alone would require the presence of authority. Understandably, archaeological traits indicative of complex social organization, control of labour, and the presence of authorities were found at this site throughout all three periods and included massive architectural projects, the division into two fortified sectors, and a large number of characteristically Haṛappan artefacts (Joshi 1990).

Such is a brief summary of archaeological traits indicative of important social transformations and the emergence of authoritative structures. The significance of these traits for broader interpretations can be discussed under four topics: size, layout, structural activity, and material culture.

***Size*:** Drastic and rapid increases in settlement size almost universally imply a significant growth in social complexity and the emergence of authoritative structures. Excavations at Dholavīra, Haṛappā, Kālibaṅgan, Koṭ-Dījī, and Nausharo have provided some data for tracing this type of changes. Other sites still lack quality data for establishing the precise time-frames of site expansions. Importantly, the founder's settlements imply the presence of strong authority and elaborate mechanisms of control by the mere fact of their existence. In other words, if Jansen's scenario of the founding of Moheṅjo-Dāṛo is correct (Jansen 1994: 271), highly sophisticated authoritative structures had to exist and to be fully functional well prior to the foundation of Moheṅjo-Dāṛo. The same applies to Surkoṭaḍā, Sutkagen-Dor, and other founder's settlements.

***Layout*:** A unique layout is one of the most evident manifestations of the Haṛappan urban phenomenon. Advance planning, the grouping of public structures, and the division into sectors are usually quoted as typical of Haṛappan sites. Each in its own way, these traits imply authoritative decisions and the existence of a complex social system. Not all of these traits however are equally present on Haṛappan sites. The most characteristic and intriguing feature is the urban segregation reinforced by the elaborate systems of internal fortifications.

Structural activity: Massive architectural projects are among the best indicators of social transformations, for they require the organization of labour, advance planning, acquisition of resources, and most importantly a good reason for construction. None of these are possible without a high degree of social differentiation — either hierarchical or heterarchical — and the existence of authoritative structures. Many Haṛappan sites conceal the remains of platforms, gates, and walls which, although less appealing in grandeur than the Egyptian pyramids or Mesopotamian ziggurats, are nonetheless monumental and labour-consuming.

Material culture: There are several types of Haṛappan artefacts, potentially indicative of authority. These include inscribed seals, inscribed objects, standardized weights, bricks of the standard ratio, precious jewellery, and the objects of long distance trade. The use of these artefacts as direct evidence for authority can be however very misleading. For example, inscribed seals have been found in Koṭ-Dījī and Allahdino; yet other traits indicate that these were minor settlements. On the other hand, the material cultures of Dholavīra and Haṛappā during the pre-Haṛappan Period or of Sutkagen-Dor during the Mature Haṛappan Period lack solid evidence of writing yet have ample evidence for the existence of authoritative structures. The matter of the fact is that on many sites authority emerges prior to or after the appearance of the aforementioned artefacts.

In sum, archaeological evidence for authority in the

Haṛappan civilization currently rests on four sets of data: size, layout, structural activity, and material culture. Yet, since the dynamics of site expansion are in many cases obscure and the traits of material culture by themselves can be quite misleading, layout and structural activity become the two key material expressions of authority. More specifically, this means that in Banawālī, Dholavīra, Haṛappā, Kālibaṅgan, Lothal, Moheṅjo-Dāṛo, Nausharo, and Surkoṭaḍā, evidence for the major social transformations, such as social differentiation, conspicuous consumption of labour, and the emergence of authority comes primarily from the idiosyncratic layout (the division in sectors) and massive architectural projects (platforms, walls, gates, moats and occasional public buildings). Besides a few public buildings, however, these traits are all facets of fortification systems, whose quintessential meaning as I have proposed above is the creation of three-dimensional and segregated worlds with restricted access and hidden monumentality. The material expression of authority thus can be described in the same terms as the meaning of fortifications. Indeed, aside from several public buildings — "granaries," the great bath, etc. — authority on many Haṛappan sites expressed itself most conspicuously in the implementation of massive public works and the segregation of space. Neither public works nor the segregation of space however had a clear utilitarian cause. As I have argued above, the construction of platforms and walls had, in most cases, an ideational rather than utilitarian significance.

The Idea of the City in the Haṛappan and Ganges Civilizations

The most revealing result of this study is that the model of the city as a combination of fortifications and authority reflects some of the historical processes that took place during the formative stages of the Haṛappan and Ganges civilizations, and consequently presents a plausible analytical device for the conceptualization of the phenomenon of the earliest South Asian city. Fortification systems of the Haṛappan and Ganges civilizations were indeed the most evident expressions of authority, and their construction was roughly concurrent with all the other changes indicative of the formation of authoritative structures. In the Ganges civilization, the sites of Ahicchatra, Atrañjikherā, Kauśāmbī, Mathurā, Vaiśālī and Śrāvastī provide sufficient data for correlating the construction of fortifications with changes in material culture indicative of major social transformations. Moreover, the archaeology of Kauśāmbī provides great potential for correlating the structural history of fortifications directly with the structural history of the buildings that may have been used by authorities; the phases of the south-western rampart and bastion can be correlated with the phases of the so-called "palace," while the phases of the Ghoṣitārāma Monastery can be correlated with the phases of the north-eastern rampart. In the Haṛappan civilization, the concurrent processes of the construction of fortifications and the emergence of authority can be traced in Dholavīra, Haṛappā and Nausharo, as well as on all the founder's sites. In Dholavīra, the earliest perimeter wall is constructed during Stage I dated by Bisht to *c*. 2650-2550 BCE. Evidence for authority begins to emerge during Periods I and II (2650-2500 BCE). In Haṛappā both authority and segregated fortifications are present at the site the latest by the Koṭ-Dījī Phase (2800 BCE). In Nausharo, authority and fortifications appear during Period ID around 2600-2500 BCE.

In some cases, one must admit, the construction of the earliest Haṛappan fortifications precedes significant social transformations, such as the emergence of authority. For example, in Banawālī, the first perimeter wall is built during Period IB dated roughly around 2600 BCE, while clear evidence for sociopolitical changes is associated with Period IC. In Kālibaṅgan the first perimeter wall is built in the beginning of Period I around *c*. 3000-2700 BCE, while major sociopolitical transformations seem to be taking place in the beginning of Period II dated to *c*. 2600-2500 BCE. In Lothal initial fortifications are built during the pre-Haṛappan Phase 1, while clear evidence for authority as well as more substantial fortifications and platforms appear during the Haṛappan Phase 2.

Nonetheless, these cases do not alter the general pattern, for it is the mutual presence of complex fortification systems and authoritative structures that marks the time of most drastic qualitative changes. Parallel and co-dependent, the processes of the formation of authority and the construction of fortifications appear to have marked the emergence of the first South Asian cities and, consequently, epitomized these cities as an idea in the minds of historical agents many years later. Remarkably, this means that the sociopolitical thinking of the historical agents hidden within mythological, conventional and religious narratives was by no means a mere fruit of imagination.

In conclusion, one must add that similarities in the processes of urbanization in the Haṛappan and Ganges civilizations proposed in this study is not a reason for postulating any direct ethnic, linguistic, religious, or cultural continuities. The South Asian civilization — whether in its most ancient or more recent manifestation — is a multi-ethnic and multi-linguistic entity, in the shaping of which an important role has always been played by interaction, external influxes and internal diversity. The uniqueness of this civilization has, to a large extent, been in the capacity to absorb, reshape, and melt down these influxes and diversities. For good reasons, Rabindranath Tagore called India "Bhāratatīrtha" and placed in the centre of the universe as a great melting pot of cultures, languages and religions. The model of the ancient city proposed here is also broad enough to accommodate a large number of very different religious, sociopolitical, and cultural traditions.

Postcript

When I delivered this paper at a conference in Dartmouth, MA, I barely knew the works of other contributors to this volume (aside from the writings of Professor Lal). Now, when I am more familiar with their writings, I would like to emphasize that I find many methods and arguments proposed in this book incompatible with the epistemology of post-Enlightenment humanistic disciplines. However, I must thank Bal Ram Singh for inviting me to this conference, as I found it to be a worthy experience.

Abbreviations

AN *Aṅguttara-Nikāya*
ASI Archaeological Survey of India
IAR *Indian Archaeology: a Review*
KA *Kauṭilīya Arthaśāstra*
LM *Lalitāmāhātmya* of the *Brahmāṇḍa Purāṇa*
Mbh *Mahābhārata*
Rām *Vālmīki Rāmāyaṇa*
VP *Vāyu Purāṇa*

Critical Editions of the Quoted Sanskrit and Pāli Texts

Aṅguttara-Nikāya, eds. Morris Richard and Edmund Hardy, London: Published for the Pali Text Society by H. Frowde, 1885-1910.

Brahmāṇḍa Purāṇa of the Kṛṣṇa Dvaipāyana Vyāsa, ed. Jagdish Lal Shastri, Delhi: Motilal Banarsidass, 1973.

Kauṭilīya Arthaśāstra, a critical edition with glossary, ed. R.P. Kangle. Bombay: Bombay University Press 1960.

Lalitāmāhātmya of the Brahmāṇḍa Purāṇa of Kṛṣṇa Dvaipāyana Vyāsa, ed. Jagdish Lal Shastri. Delhi: Motilal Banarsidass, 1973.

Mahābhārata, for the first time critically edited by Vishnu S. Sukthankar, with the co-operation of Balasaheb Pant Pratinidhi [and others] and illustrated from ancient models by Balasaheb Pant Pratinidhi. Poona: Bhandarkar Oriental Research Institute, 1927-66.

Milindapañha, being dialogues between King Milinda and the Buddhist sage Nāgasena, Pāli text, ed. V. Trenckner, London: Williams and Norgate 1880.

Vālmīki Rāmāyaṇa, ed. C.S. Patel et al., Baroda: Oriental Institute, 1960-75.

Vāyu Purāṇa, ed. Pandits of the Ānandāśrama, Poona: Āpta 1905.

References

Aboshi, Y., K. Sonoda, F. Yoneda and A. Uesugi, 1999, Excavations at Sahet-Mahet 1986-1996, *East and West* 49:119-74.

Altekar, A.S., and V. Mishra, 1959, *Report on Kumrahar Excavations, 1951-1955*, Patna: Jayaswal Research Institute.

Bajpai, K.D., ed. 1986, *Ahicchatra through the Ages*, Kanpur: Panchal Research Institute.

Bisht, R.S., 1987, "Further Excavations at Banawālī: 1983-1984", in *Archaeology and History: Essays in Memory of Shri A. Ghosh*, vol. 1, ed. B.M. Pande and B.D. Chattopadhyaya, pp. 135-56. Delhi: Agam Kala Prakashan.

———, 1998-99, "Dholavīra and Banawālī: Two Different Paradigms of the Haṛappan Urbis Forma," *Puratattva* 29:14-42.

———, 1999, "Haṛappans and the Ṛgveda: Points of Convergence", in *The Dawn of Indian Civilization (up to 600 B.C.)*, vol. 1 ed. G.C. Pande, pp. 393-442, New Delhi: Centre for Studies in Civilizations.

Bloch, T., 1904, Excavations at Basarh, *Annual Report of the Archaeological Survey of India*, 1903-04: 81-122.

Bonazzoli, G., 1979, "The Dynamic Canon of the Puranas", *Purana* 21:116-166.

———, 1983a, "Composition, Transmission and Recitation of the Puranas",

Purana 25:254-280.

———, 1983b, "Remarks of the Nature of the Puranas", *Purana* 25:77-113.

Christaller, W., 1933, *Die Zentralen Orte in Suddeutschland: Eine ŏkonomisch-Geographische Untersuchung uber die Gestzmassigkeit der Verbreitung und Entwicklung der Siedlungen mit Stadtischen Funktionen*, Jena: Gustav Fisher Verlag.

Coe, M.D., 1961, "Social Typology and the Tropical Forest Civilizations", *Comparative Studies in Society and History* 4:65-85.

Collingwood, R.G., 1946, *The Idea of History*, Oxford: Clarendon Press.

Cunningham, A., 1871, *The Ancient Geography of India*, London: Trubner.

Dales, G.F., and J.M. Kenoyer, 1991, "Summaries of Five Seasons of Research at Haṛappā (District Sahiwal, Punjab, Pakistan) 1986-1990", in *Haṛappā Excavations: A Multidisciplinary Approach to Third Millennium Urbanism*, ed. R.H. Meadow, pp. 185-262. Madison: Prehistory Press.

Deva, K. and V. Mishra, 1961, *Vaiśālī Excavations*, 1950, Vaiśālī: Vaiśālī Saṇgh.

Devi, S.M., B. Sahai, and C.R.P. Sinha, eds. 1980, *Pāṭaliputra through the Ages*, Patna: Bihar Puravid Parishad.

Doxiades, K.A., 1968, *Ekistics: An Introduction to the Science of Human Settlements*. London: Hutchinson.

Eltsov, P., 2008, *From Harappa to Hastinapura: A Study of the Earliest South Asian City and Civilization*, Boston: E.J. Brill.

Erdosy G., 1987, "Early Historic Cities of Northern India", *South Asian Studies* 3:1-23.

Fairservis Jr., W.A., 1967, "The Origin, Character and Decline of an Early Civilization", *American Museum Novitates* 2302:1-48.

———, 1975, *The Roots of Ancient India*, 2nd edn., Chicago: The University of Chicago Press.

———, 1992, *The Harappan Civilization and Its Writing*, New Delhi: Oxford and IBH Publishing.

Fustel De Coulanges, N.D., 1864, *La Cite Antique*. Paris: Hachete et Cie.

Gaur, R.C., 1983, *The Excavations at Atrañjikherā: Early Civilization of the Upper Ganga Basin*, Delhi: Motilal Banarsidass.

Ghosh, A., 1958, *Rajgir*, Delhi: Archaeological Survey of India.

Ghosh, A., and K.C. Panigrahi, 1946, "The Potteries of Ahichchhatra", *Ancient India* 1:37-59.

Härtel, H., 1993, *Excavations at Soṅkh: 2500 Years of a Town in Mathurā District. Monographien zur indischen Archäologie, Kunst und Philologie; Bd. 9*. Berlin: D. Reimer.

Jansen, M., 1987, "Preliminary Results on the 'Forma Urbis': Research at Moheṅjo-Dāṛo", in *Interim Reports: Reports on Field Work Carried out at Moheṅjo-Dāṛo*, vol. 2, eds. M. Jansen and G. Urban, pp. 9-22, Aachen: German Research Project Moheṅjo-Dāṛo.

———, 1993, *Mohenjo-Daro, Stadt der Brunnen und Kanale: Wasserluxus vor 4500 Jahren [Mohenjo-Daro, City of Wells and Drains: Water Splendour 4500 Years Ago]*, Bergisch Gladbach: Frontinus Gesellschaft.

———, 1994, "Mohenjo-Daro, Type Site of the Earliest Urbanization Process in South Asia: Ten Years of Research at Moheṅjo-Dāṛo, Pakistan, and an Attempt at a Synopsis", in *South Asian Archaeology 1993*, vol. 1., eds., A. Parpola and P. Koskikallio, pp. 263-80, Helsinki: Suomalainen Tiedeakatemia.

Jarrige, C., 1994, "The Mature Indus Phase at Nausharo as Seen from a Block of Period III", in *South Asian Archaeology 1993*, vol. 1, eds. A. Parpola and P. Koskikallio, pp. 281-94. Helsinki: Suomalainen Tiedeakatemia.

———, 2000, "The Mature Indus Phase at Nausharo: Elements of Urban Infrastructure", in *South Asian Archaeology* 1997, vol. 1. eds. M. Taddei and G.D. Marco, pp. 237-58, Rome: Istituto Italiano per l'Africa e l'Oriente.

Jarrige, J.F., 1974-1986, "Excavations at Mehrgarh-Nausharo," *Pakistan Archaeology* 10-22:63-134.

———, 1987-1988, "Excavation at Nausharo", *Pakistan Archaeology* 23:149-203.

———, 1989, "Excavation at Nausharo, 1987-1988", *Pakistan Archaeology* 24:21-67.

———, 1990, "Excavations at Nausharo, 1988-1989", *Pakistan Archaeology* 25:163-92.

———, 1993, "The Question of the Beginning of the Mature Haṛappan Civilization as Seen from Nausharo Excavations", in *South Asian Archaeology 1991*, eds. A.J. Gail and G.J.R. Mevissen, pp. 149-64.

Stuttgart: Franz Steiner Verlag.

———, 1995-1996, *Excavations at Mehrgarh-Nausharo,* Mission Archeologique Francaise au Pakistan.

———, 1997, "Les Fouilles De Nausharo Au Balochistan Pakistanais Et Leur Contributions a L'etude De La Civilisations De L'indus", in *Crai 1996*, pp. 11-67.

Joshi, J.P., 1990, *Excavation at Surkotada 1971-1972 and Exploration in Kutch,* Delhi: Memoirs of the Archaeological Survey of India, 87.

Joshi, M.C., 1989, "Mathura as an Ancient Settlement", in *Mathurā: The Cultural Legacy*, ed. D.M. Srinivisan, pp. 165-70, New Delhi: American Institute of Indian Studies.

Kalianov, V.I., 1959, ed. *Arthasastra ili Nauka Politiki,* Moskva: Izdatelstvo Akademii Nauk SSSR.

Kangle, R.P., 1963, ed., *The Kautilya Arthasastra,* vol. 2, Bombay: Bombay University Press.

———, 1965, ed. *The Kautiliya Arthasastra,* vol. 3, Bombay: Bombay University Press.

Kumar, B., 1987, "Archaeology of Pataliputra and Nalanda", *The Heritage of Ancient India;* No. 10, Delhi: Ramanand Vidya Bhawan.

Lal, B.B., 1979, "Kālibangan and the Indus Civilization", in *Essays in Indian Protohistroy*, eds. D.P. Agrawal and D.K. Chakrabarti, pp. 65-97, Delhi: B.R. Publishing Company.

———, 1979-1980, "Are the Defences of Kauśāmbī really as old as 1025 BCE, *Puratattva* 11: 88-95.

———, 1984, "Some Reflections on the Structural Remains at Kālibangan", in *Frontiers of the Indus Civilization*, eds., B.B. Lal and S.P. Gupta, pp. 55-62, New Delhi: Books and Books.

Lal, B.B., J.P. Joshi, B.K. Thapar, and M. Bala, 2003, *Excavations at Kālibangan: The Early Haṛappans (1960-1969)*, "Memoirs of the Archaeological Survey of India", no. 98, New Delhi: Archaeological Survey of India.

Lal, B.B. and B.K. Thapar, 1967, "Excavation at Kālibangan: New Light on the Indus Civilization", *Cultural Forum* IX:78-88.

Law, B.C., 1942, *Pancalas and Their Capital Ahichchhatra,* "Memoirs of the Archaeological Survey of India", no. 67, Delhi: Manager of

Publications.

Leonardi, G., 1988, "New Problems of Surface Archaeology: Sampling in Hr East Area of Moenjodaro (Pakistan)", in *Interim Report: Reports on Field Work Carried out at Mohenjo-Dāṛo, Pakistan, 1983-1986 by the Ismeo-Aachen-University Mission*, vol. 3, eds. M. Jansen, M. Tosi, and G. Leonardi, pp. 7-92, Aachen, Roma: RWTH, IsMEO.

Levy, R.I., 1984, *Mesocosm: Hinduism and the Organization of a Traditional Newar City in Nepal*, Berkeley: University of California Press.

Marshall, Sir J.H., 1915, "Excavations at Bhītā", *Annual Report of the Archaeological Survey of India*, 1911-1912: 29-94.

Mate, M.S., 1969-1970, "Early Historic Fortifications in the Ganga Valley", *Puratattva* 3:58-69.

Mccrindle, J.W., 1877, *Ancient India as Described by Megasthenes and Arrian*, London: Trubner and Co.

Meadow, R.H., J.M. Kenoyer, and R.P. Wright, 1995, *Haṛappā Archaeological Research Project: Haṛappā Excavations 1995*, Report Submitted to the Director-General, Department of Archaeology and Museums, Government of Pakistan.

———, 1997, *Harappa Archaeological Research Project: Harappa Excavations 1997*, Report Submitted to the Director-General, Department of Archaeology and Museums, Government of Pakistan.

———, 1999, *Harappa Archaeological Research Project: Haṛappā Excavations 1997*, Report Submitted to the Director-General, Department of Archaeology and Museums, Government of Pakistan.

Mukherji, P.C., 1898, *Report on the Excavations on the Ancient Site of Pāṭaliputra (Patna-Bankipur)*, Calcutta.

Mumford, L., 1961, *The City in History: Its Origins, Its Transformations, and Its Prospects*, 1st edn., London: Secker & Warburg.

Narain, A.K. and T.N. Roy, 1976, *Excavations at Rajghat, 1957/58–1960/1965, Part I: The Cuttings, Stratification and Structures*, Varanasi: Dept. of Ancient Indian History, Culture and Archaeology, Banares Hindu University.

Patil, D.R., 1963, *The Antiquarian Remains in Bihar*, Patna: Kashi Prasad Jayaswal Research Institute.

Paul, R.K., 1986, "Ahicchatra as Known through Arhaeology", in *Ahicchatra through the Ages*, ed. K.D. Bajpai, pp. 47-54, Kanpur: Panchal

Research Institute.

Piggott, S., 1950, *Prehistoric India to 1000 B.C.*, Harmondsworth, Middlesex: Penguin Books.

Possehl, G.L., 1998, "Sociocultural Complexity without the State: The Indus Civilization", in *Archaic States*, ed. G.M. Feinman, pp. 261-91. Santa Fe: School of American Research.

———, 2002, *Indus Civilization: A Contemporary Perspective*, Walnut Creek, CA: AltaMira Press.

Quivron, C., 1994, "The Pottery Sequence from 2700 to 2400 at Nausharo, Baluchistan", in *South Asian Archaeology 1993*, vol. 2, eds. A. Parpola and P. Koskikallio, pp. 629-44, Helsinki: Suomalainen Tiedeakatemia.

———, 2000, "Evolution of the Mature Indus Pottery Style in the Light of the Excavations at Nausharo, Pakistan", *East and West* 50:147-190.

Rangarajan, L.N., 1992, ed. *The Arthasastra*, edited, rearranged, translated, and introduced, New Delhi: Penguin Books.

Rao, S.R., 1973, *Lothal and the Indus Civilization*, Bombay: Asia Publishing House.

———, 1979, *Lothal: A Harappan Port Town (1955-62)*, vol. 78, *Memoirs of the Archaeological Survey of India*. New Delhi: Archaeological Survey of India.

———, 1986, *A Study of Northern Black Polished Ware Culture: An Iron Age Culture of India*, New Delhi: Ramanand Vidya Bhawan.

Roy, U.N., 1954, "Fortification of Cities in Ancient India", *Indian Historical Quarterly* 30:237-44.

Sharma, G.R., 1960, *The Excavations at Kauśāmbī (1957-1959). The Defences and the Syenaciti of the Purusamedha*, Allahabad: Department of Ancient History.

———, 1969, *Excavations at Kausambi, 1949-1950. Memoirs of the Archaeological Survey of India*, no 74. Delhi.

Singh, S.B., 1979, *Archaeology of Pancala Region*, Delhi: Adam.

Sinha, B.P. and L.A. Narain, 1970, *Pataliputra Excavation, 1955-1956*, Patna: Directorate of Archaeology and Museums.

Sinha, B.P. and S.R. Roy, 1969, *Vaisali Excavations, 1958-62*, Patna: The

Directorate of Archaeology and Museums, Bihar.

Sinha, K.K., 1967, *Excavations at Śrāvastī, 1959*, Varanasi: Benares Hindu University.

Spengler, O., 1918, *Der Untergang Des Abendlandes: Umrisse Einer Morphologie Der Weltgeschichte*, Wien und Leipzig: Wilhelm Braumṃller.

Spooner, B.D., 1913, "Mr. Ratan Tata's Excavations at Pāṭaliputra", *Annual Report of the Archaeological Survey of India* 1912-1913:53-86.

———, 1914, "Excavations at Basarh", *Annual Report of the Archaeological Survey of India*, 1913-1914:98-185.

Thapar, B.K., 1973, "New Traits of the Indus Civilization at Kālibaṅgan: An Appraisal", in *South Asian Archaeology*, ed. N. Hammond, pp. 85-104, Park Ridge: Noyes Press.

———, 1975, "Kālibaṅgan: A Harappan Metropolis Beyond the Indus Valley", *Expedition* 17:19-32.

Vogel, J.P., 1908, "Excavation at Sahet-Mahet", *Annual Report of the Archaeological Survey of India*, 1907-1908:81-131.

Waddel, L.A., 1892, *Discovery of the Exact Site of Asoka's Classic Capital of Pāṭaliputra, the Patalibothra of the Greeks, and the Description of the Superficial Remains*, Calcutta: Bengal Secretariat Press.

———, 1903, *Report on the Excavations at Pāṭaliputra (Patna): The Palibothra of the Greeks*, Calcutta: Bengal Secretariat Press.

Weber, M., 1922, *Wirtschaft und Gesellschaft. Grundriss der SocialṆkonomik.* Tṃbingen: J.C.B. Mohr (P. Siebeck).

Wilson, J.A., 1951, *The Burden of Egypt: An Interpretation of Ancient Egyptian Culture*, Chicago: University of Chicago Press.

4

The Dilemmas of Aryan Ecumene and Epicentre
Sapta-Sindhu and the Sarasvatī

Shiva G. Bajpai

> The historian always attempts to discover and explain what happened in the past; and only the explanation that is based on evidence would be valid. It is, therefore, the responsibility of the historian to refuse to engage in analyses that ignore the evidence or fail to present it.

THIS represents the views expressed by the eminent historian, Professor Eric Hobsbawm, in December 2004 at the India International Center, New Delhi. I have always held similar views regarding the profession and responsibility of the historian. Therefore, when I refuse to analyse or present many of the mainstream academic views on the ecumene and epicenter of the Ṛgvedic Aryans, I am only doing so for the reasons of professional integrity and responsibility, and not for a lack of appreciation of their sincerity.

The problem of the identification of the earliest region of the Aryan ecumene or homeland including its epicentre in Bhārat (India) has been an intractable one despite the endeavours of international scholarship for nearly two centuries. The main reasons for this intractability have to do with the global, albeit Eurasian, dimensions of the Aryan question, and its corollary, the theory of Aryan invasion (now called "migration") of India on the one hand and, on the other, the presumptive non-Aryan characterization of the "Haṛappan Culture" or the Indus-Sarasvatī civilization first discovered in the 1920s. The resultant mythic reconstruction of historical processes by modern academicians and scholars accorded an amazing role to the exploits of the allegedly alien Aryan people, thus accounting for the demise of the splendid urban Haṛappan culture as well as the beginning of a new rural Vedic culture in *c.* 1500 BCE in north-western India. Although recent archaeological discoveries and other scientific studies including the genetic DNA research have chipped away at the very foundations of such a reconstruction of historical processes, the establishment Indologists both in India–South Asia as well as abroad nevertheless tenaciously cling to their baseless theories by drawing on puzzling features of Eurasian Aryan archaeology and Indo-European linguistics, thereby preventing a correct and meaningful reconstruction of India's early history.

The dilemma of the Aryan ecumene stems from the larger Aryan phenomenon, but it centres on the identification of the Sarasvatī River plain, the epicentre of the R̥gvedic culture and the delineation of Sapta-Sindha or Sindhavaḥ, the country of the Vedic Aryans. Central to determining the epicentre and the ecumene is the question of the correct identification of the Sarasvatī, the most celebrated river in the *R̥gveda* and the entire ancient Indian historical tradition. According to the Vedic testimony confirmed by the cumulative archaeological, geological and other scientific evidence both the Indus and the Sarasvatī were independent rivers that separately flowed into the western ocean. The R̥gvedic evidence categorically describes the mighty Sarasvatī as "flowing from the mountains to the sea" (*R̥V* 7.95.2). The epico-Purāṇic evidence and the ancient Indian historical tradition corroborate the fact of the Sarasvatī independently flowing into the ocean. Thus the interpretation of the term Sapta-Sindhavaḥ by the establishment Indologists as the Indus and its seven tributaries is definitely wrong when it excludes the Sarasvatī as a separate river by equating it with the Indus (for example, Griffith in fn.2 of *R̥V* 6.61; Allchin's ridiculous translation as "Seven Indus-es), or includes it as an eastern affluent of the Indus for which there is no evidence. Moreover such an interpretation contradicts what is explicitly stated in the *R̥gveda* about the Sarasvatī River. Further, the gratuitous statements as to the Sarasvatī forming the eastern frontier of the Sapta-Sindhu Region are misleading because, in addition to leaving out the region between the Dr̥ṣadvatī and Gaṅgā, these scholars avoid confronting the fact that the Sindhu of Sapta-Sindhavaḥ does not stand for the Indus river at all; rather it denotes "river" in a generic sense. Thus Sapta-Sindhavaḥ stands for "The Land of Seven Rivers" which, as I would argue, originally designated the region of the Sarasvatī and its tributaries and later encompassed the vast country between the Gaṅgā in the east to the Indus including its tributaries, especially the Kubha (Kābul) extending to the Hindu-Kush mountains in the north-west. The *R̥gveda* itself describes the Sarasvatī by the epithet Sapta-svasā, "having seven sisters or being one of the seven sisters" (*R̥V* 6.61.10) and Saptathī Sindhu-mātā (the seventh mother of rivers, *R̥V* 7.36.6). The ancient historical tradition also recalls the seven-sistered Sarasvatī River. While there may be difference of opinion as to the identification of the Sarasvatī's tributaries, the *R̥gveda* does explicitly name at least two: the Dr̥ṣadvatī and the Apayā in modern Haryana state. It is generally believed that both the Sutlej in the west and the Yamunā in the east or their significant branches at sometime joined the Sarasvatī River. It is the Sarasvatī, and not the Indus, which received the most attention and praise not only in the

Ṛgveda but also in the entire ancient Indian historical tradition. The sacred Sarasvatī was already lauded in the *Ṛgveda* as "the best of the rivers, the best of the mothers and the best of the goddesses (*ṚV* II.41.16)." Certain diehard Indologists notwithstanding, there is a growing consensus among the scholars that the Ṛgvedic Sarasvatī was located between the Yamunā and Sutlej (*ṚV* X.75.5) and it generally followed the course of modern Sarasvatī-Ghaggar-Hakra-Nara to the Rann of Kutch into the western ocean. The geologists have also discovered the glacial sources of the Sarasvatī and the archaeologists have identified about 70 per cent of all the sites of the various phases of the Haṛappan culture on its banks and those of its tributaries. The chronological span of these archaeological sites that would be part of the Vedic age extends from the fifth to the second millennium BCE (B.B. Lal, 2002, The *Sarasvati Flows on the Continuity of Indian Culture*, New Delhi: The Aryan Books International).

The *Ṛgveda* is likewise unambiguous about locating the epicentre of the Vedic culture in the land between the Sarasvatī and its eastern tributary the Dṛṣadvatī. It is described as "the navel of the earth" (*nābhā pṛthivyā*; *ṚV* 3.2.4) and the most excellent or greatest place on earth (*vara ā pṛthivyā*, *ṚV* III.23:4; 53:11) It is the holy land and served as the altar of many Vedic sacrifices as well as the seat of the first kingship of Manu. The sovereignty of the celebrated Nahuṣa and his descendants was inaugurated in the auspicious locality between the Sarasvatī and the Apayā; This was also the site of the imperial sacrifices including the Horse sacrifice of Sudāsa, the victor of the famous Battle of Ten kings. This region also constituted the heartland of Kurukṣetra region, the locus of Vedic imperial polity and religio-cultural personality. It was covered with numerous pilgrimage sites. Because the geo-cultural and geopolitical identity of the Aryans was anchored to this blessed land, it acquired the epithets of the Divine Land (*Brahmāvartta*) and the Field of Righteousness (*dharmakṣetra*) in succeeding centuries.

While the western boundaries of the Vedic epicentre, Brahmāvarta did not change beyond the Sarasvatī River, those of the country Saptasindhu did expand over time both westward as well as eastward. According to the *R̥V* X.64, the Sarasvatī, the Sarayū, and the Sindhu each had seven affluents. The Sarayū was the name of the combined stream of Vitastā, Askini, Paruṣṇi, and Vipāśā. The western tributary of the Indus was Kubha (Kabul), thus extending the frontier of Saptasindhu region to the Hindukush Mountains. In the east it extended into the western Gaṅgā Plain. The celebrated Nadī-stuti of the *R̥gveda* (*R̥V* X.75) clearly defines the frontiers of R̥gvedic Aryan ecumene, Sapta-Sindhu as extending from the Gaṅgā in the east to the Indus with its tributary Kubha in the west. The dynamics of cultural and political expansion of the Sarasvatī-centred Sapta-Sindhu are dimly but surely revealed in the *R̥gveda* and profusely recalled in the epico-Purāṇic historical tradition. The geopolitical consequences of the Battle of Ten Kings are echoed in the Nadī-stuti. More importantly, however, were the religio-cultural ascendancy of the Sarasvatī region and the desire of peoples of other regions to identify themselves with it for the sake of religio-cultural status and legitimacy. That the quest for religio-cultural legitimacy was a compelling motive is not only reflected in the Vedic and epico-Purāṇic sources but also in the Buddhist literature as well. The analogous entities were, however different: Sapta-Sindhu in the Vedic period and Madhyadeśa (Central Region) in the Buddhist period. This original epicentre of the Aryan culture continues to be part of the most holy land of all the Indic religions.

Geographically the Vedic ecumene, Sapta-Sindhu covered

the same vast region, as did the Haṛappan culture of the fourth-third and second millennia BCE. While there has been considerable theorizing over the reasons for the decline and demise of the Harappan culture, there is no uncertainty as to the principal cause of the decline and dislocation of the early Vedic culture. It was due to the drying up of the perennial mighty river Sarasvatī. The catastrophe is documented in the later Vedic literature as well as the ancient historical tradition. The lost Sarasvatī at Vinaśana was not a myth. It was a historical fact as revealed by archaeology at Kalibaṅgan, a major city abandoned on account of the loss of the river water. It happened chronologically around 2000 BCE.

My identification of the Aryan ecumene and the epicentre of the R̥gvedic culture eliminates the rampant confusion in the extant scholarship in that it accords the proper and accurate place to the Sarasvatī in the Sapta-Sindhu region and defines the expanded western and eastern frontiers of the Aryan ecumene as a result of religio-cultural and political dynamics of historical development. Both geographically and chronologically, determined on the basis of the drying up of the Sarasvatī River in *c.* 2000 BCE, the R̥gvedic culture overlaps the Haṛappan culture. The conclusion, therefore, is unavoidable that we are, in fact, dealing with one and the same people and their culture with a diversity of features and regional variations. The implications of this identity on the reconstruction of early history of India are incalculable. We are now at the threshold of correctly re-writing the new history of early India–South Asia and by extension, providing the basis for a new approach to the larger Eurasian Aryan question.

Discussions

1. What about Sarasvatī that is in the Allahabad but it is not the one that is in the *Ṛgveda*?

   The Sarasvatī that is believed to join the Gaṅgā by a subterranean channel along with the River Yamunā to form the sacred Triveṇī confluence at Allahabad recalls the time when the Yamunā or one of its major channels joined the Sarasvatī in the Ṛgvedic age. However, conversely it is the Sarasvatī that is traditionally believed later to join the Gaṅgā and the Yamunā in order to form the Triveṇī *saṅgama* (the confluence of three rivers) endowing the new place with holiness and sanctity, which it alone could confer because of its own Vedic eminence and glory. It is, in fact, the Yamunā's historic association with the holy Sarasvatī that is apparently being recalled to enhance the sacredness of the confluence. Since it was the Sarasvatī that was the most exalted and sacred river eulogized as *naditame* (the best of the rivers), *ambitame* (the best of the mothers) and *devitame* (the best of the goddesses) in the Ṛgvedic age, its association with the Gaṅgā symbolized the transfer of all the sublime features of her greatness to the Gaṅgā, which eventually appropriated all her historic attributes and epithets. In fact, in time the Gaṅgā came to occupy the same central place in Indian history and culture as did the Sarasvatī in the Ṛgvedic age.

2. The question arises, what is, in fact, the Saptasindhu?

   Ṛgveda clearly describes the Sarasvatī, by terms, *saptasvasā sujuṣṭhā* and *saptathī sindhumātā*. So, we know that *sapta* (seven) is definitely used for the river Sarasvatī. This identified the original Saptasindhu with the Sarasvatī region, which was the heartland of the

Vedic culture. Within the Sarasvatī river valley the Saptasindhu term and designation must have become popular in a regional sense. And we see that some time during the political process of expansion and integration, the word Saptasindhu was both extended and appropriated by others as well. The evidence that is available to me is in the *Ṛgveda, Maṇḍala* 10.64 where the three river systems, namely, the Sarasvatī, the Sarayū, and the Sindhu are clearly described, each comprising seven rivers. This means that the idea and the designation of Saptasindhu have expanded westward. When we come to the *Nadīstuti* (*ṚV*. 10.75) then we have another version of Saptasindhu that extends from the Gaṅgā in the east to the Hindukush Mountains in the north-west because the Khubha (modern Kabul River) is mentioned as a western tributary of the Indus. So there are three stages of expansion that can be noticed historically. Therefore, the vast expanse of the term Saptasindhu that originally meant only the Sarasvatī valley was ultimately extended to all the regions up to the Hindukush Mountains. I did point out already that in all the enumeration of these rivers, whether it is in the *Nadīstuti* or *Maṇḍala* X.64, they are all counted from the east to the west, thereby making the direction very important for any historical reconstruction.

Now within this region, I tried to locate the core of this culture. The text of the *Ṛgveda* itself tells us about the core region that lay between the Dṛṣadvati and the Sarasvatī, both of which have now been identified. Within this core region, there was also a sacred spot named Manusa, near the Apaya River, which is a tributary of the Sarasvatī. The term used for the core region in the *Ṛgveda* is "Nābhā-pṛthivyā" and "Vara ā pṛthivyā" which is mentioned in *ṚV*, III.28 and elsewhere. It is not only the excellent place on earth but also is Nābhāpṛthivyā that is the navel of the universe or the centre of the earth. That kind of terminology or description was not used for any other locality in the entire Vedic literature. It clearly tells us where the centre was. It was located in the region of the Apaya between the Dṛṣadvatī and the Sarasvatī rivers.

Earlier term used for this region was Kurukṣetra, but by the time we come to the age of the *Manu-Smṛti*, it is not a geo-political evolution that was central to popular tradition but is was the sanctity, sacredness, holiness that was the crucial concern. That's why in the *Manu-Smṛti* we have the term Brahmavarta — the Divine Land — for it. And that concept persisted in various later historical traditions. Thus Saptasindhu then extended from its originally Sarasvatī river plain, to western Punjab region and finally to the entire country from the Gaṅgā all the way to the Kabul river.

3. The next question is when did it all happen?

The Sarasvatī river dried up about 2000–1900 BCE at Kālībaṅgan, the big site on it that was abandoned. We are talking about the time when Sarasvatī was a full flowing river. The later texts clearly tell us that the river dried up. From the time the *Pañcaviṁśa Brāhmaṇa* and the *Mahābhārata* the tradition is unanimous on this issue of the drying up of the mighty perennial river Sarasvatī. So the drying up time is roughly around 2000 BCE. Now the core of Ṛgvedic culture Nābhāpṛthivyā/Vara ā pṛthivyā/Kurukṣetra/

Dharmakṣetra or Brahmavarta was anchored on the Sarasvatī. In various hymns of the *R̥gveda*, especially 6.61, we find the kind of dedication these great sages have to the river and the land in its plain, that it could be called an expression of proto-nationalism and religio-culturalism. It is apparently a forerunner of the noble sentiments expressed for the country as a whole in the Pr̥thvī-Sūkta of the *Atharvaveda*. The *R̥gveda*'s large part belongs to *c*. 2000 BCE and before it. If it is that way, then the R̥gvedic culture & Haṛappan culture fall in the same time span.

Conclusion

It is irresistible to conclude that the two cultures, the Vedic and the Haṛappan, were one and the same but not mono-linguistic, monolithic, or mono-ethnic. From the available data, it seems that we can't avoid the conclusion that the two cultures overlapped and they were part of one and the same culture milieu. The sources or materials available are from archaeology and the literature especially, the *R̥gveda*, though we don't have all its recessions and we do know that much has been lost. Given the coincidence of convergence of literary, archaeological, geological, and other scientific data, it can't be denied that the two cultures, the Vedic and the Haṛappan, were not one and the same representing various aspects of the same phenomenon in the same space and time of our history.

5

The Aryan Myth in Perspective
History, Science and Politics

N.S. Rajaram

It is now more than a century since the Aryan Invasion Theory (AIT) made its way into history books and encyclopaedias the world over, as the basis for the history of ancient India and the source of the Vedic civilization. Though linguistic in origin, the climate in which it evolved — dominated by British colonialism and German nationalism — ensured that it soon acquired a political and even biological form, giving rise to such notions as the Aryan race and the Aryan nation. Government departments in British India like the Anthropological Survey mixed up physical appearance and character traits and made it a tool of divide and rule.

Because of its European origin and orientation, there were attempts to shift the origin of the Vedic Civilization and its language to sources in lands closer to Europe. This gave rise to an academic discipline called Indo-European studies, devoted to exploring the origin of Europeans, their language and culture. A major result of this approach has been to make India and its culture including the Vedas to be of non-Indian origin. The Aryan invasion (or migration) has been the lynchpin of this discipline.

While the defeat of Nazi Germany and end of European colonialism put an end to the political needs of these theories, they have survived in Western academia because of the heavy investment that scholars have made in Indo-European studies. Recent findings in science, particularly in population genetics have delivered a mortal blow to the AIT. This has led its proponents to resort to propaganda and political lobbying to save it by overturning scientific and historical facts.

This campaigning, like during the recent controversy over the revision of California schools curriculum, is only the latest manifestation of the kind of struggle that is waged whenever new discoveries overthrow old ideas. The most famous of these took place in the time of Galileo. In the end, the supporters of Indo-European studies are no more likely to succeed than Galileo's opponents, who too had the support of powerful political and religious interests. Ultimately, it is truth not personalities that will prevail though the battle for truth is likely to be prolonged. It is best to take a long-term view and prepare the ground for a new generation of researchers.

Background: A Myth that Refuses to Die

When judged by evidence and logic, the various Aryan theories, especially the AIT must be regarded one of the weakest intellectual exercises in recent history — an intellectual failure of the first magnitude. But if longevity and capacity for survival are measures of success, then the Aryan myth — it is hardly a theory — must be counted among the most successful. A product of speculations in comparative linguistics, influenced by German nationalism and British imperialism, it has continued its influence in academia and beyond for well over a century. Even today, when the whole foundation has collapsed, it has not lost its capacity to influence events, of which the recent controversy over proposed changes in what is taught in California schools is only the latest example.

How are we to explain this and what needs to be done to ensure that such a pathological situation does not persist indefinitely into the future? These are weighty questions that have to be addressed at several levels — factual, educational and political. They clearly lie beyond the scope of a single article like the present one. So what is done here is to place it in perspective by looking at the present debate and turmoil as a natural human reaction whenever there is a fundamental shift in world-view, as happened in the time of Galileo. We begin by looking at the latest scientific and historical facts pertaining to the Aryan myth.

Aryan Myth Fostered in "Special Conditions"

It is useful to look at the "special conditions" (as Huxley called it) that led to the Aryan invasion being foisted as the central dogma in ancient Indian history and historiography. This forces us to come to terms with the scientific evidence that will enable us to see this unfounded yet pernicious myth in its true light.

The notion that Indians are one branch of a common stock of people who lived originally in Central Asia or in the Eurasian steppes arose in the late eighteenth century. It began as a linguistic theory to account for similarities between Sanskrit and classical European languages like Greek and Latin. From this modest beginning it soon acquired a life of its own when scholars, especially in Germany, concluded that Europeans and ancient Indians were two branches of a people they called Aryans and later as Indo-Europeans. A whole new academic discipline calling itself Indo-European studies came into existence whose very survival is now at stake.

The Aryan theory, which began life as a linguistic theory soon acquired a biological form. Scholars, mostly linguists, began to talk about not just Aryan languages, but also an Aryan race. Since Indology had its greatest flowering in nineteenth-century Germany it is not surprising that racial ideas that shaped German nationalism should have found their way into scholarly discourse on India. The Indo-European hypothesis and its offshoot of the Aryan invasion (or migration) theory came to dominate this discourse for over a century. The German-born Oxford linguist Friederich Max Müller was the most influential proponent of this theory.[1]

It is important to recognize that the people who created this theory were linguists, not biologists. Scientists, including German scientists had little use for it. As far back as 1939, Sir Julian Huxley, one of the great natural scientists of the twentieth century observed:[2]

> In 1848, the young German scholar Friederich Max Müller (1823–1900) settled in Oxford. . . . About 1853 he introduced into the English language the unlucky term *Aryan* as applied to a large group of languages. . . .
>
> Moreover, Max Müller threw another apple of discord. *He introduced a proposition that is demonstrably false.* He spoke

---

1. He later repudiated the racial aspect of the Aryan theory insisting that it was entirely linguistic. This though was due to political developments in Europe, notably German unification following the Franco-Prussian War and the emergence of Germany as Britain's greatest rival. Max Müller, originally a staunch German nationalist, had to renounce his Aryan race theory to save his position at Oxford. For details see Navaratna Rajaram and David Frawley, *Vedic Aryans and the Origins of Civilization*.

2. Oxford Pamphlet No. 5, OUP: p. 9. See also Navaratna Rajaram and David Frawley *Vedic Aryans and the Origins of Civilization*, New Delhi: Voice of India, p. 37.

> not only of a definite Aryan language and its descendants, but also of a corresponding "Aryan race." The idea was rapidly taken up both in Germany and in England. (Ibid.)

Here is what Huxley had to say regarding the scientific view at the time (1939):

> In England and America the phrase "Aryan race" has quite ceased to be used by writers with scientific knowledge, though it appears occasionally in political and propagandist literature. . . . In Germany, the idea of the "Aryan race" received no more scientific support than in England. Nevertheless, it found able and very persistent literary advocates who made it appear very flattering to local vanity. It therefore steadily spread, fostered by *special conditions*. (Emphasis added).

These "special conditions" were the rise of Nazism in Germany and British imperial interests in India. While both Germany and Britain took to the idea of the Aryan race, the courses taken by this racial theory in the two countries were quite different. Its perversion in Germany leading eventually to Nazism and its horrors is too well known to be repeated here. The British, however, put it to more creative use for imperial purposes, especially as a tool in making their rule acceptable to Indians. A BBC report admitted (6 October 2005):

> It [AIT] gave a historical precedent to justify the role and status of the British Raj, who could argue that they were transforming India for the better in the same way that the Aryans had done thousands of years earlier.

That is to say, the British presented themselves as a "new and improved brand of Aryans" that were only completing the work left undone by their ancestors in the hoary past. This is how the British Prime Minister Stanley Baldwin put it in the House of Commons in 1929:

> Now, after ages, . . . the two branches of the great Aryan ancestry have again been brought together by Providence. . . . By establishing British rule in India, God said to the British, "I have brought you and the Indians together after a long separation, . . . it is your duty to raise them to their own level as quickly as possible . . . brothers as you are. . . ."

Need we say more? Today it is sustained by "special interests" rather than special conditions that no longer exist. These interests include political chauvinism in India and the survival of Indo-European studies in Western academia. It is only a matter of time before this vestige of colonial politics disappears from the scene making way for a more objective approach to the study of ancient India. This is already happening. In the interim, the kind of dispute and controversy witnessed in California are only natural.

On the scientific side, the emergence of molecular biology and the growth of population genetics in the second half of the twentieth century have delivered the *coup de grace* to this pseudo-discipline. The story that science has to tell us is very different from what had been believed for well over a century. What follows is a summing up of the current state of knowledge of human populations inhabiting the world today. We begin with a brief summary of human population genetics.

Genetics on Inherited and Acquired Traits

The Aryan invasion (or migration) theory is only one of several theories created during the European colonial period. Most of them start with the belief that civilizations in different parts of the world began with a massive migration from a central homeland. This belief is usually presented in terms of arguments based on the physical appearance of different population groups. Skin and eye colour get extraordinary attention and importance in this "science." The emergence of genetics, which is the study of inheritance, has discredited the whole approach and all of its conclusions.

Two key concepts play a fundamental role in the scientific study of populations, including human populations: genotype and phenotype. Genotype is what we inherit and phenotype is what is observable. The most common error is to confuse the phenotype, or an observable feature like skin colour for an inherited trait (genotype) without taking note of the environment in which it evolved.

Here is the key issue: any phenotype (observable feature) is the result of the interaction between the genotype (inherited factors) and the environment. The same genotype can produce different phenotypes in different environments, or even if the environment changes over time as almost all environments do. *This is why people in different parts of the world look different even though all of us are descended from Africans.* By 'environment' we mean external factors that include food habits and diseases that result in adaptation as well as the elimination of those unfit to survive. (This is called natural selection, but can also be called natural elimination).

Most changes brought on by the interaction between inherited features (genotype) and the environment take thousands to tens of thousands of years, if not more. A phenotype (like skin colour) that we observe in an individual or a group today is the result of this long evolutionary history. To disentangle a specific original trait from features observed today is next to impossible since the environment has also changed with the phenotype. For example, Europeans today, whose ancestors came from South Asia some 40,000 years ago, most likely look quite different from how their ancestors did when they arrived in Europe.

To compound the difficulty, differences between individuals within a group are always greater than the differences between different groups. That is to say, human beings now inhabiting the world are extraordinarily close, genetically speaking, though they exhibit great variability in observable traits (phenotypes) like physical appearance. They are a complex mix of inheritance and environment. This fact makes it virtually impossible to trace the origin of any population based purely on physical appearance since the environment in which it evolved cannot be recreated. This means we have to find some inherited traits that have been preserved over very long periods and hopefully less sensitive to environmental changes.[3]

Harvard geneticist Lewontin puts it this way:

> Reconstructing the evolutionary past of the human species is almost as difficult as predicting the future, although both are common exercises that biologists engage in, especially when they address a nonscientific public.[4]

In using genetic data to study ancient populations and their migrations, all we can do at this time is to look at some traits that are *not affected* — or at least preserved to some extent — by environmental changes and study their distribution among different human groups. It is important to note that this *cannot* be a phenotype or a superficially observable feature like skin colour, which is the result of interaction between what is inherited and the environment.[5]

---

3. There are further complicating factors like mutation and genetic drift that need not concern us here.

4. Richard Lewontin, *Human Diversity* (2000), New York: Scientific American Library, p. 163.

5. Skin colour tends to get darker as we move closer to the equator and lighter as we move towards the poles. This is the result of natural selection. Human pigmentation has evolved to be dark enough to prevent sunlight from destroying the nutrient called folate but light enough to foster the production of vitamin D. →

A particular trait that we choose as characterizing a population group is called a genetic marker. One such marker that has proven useful is the M17 genetic marker. It is common in India and in adjacent regions but becomes increasingly rare as we move westward into Europe. This, combined with the fact that Indian carriers of M17 are genetically more diverse than European carriers shows that the Indian population is older than the European.[6]

Space, Time and Genes

Population geneticists have identified two objects that carry genetic information that is passed on from generation to generation. They are the mitochondrial DNA (mtDNA) and the Y-chromosome. mtDNA is inherited through the female line (passed on from mother to daughter) while the Y-chromosome is transmitted through the male line. There are individual quirks in these cells that are specific to regions like Africa, India, South-east Asia and so forth. These are the genetic markers we look for. Mapping them allows us to study the possible origins of different population groups now inhabiting the globe. For example, we know that all humans living in the world today are descended from a relatively small African population because

---

→ The fact that we see wide variation in skin colour in India and Europe is evidence that they have lived there long enough for natural selection to work and therefore not recent migrants.

6. It is a basic law of population genetics that older a population group, more genetically diverse it is. Africa is genetically the most diverse continent because it contains the oldest humans. In contrast, Native Americans are the least diverse because they are more recent comers to the region. (This does not apply to countries like the United States and Australia that are composed for the most part of recent immigrants. They have not lived long enough for evolution to work.)

Africa contains almost all the genetic markers found in other parts of the world, but the reverse is not true.[7]

Following more than a century of research in genetics, especially molecular genetics, it is becoming possible to trace the origins of different population groups in the world. It is important however to approach it with care because it has some pitfalls. In particular, since all humans living in the world today have 99.98 per cent of their genes in common, almost any two groups can be found to be genetically similar. Failing to recognize this has led to absurd conclusions like the claim that upper caste Indians are of European origin, who "imposed the oppressive caste system" on the indigenous population (there is no oppressor gene).

The error here lay in assigning biological causes to a man-made classification like caste. Nature, however, does not recognize man-made boundaries. Similar claims can be made for religion — finding a genetic basis for Christianity. Taking this a step further, one may identify Catholic genes, Protestant genes, and presumably even Mormon genes in Salt Lake City, Utah, the home of the Mormon Church, where the claim about genes and caste was first made.[8]

Similarly impossible claims have been made about language, social habits and the like that can have no biological basis. The error consists in mistaking the phenotype for a

7. This means that the genotype responsible for fair skin and light eyes that is common in Europe is present in Africa but does not come into play because of the tropical environment. (This is an oversimplification that ignores mutation, but will do here.)

8. M. Bamshad, et. al. 2001, "Genetic Evidence on the Origin of Indian Caste Populations", *Genome Research* 11, pp. 994-1004. (This article has a chequered history. When Rajaram pointed out the fallacies in the article to the editor of *Genome Research*, he responded that he was not the one responsible for its publication!)

purely inherited trait or genotype. In addition, some workers have tried to use genetics to justify their own pet beliefs and theories like the Aryan invasion. This has led to absurdities like one group claiming that only males migrated (more of which later) while another claimed only females did! Obviously both cannot be true, but both can be false.

After some initial hiccups, the definitive statement about the genetic composition of the Indian population was summarized as follows by researchers led by Luigi Cavalli-Sforza:

> Taken together, these results show that Indian tribal and caste populations derive largely from the same genetic heritage of Pleistocene southern and western Asians *and have received limited gene flow from external regions since the Holocene.* The phylogeography [neighbouring branches] of the primal mtDNA and Y-chromosome founders suggests that these southern Asian Pleistocene coastal settlers from Africa would have provided the inocula for the subsequent differentiation of the distinctive eastern and western Eurasian gene pools. (Emphases added.)[9]

Noting that mtDNA is carried by the female line, while Y-chromosome is passed on through the male line, what this means is that the Indian population is largely indigenous in origin and has received negligible external input (gene flow) since the end of the last Ice Age (Holocene). This means that various migration theories like the Aryan invasion in 1500 BCE simply cannot be true.

The Oxford geneticist Stephen Oppenheimer is more specific and also more emphatic, focusing on the M17 or the

---

9. T. Kisilvid, et. al. "The Genetic Heritage of the Earliest Settlers Persist Both in Indian Tribal and Caste Populations", 2003, *American Journal of Human Genetics*, 72: pp. 313-32.

so-called 'Caucasoid' (politically correct for "Aryan") genetic marker:[10]

> . . . South Asia is logically the ultimate origin of M17 and his [*sic*] ancestors; and sure enough we find highest rates and greatest diversity of the M17 line in Pakistan, India and eastern Iran, and low rates in the Caucasus. M17 is not only more diverse in South Asia than in Central Asia, but diversity *characterizes* its presence in isolated tribal groups in the south, thus undermining any theory of M17 as a marker of a "male Aryan invasion" of India.

So there was no Aryan invasion — by males or by females. This also means that the tribal or the so-called "indigenous' populations of India are not any different from the people making up the bulk of the Indian population, which is what Cavalli-Sforza and his colleagues also found. As Oppenheimer observes, genetics is quite specific on this point.

> One age estimate for the origin of this line in India is as much as 51,000 years. All this suggests that M17 could have found his [*sic*] way initially from India or Pakistan, through Kashmir, then via Central Asia and Russia, before finally coming to Europe. (Ibid).

It is worth noting that this is the *exact reverse of the scenario postulated by various invasion/migration theories including the Aryan invasion theory.* This is not by any means the last word on population genetics, but new findings are unlikely to salvage these nineteenth-century theories or their modern incarnations founded on beliefs and political needs.

Conclusion: From Galileo to Max Planck

Seen against this background of evidence from a wide range of sources — from natural history and genetics to literary and

10. Stephen Oppenheimer (2003), *Out of Eden: The Peopling of the World*, London: Constable, p. 152.

archaeological records — the idea that the Indian civilization developed in a few centuries, seeded by small groups of invading (or migrating) "Aryans" from the Eurasian steppes cannot be taken seriously. But this is only in hindsight. The fact is — it *was* taken seriously, and even today, when one would expect a more enlightened attitude towards facts and evidence than what prevailed in the nineteenth century, various devices are being employed to somehow prevent it from collapse. The recent controversy over the proposed changes in the California school curriculum is only the latest episode in this ongoing battle to replace these theories with a new approach based on facts and logic.

This phenomenon of an established order resisting change has a long history. Even in the exact sciences, change rarely takes place without a struggle. The most famous of these is probably Galileo's struggle with the church leading to his Inquisition. History books present this as a classic case of religious dogma against science, and point to Galileo as the victim of the struggle of knowledge against dogma and superstition. This is a serious distortion of the true nature of the conflict. What Galileo challenged was not the authority of the Church — he was a believing Catholic — but the world-view of his contemporaries. This world-view held that the empirical method and mathematics — both products of the human mind — could not be applied to the study of the heavens, which they held was the creation of God. According to them it was only theology that could explain the heavens — not experiment and observation, much less mathematics.

This is an important point frequently lost in the oversimplification involved in seeing Galileo's persecution as a case of science against religion. His adversaries, who prominently included Cardinal Bellarmine, saw themselves as scientists. It was only when they failed to defeat him in the scientific arena that they resorted to influencing religious and political authority represented by the Vatican, then the paramount power in Italy. More than religion, Galileo's challenge was to theology as the pre-eminent tool in the study of the world. We now see mathematics as the queen of sciences. In Galileo's time, that position was held by theology. According to Galileo, "the universe is written in the language of mathematics." This was something that philosophers (i.e. "scientists") like Cardinal Bellarmine would never concede. To them, the universe was God's creation and only theology was the legitimate tool.

To a historian of science, there is a remarkable similarity between the attitudes of theologians in Galileo's time and of philologists and anthropologists in our own. They cannot accept the fact that the very foundation of their discipline has collapsed. Natural history and genetics have demolished their theories as well as their methods. And like Galileo's adversaries, they too have chosen to resort to politics and propaganda, though the forces they invoke lack the authority of the church in Galileo's time.

Progress, however, is not a respecter of position and prestige. It is unlikely that the proponents of the Aryan theories will be able to turn the clock back or stem progress. What can we expect? Will they recognize that their positions are doomed and learn new facts and master new methods? Highly unlikely. Max Planck, one of the founders of quantum physics that went on to revolutionize physics once observed:

> An important scientific innovation rarely makes its way by gradually winning over and converting its opponents: it rarely happens that Saul becomes Paul. What does happen is that its opponents gradually die out and that the growing generation is familiarized with the idea from the beginning.

If history is any guide, it will be no different with the Aryan theories. We are unlikely to convert the existing adherents: they have too much invested in it, and too set in their ways to change. The most we can expect from them is old wine in new bottles — like AIT being served up as the Aryan "influx" theory instead of the Aryan "invasion" theory. Time and progress will take care of them. What we should be focussing on is the next generation of researchers and paving the way for their work. We should be devoting our time and energy less to fighting these ghosts from the past and more to building a foundation for the younger generation. We can begin by highlighting the importance of some crucial factors like ecology and climate change that have been all but ignored by historians and anthropologists for over a century. We can also emphasize the importance of multidisciplinary approaches that combine science and literary records.

In summary, returning to the present situation, let us accept this well established scientific fact: outside of Africa, South Asia contains the world's oldest populations, and modern Europeans are themselves among the peoples descended from migrants from India, going back more than 40,000 years. There exist ample materials from diverse sources ranging from natural history and archaeology to literature and astronomical records that testify to this. Let us study them and learn about the people who created them without resort to labels and stereotypes like "Aryan" and "Draviḍian." Our time horizons should also change from centuries to millennia, and even tens of millennia. We need to understand more about the impact of climate change, especially during the transition from the Ice Age to the Holocene. (The Holocene is the present interglacial or warm period in which we are living). This should be the starting point for studying history in the Holocene or the post Ice Age period.

6

Aryans and Ancestral Angst
The Obligation of Identity Construction

Yvette C. Rosser

THE volatile nature of national identity formation implicates the politics of historiography and impacts the writing and rewriting of historical narratives. Certainly the "rewriting of history" is not unique to India, "history battles" are being waged from Israel and Palestine to the Balkans and the countries of the former Soviet Bloc. In the USA, during the "History Wars" in the late 1980s and 1990s, educators and intellectuals from the liberal left and conservative right fought tit for tat battles in the op-ed pages of major newspapers. As Sam Wineburg colourfully describes in his recent book, *Historical Thinking and Other Unnatural Acts*,

> The choice between the two seemed absurd but this was exactly what the debate about national history standards had become, "George Washington or Bart Simpson," asked Senator Slade Gorton (R-Wash.) during the 1995 Congressional debates on this subject: Which figure represents a "more important part of our Nation's history for our children to study?"[1] To Gordon, the proposed

1. Cited in Wineberg from: Gary B. Nash, Charlotte Crabtree, and Ross E. Dunn, *History on Trial: Culture Wars and the Teaching of the Past* (New York: Knopf, 1997), p. 232.

> national standards represented a frontal attack on American civilization, an "ideologically driven anti-Western monument to politically correct caricature." The Senate, in apparent agreement, rejected the standards 99-1.[2]

Which history we will teach our children becomes more important than why or how history is taught.

The rancour that was exchanged during this debate over the U.S. National History Standards[3] is indicative of the seriousness with which proponents of each school of thought view their mandates, as if their very survival was at stake. As Sam Wineburg describes, "In the barroom terms befitting such a brawl, those who wrote the standards were traitors, those who opposed them, racists." Senator Bob Dole, the 1996 Republican presidential candidate stated that the "national standards were the 'handiwork of people worse than external enemies'." Those supportive of the new National History Standards pointed out that these kinds of paranoid comments were "driven by latent fears over a diverse America in which the 'new faces [that] crowd[ed] onto the stage of history ruin the symmetry and security of older versions of the past'."[4]

In Indian historiography a similarly contemptuous mêlée has erupted around what would otherwise seem like a rather dry intellectual debate among antiquarians discussing the distant past — regarding questions about the origin, or geographical homeland of the Vedic Aryans. Were they, as colonial era and Marxist historians have long claimed, nomadic tribes originating in the Russian Steppes who came into the subcontinent over the Khyber Pass in successive waves,

---

2. Wineberg (2001), p. 3.
3. The standards were intended to be recommendations, not required.
4. Wineberg (2001), p. 4.

beginning around 1700 BCE, where they encountered and possibly conquered and displaced a sedentary Indus Valley, perhaps Draviḍian culture? Or were the Aryan family groups indigenous to the Saptasindhu region of north-western India, as many archaeologists and other scholars of Vedic literature propose?

European philologists "discovered" the rich literary Sanskrit tradition at the end of the eighteenth century; and during the nineteenth century constructed the theory of the Aryan invasion based on their study of the etymology of common roots of words, which they claim came from a proto-Indo-European parent language German and British Indologists mined Vedic literature looking for clues that could prove the Aryans originally came from outside of the subcontinent. It was reasoned that such a sophisticated language, related to but more refined than Latin, must have come into India from a common proto-Indo-European source. According to this line of thinking, from its pristine Vedic form, Sanskritic culture gradually degenerated into Hindu idolatry and ritual. Conveniently, the Aryan invasion provided a pattern of conquests by outsiders, which helped to justify colonial rule over a land that had always been subjugated by foreigners — first the Central Asian Aryans, followed by the Hūṇas and other groups most notably Turks and Afghans, and finally the Europeans. In this way, India was seen as a derivative civilization, always in need of stimulation from outsiders to progress.

The Aryan Invasion Theory has been widely disseminated for over two centuries and still features prominently in most high school and college level world history textbooks in the USA and, notably, in India. It also figures prominently in countries such as Pakistan where the textbooks describe the Aryans as fair skinned invaders who brought the evil caste system to the area that is now Pakistan and enslaved the indigenous dark-skinned Draviḍians, who were the original residents of the Indus Valley sites. Almost all Pakistani textbooks add a warning that the descendants of the Aryans (Hindu dominated India) would, if given a chance, also enslave the Muslims of Pakistan. Many contemporary scholars, both in the West and in India, also embrace the invasion narrative, though in a more politically correct, and less overtly nationalistic tone than in Pakistan.

There are, however, many scholars who refute the Aryan Invasion Theory and have called into question the methodologies of the Western philologists and their modern and post-modern counterparts, the Indologists. Lining up in opposing positions, the "inside India" proponents claim that the theories of Indologists were constructed with a political agenda from an unequal relationship of power — from a position of cultural and economic hegemony. It is argued that scholars who are strongly opposed to considering an indigenous origin for the Sanskrit language employ Euro-centric colonial era paradigms in their analyses, which overlook not only the archaeological record, but misread and ignore important references from Vedic literature.

Employing alternative research methodologies and reevaluating passages from the Vedas, scholars who are questioning the Aryan Invasion/Migration[5] Theory have found considerable flaws in the early Indological interpretations. By computing ancient astronomical correlations based on the procession of the equinoxes with

---

5. Over the past twenty years many scholars, such as the well-known Indian historian Romila Thapar, have revised the invasion theory and now advocate the Aryan Migration Theory — that the Aryan tribes came as nomadic pastoralists in waves over the course of several centuries.

seasonal astrological references in the *Ṛgveda*,[6] and bringing into consideration the vast data that has emerged in the past few decades from archaeological discoveries at sites along the bed of the dried up Sarasvatī River and across large areas of northern India and the Gujarātī coastal area, scholars have seriously challenged the Aryan Invasion/Migration Theory.[7]

These proponents of an inside India origin for the Aryans have suggested that the civilization that created the cities, trading routes, and seaports of the Indus/Sarasvatī culture were in fact the same cultural group whose predecessors produced the Vedas and are thus the ancestors of the "Haṛappans" and by extension, ancestors of the contemporary inhabitants of the Indian subcontinent. This of course could only have occurred if the writing of the Vedas was associated with the Indus/Sarasvatī civilization. Such a theory pushes the dates of the Vedas back several thousand years from what was assumed by traditional Indologists, who dated them from around 1200 BCE.[8]

---

6. *Astronomical data and the Aryan Question*, http://www.hindunet.org/saraswati/aryan/koenraad1.html

7. "Dr. B.R. Ambedkar, famous for his work on the Indian Constitution, as well as his campaign in support of the nation's dalit/harijan/vanavasi communities noticed the racial overtones underlying the theory and described the British espousal of the Aryan Invasion theory in the following words: 'The theory of invasion is an invention. This invention is necessary because of a gratuitous assumption that the Indo-Germanic people are the purest of the modern representation of the original Aryan race. The theory is a perversion of scientific investigation. It is not allowed to evolve out of facts. On the contrary, the theory is preconceived and facts are selected to prove it. It falls to the ground at every point.'" From: http://members.tripod.com/~INDIA_RESOURCE/sahistory.html

8. It is well known that the scholars of the eighteenth and nineteenth centuries assumed that the earth was created in 4000 BCE, based →

Reinterpreting dated data, and applying new theories and technologies to old historical problems is the usual and accepted methodology of the history profession and serves to further research. The same rethinking of chronology is going on among Egyptologists as they apply new laboratory tests to mortar samples from pyramids and other techniques that can help date the structures more exactly. Even in the field of Egyptology there are wide discrepancies among competing theories. The great difference between Indology and Egyptology is that the vast majority of Egyptians do not have spiritual connections and extant ritual practices that tie them to the ancient religions of the Pharaohs, whereas contemporary Hindu-Indians trace their religious traditions directly to the Vedas and many of their customs, such as the fashions of females to wear bangles and put vermillion in the parts of their hair were also popular 5000 years ago in the Indus/ Sarasvatī civilization.

When it comes to the Aryan Invasion Theory, well-established tenured Indologists have little patience for challenges to their century-long claims of an outside India origin for Vedic Sanskrit. Quite often, in this debate, rather than calling methodologies and textual references into question, a common response against arguments supporting an inside India origin of the Aryans, as strange as it may seem, is to politically discredit the research by accusing the scholars of fascism and or hyper Hindu-centric nationalism, irregardless of who is presenting the data or what data they have presented. If Hindus themselves were not concerned about this issue perhaps the opposing debate would be far more dispassionate without the personal attacks based on the

→ on Biblical dating. They extrapolated backwards to date the Vedas. Obviously the earth is billions of years older.

perceived need of post-modernity to deconstruct *dangerous* identity politics.

It is widely assumed by many Indologists that the vast majority of scholars who question the invasion paradigm are Hindu nationalists, whom they derisively refer to as "Hindu Fundamentalists." This seemingly automatic response — unquestioningly labelling scholars as "fascist" sympathizers — simply for asking penetrating questions and posing alternative solutions to an old historical problem — is a common tact within the hotly contested politicized debate over the content and meaning of ancient history in India. However, there are numerous Western and non-Hindu scholars who are also rethinking the plausibility of the invasion theory, and even they are accused of supporting the political agenda of ultra-right-wing Hindu super nationalist politically motivated scholars. What makes this particular debate so remarkable, besides the vivid and hot hyperbole, is the sheer remoteness of the historical narrative in question.

A simplistic polarized understanding — racist/humanist, patriot/traitor — emerges from dogmatic attachment to a particular historical perspective. This attitude of "you're either with us or against us" that was popularized by President George W. Bush after the terrorist attacks of 11 September 2001, was also expressed by Senator Bob Dole on the floor of the U.S. Senate in 1995 during his very vocal and hyper patriotic condemnation of the multicultural stance he perceived in the U.S. History Standards. This either/or compartmentalization completely ignores the dynamic role of contesting historiographies.

The debate over the Aryan Invasion Theory plays out in India in an almost identical pattern, where many scholars, including Euro-Americans and Indian leftists, have labelled those who question the Aryan Invasion Theory as Hindu fundamentalists, also referred to by the pejorative term Saffronites, in reference to the ochre colour of a saint's robes and the flag used by the RSS.[9] Scholars who are personally committed or professionally attached to the Aryan Invasion/ Migration Theory[10] are quick to accuse proponents of the Indigenous Aryan Theory of promoting racism, rabid nationalism, xenophobia, and other social ills. They claim that if the Saffronites succeed in proving that the Aryans were not outsiders, it will make it easier to vilify Indian Muslims as foreigners.[11]

An article that appeared in an Indian magazine *Frontline*[12] reporting about the 61st session of the Indian History Congress (IHC), held in Kolkata from 2 to 4 January 2001, expressed "concern over attempts to distort history in school textbooks and thus subvert secular education." The well-known Marxist historian, and eminent scholar from Aligarh University, Professor Irfan Habib is quoted in the article where, in mocking tones, he evaluates the historical debate,

9. Rashtriya Svayamsevak Sangh (RSS) — literally, National Voluntary Service Society, a Hindu nationalist organization founded in 1924, known to be one of the largest service organizations in the world.

10. Some scholars refer to this theory as the Aryan Invasion Theory, others call it the Aryan Migration Theory.

11. Ironically, many caste conscious (read: colour conscious) Hindu elites in India also support the Aryan invasion theory because they prefer to see themselves as racially distinct from indigenous groups, therefore an Indo-European homeland makes them feel more Caucasian, that they consider to be racially superior to a darker hue of skin tone which they associate with south Indians and tribal peoples. This type of skin tone-based racism can be found in all societies and even within families.

12. "Concern over distortions", by Suhrid Sankar Chattopadhyay, vol. 18, issue 02, 20 January–2 February 2001. *Frontline* is well known for its staunch opposition to the Sangh Parivar. The editor,

→

> According to the Sangh Parivar,[13] the Aryans did not come to India, they were from north India, in fact, more specifically, from Punjab, Haryana and western Uttar Pradesh. This is ridiculous, and it has reached such a point that whoever says that the Aryans came to India are labelled racists and those who say that they were from India are hailed as patriots.

Those who support the Aryan Invasion Theory, such as Professor Habib, are conversely labelled neo-colonial and anti-national, and as he mentioned, "racists" by scholars "hailed as patriots" who support the indigenous Aryan model. According to those so-called patriots, historians like Professor Habib are still clinging to old theories, refusing to take note of new discoveries, blinded by a legacy of "neo-colonial mindsets" and "pseudo-secular vote bank politics."

Scholars who share Professor Habib's view that an inside origin of the Aryans is "ridiculous" refer to the advocates of that theory as racists, and other pejorative terms, and against the basic secular, socialist, pluralistic ethos of India. In this high pitch discourse there is very little discussion of evidence based on research, and the rhetoric is diverted to personal attacks and slander. Both camps inevitably label the other anti-national.

Racists and patriots are fighting a contemporary academic battle over an interesting, but remote historical question. Professor Irfan Habib finds the idea of indigenous Aryans to be ridiculous and could have continued his list of dyads to include other pairs of ideologically opposing positions —

→ N. Ram is a pro-Chinese Marxist, as can easily be seen from his editorials.

13. The group of organizations, including the RSS, the BJP, and the VHP, that promote a Hindu-centric perspective of Indian history and culture.

obscurantist/scientific, traditional/modern, revivalist/progressive. The politically charged nature of this debate has provoked normally sophisticated and erudite Sanskrit scholars, even at institutions such as Harvard,[14] to insinuate that supporters of the "Autocthonous Aryan" theory are fascists or at best New Age adherents to neo-Hindu obscurantism.[15] However as the following quote from a scholar of Sanskrit from Athens, Greece points out, not all who question the Aryan Invasion Theory are Hindu nationalists and there is, more importantly, room for doubt and scholarly discourse.

> The situation whereby the Aryans are indigenous and compose the bulk of the (*Ṛgveda*) in the 4th millennium in *Saptasindhu* is a very ṣimple one and in harmony with the archaeological data in the region. Scholars who think that this simple situation is at odds with their linguistic theories need do no more than re-examine these theories, which necessitate the further theory of the Aryan immigration, which theory generates complexities and problems and is in conflict with the data of archaeology. After all it is not as though these linguistic theories are without problems of their own or that in their present form they harmonize with archaeological data anywhere else in the Eurasian belt involved.[16]

The philologists are ready to defend the Indo-European forts and fight it out with the archaeologists, whom they have

14. Professor Michael Witzel, a Sanskrit professor at Harvard University is one of the most fervently politicized advocates of the migration theory.
15. See *Frontline*, December 2000.
16. From internet correspondence of Nicholas Kazanas, a Sanskritist from Athens, Greece, *The RV Date = a Postscript* an answer to Michael Witzel's comments about the Aryan Invasion and the Indus Valley civilization. (Used with permission "Nicholas Kazanas" <aroik@comvos.net>)

dubbed Hindu nationalists. These philologists and professors of South Asian Studies are not just non-Hindu Indians, such as Irfan Habib, or "secular or pseudo-secular" Indians, such as Romila Thapar, who are passionately opposed to reopening the verdict on this antiquarian question, Euro-American scholars are equally threatened and have drawn their ideological battle lines. Kazanas continues,

> Instead of emitting such strident emotional cries and witch-hunt slogans, Prof Witzel and his followers had better re-examine their unfounded linguistic assumptions and recall the words of Edmund Leach (published in 1990),[17] who was neither an Indian nationalist technocrat, nor a New-Age writer, but a solid, mainstream pillar of the academic establishment. He wrote: "Because of their commitment to a unilineal segmentary history of language development that needed to be mapped onto the ground, the philologists took it for granted that proto-Indo-Iranian was a language that had originated outside either India or Iran. From this we derived the myth of the Aryan invasions." Then that provost of King's College, Cambridge, added that to shift the Aryan invasion theory, which he dismissed contemptuously, "is like trying to cut down a 300-year-old oak tree with a pen-knife. But the job will have to be done one day."

It is amazing that a vignette from the ancient past can arouse such passion among what are often stereotyped as a rather dull lot: social scientists and humanities scholars. Though a historical study of evidence about a people who lived 5000 or 7000 thousand years ago would not seem a likely source of such heated polemics, when it comes to identity formation and laying claims to a biological biography tied to a sacred geography, no other discipline seems to elicit such acrimonious

17. Leach, Edmund "Aryan Invasions over four millennia" in *Culture through Time*, ed. E. Ohnuki-Tierney, Stanford: Stanford Univ. Press, 1990, pp. 227-45.

and passionate debates as does historiography.

With due acknowledgement of the virulence with which many Marxist/Westernized/anti-Hindu Revivalist scholars argue their perspective and the importance that they place on maintaining a certain point of view, it is also a given that debate is the source of discovery in the field of historiography. It is this dynamic nature of the discipline that is at the heart of true historical research — an ultimately very democratic process that is constantly pushing the envelope of knowledge by illuminating little known facts and presenting alternative interpretations.

Very often scholars outside the field make breakthrough discoveries that create a framework or timetable upon which historical hypotheses can be re-explored and articulated. Except in the case of top-down force-fed historical distortions, such as those imposed on the German people by the Nazis and the Russian people by the Soviets, most alternative historiographies arising from the scholarly population are an expression of changing identities or contesting perceptions of the past.

Changing historical perspectives are not unique to Indian history. For years French history textbooks ignored "France's collaboration with its Nazi occupiers" but since "the mid-1970s, spurred by scholarly histories, the spread of new historical methods and the rise of a less tainted and more curious generation" French textbooks "began to deal more honestly with World War II."[18] Sometimes some historical interpretations may swing too far to the left and seek to validate a vulgar unfolding of society according to Karl Marx. Other times history may be skewed as it is adjusted to

18. "Teaching Myths and History", *The New York Times*, Editorial, 17 February 1998, p. A22.

accommodate more nationalist interpretations — history can be used to validate almost anything depending on how you use it.

The historical narratives of some nations, such as Japan and Germany, are scrutinized by foreigners, whereas other nations are allowed to eliminate unpleasant facts and elide nasty historical events. For instance, there is little international pressure exerted on the internal affairs of the education ministry in Turkey to express remorse in their school textbooks regarding the massacre of Armenians. Tibetans, and Tibetophiles in the international community, obviously have no leverage and indeed not any possibility of pressuring the education ministry of the People's Republic of China to include an apologetic appraisal of the negative impact the Chinese occupation has had on Tibetan culture.

Some genocidal tales or subaltern revolutions become proper topics for academic discourse and find voice in popular histories. Other cultural cataclysms and demographic decimations are simply swallowed by time as too impossible to believe or perhaps seemingly irrelevant. Or importantly, as in the case of what has been termed the "Hindu Holocaust,"[19] sometimes topics are so charged with contemporary antagonisms leading to potential for inter-group violence, that they are shunned as an improper subject for academic discourse.

History is written to suit real politics and the sensibilities of the modern age, as Michel Rolph Trouillot observes in *Silencing the Past*,

19. The Islamic invasions of the subcontinent resulted in the forced migration of millions of Hindus over the Hindukush mountains, and the destruction of hundreds of temples, schools, and libraries.

> When reality does not coincide with deeply held beliefs, human beings tend to phrase interpretations that force reality within the scope of these beliefs. They devise formulas to repress the unthinkable and to bring it back within the realm of accepted discourse.[20]

The controversy regarding whose paradigms and whose historical narratives become standardized and whose are discarded is a topic that often becomes a passionate political issue. Conflicting historiographical orientations are hotly debated as we engage the changing face of the past with the tools of the present.

The following long quote from Ananda Wood, an independent Indian scholar living in Pune,[21] articulately expresses the dynamic uncertainty of competing analyses of Indian historiography,

> One thing that occurs to me about the teaching of history is that teachers should not be afraid to say to their students: "We don't know." This applies in particular, in a rather big way, to the Vedas and the Indus civilization. In the present situation, I think it's best to say to students:
>
> Some scholars suggest that the Vedas were composed by immigrants who came into India at the end or soon after the Indus civilization, around 1,500 to 1,000 BCE. And others suggest that they were composed by the inhabitants of the Indus civilization as it developed, starting perhaps as early as 6,500 or 6,000 BCE. But the truth is that there isn't

---

20. Trouillot, *Silencing the Past*, p. 72.

21. Ananda Wood, whose father was "English, of Irish stock, and whose mother was a Parsee," has a bachelor's degree in mathematics and theoretical physics from Cambridge University, and a doctorate in anthropology from University of Chicago (with field research in Kerala, India). This quote is taken with permission from a personal e-mail communication.

> conclusive evidence for either picture. So there is a huge uncertainty, of 5,000 years, in the age of the Hindu tradition. That uncertainty affects our entire dating of ancient and classical Indic traditions. Modern scholars have tended to dismiss traditional datings as absurdly mythical exaggerations, but it may be that the traditional datings are not quite so wrong at all.
>
> Of course, such an admission of gross ignorance comes very hard to many teachers: especially in India, where attitudes tend to be polarized between old-fashioned authoritarianism among the traditionalists and brattish assertiveness among the 'liberals.' Moreover, for those teachers who do bite the bullet and admit the gross uncertainties of Indian history, the admission will of course raise some very tough questions to be answered about the nature and course of Indian history.

As can be seen from the report below, instead of taking Ananda Wood's advice, educators often ignore the issue:

Denial Is Not a River in India

On 11-12 March 2006, the Foreign Policy Research Institute's International Education Program hosted forty-four teachers from across the USA for a "weekend of discussion on teaching about India" at the University of Tennessee at Chattanooga. See the FPRI report "Teaching About India" (vol. 11, no. 2) : http://www.fpri.org/footnotes112.200604.kuehner.teachingindia.html

Among the presenters, Richard H. Davis of Bard College spoke to the teachers about early Indian history suggesting several "teachable moments" for high school students in the study of South Asia. The first era that he identified was the ancient "urban civilization" in the Indus Valley. Davis gave a synopsis of the archaeological discoveries made in the 1920s, when scholars "realized they'd discovered a lost civilization, a complex, literate, urbanized, centrally organized society that covered an area larger than present-day Pakistan." Davis mentions that this culture had carried on "long-distance trade with Mesopotamia" and had survived many centuries. He concludes however that the Indus civilization was "entirely lost," and poses the question, "Why did it end between 1900-1700 BCE?"

Davis answers his own rhetorical query myopically, referring to "*one* of the earliest hypotheses" that was formulated by nineteenth-century European Indologists who claimed that there was a "*conquest* by a new group of horse-riding *invaders*" (emphasis added). Though Davis tells the teachers that "no evidence of this [invasion] has been found," after highlighting the discredited theory, he doesn't bother to mention the many archaeological discoveries made since the 1940s that have provided significant data leading scholars to formulate new theories concerning the Indus Valley Civilization and the Aryans. Davis states that "no evidence (supporting the conquest by invaders after 1700 BCE) has been found," but he strangely doesn't offer any alternatives. He mentions the archaeology of the 1920s but completely ignores the detailed excavations completed during the last half of the twentieth century. He thereby short-changes the teachers and their students, who are deprived of recent research that has analysed and deconstructed the very same theory he initially mentioned but quickly debunked for no stated reason. Davis then goes on to rely on this very same questionable theory as the basis of his further historical trajectory.

This is the same convoluted, oxymoronic methodological approach that is used in World History textbooks, which first question the colonial invasion theory and subsequently base the historical narrative about ancient India on a series of violent invasions that seem never to have happened. Though the romantic theory of chariot-driving, horse-riding Aryan invaders was discarded long ago, its trajectory is still assumed as the basis of the chronological historical narrative of ancient India. N. Kazanas, a Sanskrist and director of Omilos Meleton in Athens, observed in his article "The AIT and Scholarship," that regarding the origins of Hinduism and the historiography of ancient India, the "substratum thinking is invasion and conquest."

At the Foreign Policy Research Institute (FPRI) workshop for secondary educators, as in most High School World History textbooks, ancient Indian history is explained by retaining the discarded model of an Aryan ingress into north-west India. As Davis explained to the teachers,

> The years 1300-1000 BCE saw the rise of the Indo-Aryans, new groups of nomadic, pastoral, cattle-keeping people who appeared in the north-west areas of South Asia. These were not agriculturalists or city people, and they left little behind. But when urban civilizations re-emerged in South Asia centuries later, these Indo-Aryans were the dominant social group.

This telling of ancient India is based on the assumption of an ingress of nomadic pastoral people from Central Asia into the Subcontinent. The presumed arrival of these uncultured outsiders forms the substratum of all Indian historical narratives. Even though this hypothetical migration/invasion theory remains unverified, it is not discarded after it is deconstructed, but allowed to stand, questioned but intact, forming the bedrock of all subsequent Indian history.

Ignoring contemporary scholarship and perpetuating a lopsided presentation, in 2006 the FPRI organized a high profile conference on "Teaching about India" yet none of the sessions referred to the changing paradigms in the teaching of Indian history and culture. The paradigm is changing but the mainstream scholars employed to teach about India don't mention the dramatic theoretical shift in the coverage of the history of ancient India. Denial won't change the inevitable though it can delay its arrival.

There is a revolution going on regarding the teaching of India. However, this metamorphosis is not even alluded to in educational events such as the FPRI designed to teach about India. This oversight is not because of ignorance. The academic movement is gathering momentum; even Davis mentioned that the accepted theory had been overturned but he just didn't bother to explain why or how. He didn't engage the issues.

The University of Tennessee at Chattanooga Asia Program, who co-sponsored the conference, was the publisher of the 2001 edition of the journal *Education Asia*, which addressed problems in the teaching of India. The FPRI should have touched on this highly relevant trend, exemplified by the changing paradigm regarding the Aryan Invasion/ Migration.

There is a very ironic reason that the counter arguments invalidating the Aryan ingress theories are ignored. These cutting-edge changes go against the long-held perspectives of mainstream Indologists, theories upon which they, and their mentors, have based their careers. Many contemporary specialists of India studies vilify, demonize, or simply ignore those whose work questions or negates certain pet theories. This dismissive approach is exemplified by the disdain that many historians of ancient India show for archaeology. The work of B.B. Lal, known as the father of Indian archaeology, disproves the Aryan Invasion/Migration Theory, yet his work is maligned or ignored. At the very least, scholars such as Davis should explain that the AIT has been questioned mainly through the work of archaeologists. Though central to the debate, this important detail is ignored.

There are contemporary scholarly efforts working consistently to change the convoluted paradigms upon which the study of ancient Indian history has been erroneously constructed. Paradoxically, the work of scholars such as B.B. Lal can be ignored precisely because the ancientness debate has been dreadfully politicized. Ironically, the work of Indian archaeologists has been so thoroughly vilified by scholars such as Professor Michael Witzel at Harvard, that other scholars can easily ignore the evidence unearthed from the ancient Indus/Sarasvatī Valleys. In this paranoid milieu, ground-breaking work such as Sankrant Sanu's impact on Encarta is seen as a threat instead of a conscious, articulate, observant insider's contribution to the field. Paradigm shaking work has been pejoratively politicized and dismissed. This strategy of denial can't last forever. (See: *Are Hinduism Studies Prejudiced? A Look at Microsoft Encarta* http://www.sulekha.com/blogs/blogdisplay.aspx?cid=4499)

Strangely, many scholars at top notch educational institutions in the USA, such as Michael Witzel at Harvard, demonize those who are engaging and eliminating the biases in the teaching of India. Or as in the case of FPRI, simply ignore the strides that are being made in the reinterpretation of Indian culture and a new understanding of the chronology of India's history. The paradigm is shifting, slowly but steadily, and on the near horizon there is a significant academic metamorphosis in the study of India. From the entrenched colonial model to a new holistic, multi-perspectival reinterpretation that reflects origins and connections, the mould is breaking and a new model of Hindu studies is emerging.

Unfortunately, the paradigm shift causes fear, so it's ignored. But it is the model of the future and one day soon, in the narration about India's history and cultures, the "indigenous" approach will be non-controversial, respected and accepted as intrinsic to the understanding of Hinduism. Soon, this approach will be part of mainstream scholarship without the subtle and pervasive negative slant or incomplete coverage now allotted.

There is inevitably a backlash created by a paradigm shift among those who are dedicated or attached to the earlier paradigm. We all know what happened to Galileo, he had to recant that the earth was round. This reluctance to accept new paradigms (new information) has been seen throughout history and in many disciplines. For example, research in neuroscience in the mid-1970s discovered that the central nervous system could affect the immune system, and the new science, psychoneuroimmunology was born. Even with continuing research studies confirming these findings, providing further evidence that not only the brain, but what we think and feel affects the immune system, it was not until 20 years later that textbooks in the health care field began to include psychoneuroimmunology and the power of the body-mind connection to affect health. The changing theory of the Aryan invasion has similar transformative potential accompanied by foot-dragging resistance.

Doing Historiography

An honest approach to the problem of not knowing all the facts about certain historical events is to tell students that there is uncertainty and teach them that they can use the tools of the present to unlock the mysteries of the past. Instead of dismissing data that does not fit an earlier hypothesis, teachers can lead their students through an interactive investigation into what we know and don't know about ancient India. Students can be encouraged to investigate the complex and competing web of parallel and opposing, complementary and conflicting theories. The ingress by Central Asian peoples was initially referred to as the AIT, though in the past few decades, scholars have adjusted and reformulated the theory, which they now refer to as the Aryan Migration Theory (AMT). There are other scholars who have looked at the data from different perspectives, and have formulated several theories, including, but not limited to Out of India Theory (OIT) and other explanations, that argue against the probability of an Aryan Invasion/Migration Theory.

By juxtaposing information from various sources, such as linguistic, archaeological, literary, astronomical, historical, and genetic studies, an exercise in "Doing Historiography" can examine the divergent materials concerning the Aryan Invasion/Migration Theory. This would enable students to investigate this academic theory — and make their own hypotheses as to whether they think that the Vedic Aryans originated somewhere near the Russian Steppes. Or perhaps they were from somewhere in the north-western part of the subcontinent in present-day Pakistan or perhaps near Gujarat or Haryana. Were the Aryans a pastoral, nomadic people who entered into the subcontinent some time between 1800 BCE and 1200 BCE? Or were the Aryans indigenous to the subcontinent and related to the builders of the Indus Valley/ Sarasvatī River civilization?

This sort of objective methodology presents the pros and cons from a variety of sources and areas of interest. Students can evaluate the data through group work, debates, graphics, and other co-operative activities. The facts in the case can be listed and referenced. This comparative process allows the students to examine facts supporting the Aryan Invasion/ Migration Theory and facts that disprove it. The students can develop a chart listing pro and con evidences referenced from scholars with quotes, maps, and other data. This chart can provide a compilation of information highlighting details from "both sides of the debate." As they review the data on the chart, the students will compare and contrast, categorize, evaluate, and make inferences to complete the activity. They will make lists: pro, con, and undecided. They can compare facts, discuss the evidence in groups, debates, and other pedagogical processes. They can then present their conclusions. This learning process stresses intellectual analytical skills, as well as historical competency. Students can analyse the data using various strategies, such as a Venn diagram to represent the relationships of cultural artefacts — charts and graphs can be constructed to show similarities, trends, and differences.

This type of pedagogical process develops higher level thinking skills as well as intellectual tools enabling historical knowledge. The process of using the Aryan Invasion question to do historiography is based on educational standards such as:

- Students distinguish fact from opinion in historical narratives and stories.
- Students distinguish relevant from irrelevant information, essential from incidental information, and verifiable from unverifiable information in historical narratives and stories.
- Students assess the credibility of primary and secondary sources and draw sound conclusions from them.
- Students detect the different historical points of view on historical events and determine the context in which the historical statements were made (the questions asked, sources used, author's perspectives).

- Students understand and distinguish cause, effect, sequence, and correlation in historical events, including the long- and short-term causal relations.
- Students explain the sources of historical continuity and how the combination of ideas and events explains the emergence of new patterns.
- Students recognize the role of chance, oversight, and error in history.
- Students recognize that interpretations of history are subject to change as new information is uncovered.

For references showing various sides of the AIT debate, see: http://www.eastwestcultural.org/public/amt/amt-internet.html

Evidence supporting the Aryan Evidence nullifying the Aryan Invasion/Migration Theory.

Students learn more if given the opportunity to figure things out, rather than being told what to think. Historians and other scholars must keep their minds open when confronted by alternative theories and new ideas. In this way, the scholarly discipline is envigorated and renewed.

7

The Mahābhārata War
Its Date on the basis of Astronomical References

B.N. Narahari Achar

A compelling derivation of the date of the Mahābhārata war is made on the basis of astronomical references in the epic, which number more than one hundred and fifty. Although the astronomical references are found scattered throughout the epic, those pertaining to the war are found in Udyoga and Bhīṣma Parvas and have been characterized as confusing and self-contradictory. Contrary to this general belief it is shown that the astronomical references in the Bhīṣma Parva are systematic and are in accordance of a Vedic tradition of astrological omens described in *Atharvaveda* and its Pariśiṣṭas, and refer mostly to comets. The true planetary positions are in agreement with those described in Udyoga Parva. These include (i) Śani at Rohiṇī, (ii) lunar eclipse on Kārttika *pūrṇimā* (iii) solar eclipse at Jyeṣṭha. These together with retrograde motion of Mars before reaching Jyeṣṭha lead to a unique date, 3067 BCE for the war. The same date had been proposed earlier by Professor Raghavan. The astronomical events described in the epic are demonstrated with star maps simulated using planetarium software. The consistency of this date with various traditional reckonings is discussed. This date then forms the sheet-anchor for the chronology of Bhārata.

I. Introduction

THE importance of the date of the Mahābhārata war for the chronology of India cannot be overstated. In the opinion of Pusalker,[1] the Mahābhārata war is the central landmark in Indian traditional history and fixing the date of the event will give a starting point for settling dates of events occurring before and after it. According to tradition, as declared in the epic itself, the war between the Kauravas and Pāṇḍavas took place at the junction of *Dvāpara* and *Kali yugas*,[2] around 3000 BCE. Bhāratīyas never had any doubt about the historicity of the event and have been celebrating the anniversaries of certain events connected with the epic such as Gītājayantī and Bhīṣmāṣṭamī for centuries. However, when Western scholars began to study the epics with interest from a "rationalist historic" point of view, doubts were expressed about the war ever having been a historic event. Some granted that the event was historic, but only a family feud, which was exaggerated to epic proportions and expressed doubts about its date. Western scholars,[3] while acknowledging that unlike other ancient civilizations, the ancient traditions in Bhārata have been preserved without a break down to the present day, have generally argued that Bhāratīyas lack a sense of history and that there is a dearth of "historical texts" in Bhārata that contain records of dates and events. These scholars have discounted the fact that two of the great epics of the world, *Rāmāyaṇa* and *Mahābhārata* are traditionally regarded as *itihāsas*, i.e. historic texts and that there are in addition, a host of supporting texts in the form of Purāṇas. Ignoring the fact that

---

1. Pusalker (1996), p. 272.
2. *antare caiva saṁprāpte kali dvāparayorabhūt*
   samantapañcake yuddhaṁ kurupāṇḍava senayoḥ II — *MBh* I.2.9
3. A.L. Basham (1953), *The Wonder that was India*, New York: Grove Press Inc., p. 4.

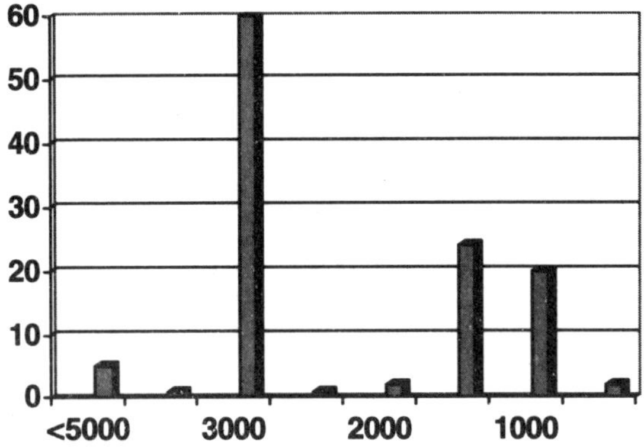

fig. 1: Distribution of the number of authors and the dates (in BCE years) proposed based on all methodologies.

Bhārata has its own sense of history and its purpose,[4] the scholars have systematically misrepresented the chronology of Bhārata so as to fit some misguided theory.[5] A plethora of dates derived on the basis of a number of diverse methodologies and with no consensus, have been proposed. More than 120 research papers and books have been published on the topic of the date of the Mahābhārata war.

Fig. 1 displays the distribution of dates ranging from ~5000 BCE to 600 BCE and the number of authors[6] proposing the dates on the basis of various methodologies such as linguistics, archaeology, astronomy, Purāṇic genealogies, etc. Most of the Indian scholars prefer the date ~3000 BCE, most of the Western scholars showing a preference for the much later dates around 1500 BCE-1000 BCE. A number of authors have determined the

---

4. *dharmārtha kāma mokṣāṇāṁ upadeśa samanvitaṁ* ।
   pūrvavṛttaṁ kathāyuktaṁ itihāsaṁ pracakṣate ॥

5. The so-called Aryan Invasion Theory or AIT, now thoroughly discredited.

6. Sathe (1983), p. 8.

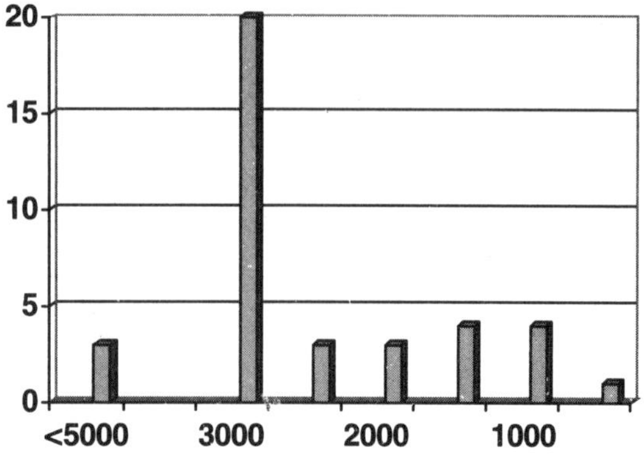

fig. 2: Distribution of number of authors and the dates (in BCE years) proposed on the basis of astronomical references

date of the war on the basis of astronomical references[7, 8] found in the epic itself. However, it has not been possible to arrive at a definite date on the basis of astronomical references either. *Fig.* 2 shows the distribution of dates from more than forty scholars who have made use of the astronomical data. It is clear that there is as much variation in the dates based on astronomical references alone as the dates based on diverse methodologies. Practically every scholar has criticized the astronomical references in the epic as conflicting and self-contradictory, so that no satisfactory and acceptable result can be obtained from these data.[9]

A new research tool in the form of Planetarium Software[10] has recently become commercially available. These software can project the view of the sky at any time and place on the world from about 4700 BCE to about CE 10000 and the author has successfully used these products to study the astronomical references in the Vedic texts and in the epic

7. Dikshit (1966), p. 118.
8. Kane (1958), vol. III, p. 902.
9. Pusalker (1996), p. 272.
10. *Sky and Telescope* (2001), p. 72.

Mahābhārata. The purpose of this essay is to present the results of a research programme carried over a period of about five years to determine the date of the Mahābhārata war on the basis of the astronomical references in the epic and their simulation using the planetarium software. It will be shown that contrary to the general belief, the astronomical references in the Bhīṣma Parva and Udyoga Parva, which constitute the astronomical references most pertinent to the war, form a very consistent set and in the context of omens as indicating impending calamities, agree closely with the tradition of omens in *Atharvaveda* and its *ariśiṣṭa*s. The astronomical references lead to a unique date for the war, 3067 BCE and all other astronomical references in the epic are consistent with this date. This date had also been proposed earlier by Professor Raghavan.[11] This date forms the sheet-anchor for the chronology of Bhārata.

The plan of this article is as follows. A brief description of the salient features of the planetarium software products commercially available will be discussed. The limitations of the simulations are also discussed. The set of astronomical references in the Udyoga and the Bhīṣma Parvas are discussed. The consistency of the references within the Bhīṣma Parva is discussed. It is shown that most of the astronomical references in this set pertain to comets and that the few truly planetary references are identical to the ones in Udyoga Parva and that these common references lead to the unique date of the war. The consistency of the other astronomical references in the epic is illustrated by star maps generated by the planetarium software. In the final section there is a consolidation of the traditions of *Bhāgavata-Purāṇa*, Saptarṣi Era, and beginning of Kali Yuga.

11. Raghavan (1969), p. 31.

The Planetarium Software

The term planetarium software refers to a collection of computer programmes which can generate and display on the screen of a computer monitor thousands of stars and other heavenly objects as seen in the sky at any given location and at any given date and time (between 4713 BCE and CE 9999), all at the touch of a mouse. These software programmes draw from the most up to date star catalogues and are based on the current theories of planetary and stellar phenomena. They are routinely used for telescopic applications both in manual and computer controlled modes of operation, for they can project at which part of the sky and what time a desired object becomes visible in the sky and direct the telescope accordingly. They are also used for satellite tracking applications routinely. Details of such applications are available in the instruction manuals. Literally hundreds of such programmes are available in the market to suit any need for astronomical applications. There are several popular products commercially available:[12] The Sky, SkyMap Pro, Red Shift, Cybersky, Starry Night, etc. for PC applications and Voyager for McIntosh applications. These software products can also be used as tools of research in exploring ancient astronomy as has been shown by the author in some recent publications.[13] The author has found SkyMap Pro to be most suited for current applications, but has used Red Shift, Cybersky and, occasionally, The Sky as supplementary tools. The author also has found useful another computer programme,[14] Pancang2, which can calculate *tithi* and *nakṣatra* for any day on the Gregorian calendar. This programme has been used only as a check and has not been used for any calculations other than for verification purposes.

---

12. *Sky and Telescope* (2001), p. 72.
13. Achar (1999), p. 2.
14. Yano and Fushumi.

The simulations provided by the planetarium software are extremely reliable and they are based on the most recent star catalogues and planetary information. However, some caution has to be exercised in using these programmes to compute eclipses at dates going back several thousands of years in time. Let us assume that the periods of planets and the moon are known accurately to six decimal places, say for example. The sixth place is somewhat uncertain. When the data is extrapolated to 3000 BCE, a time span of 5000 years, some 60000 revolutions of the Moon would have been considered, but only 200 revolutions of Saturn. The accuracy of the last decimal place is very important for the Moon, but not for Saturn. Thus in a simulation corresponding to 3000 BCE, the extrapolated position of Saturn is very reliable, but that of the moon is somewhat uncertain. This becomes evident in simulating the exact moment of new moon, for example. There is a spread of about 12 hours among the times for the new moon given by the SkyMap Pro, Redshift and Cybersky. That given by The Sky is off by seven days! There are other factors to be considered. This has to do with the slowing off of earth's rotation by about one millisecond per century. This is small, but introduces an uncertainty of about 12 hours in the occurrence of an eclipse when extrapolated to 3000 BCE. This means one cannot calculate the occurrence of a solar eclipse within an accuracy of several hours. This would in turn cause the location of a total solar eclipse also uncertain. It should be emphasized here that the occurrence of the solar eclipse itself is quite certain, but what is uncertain is the exact location where it occurs. In view of this, it would be difficult to choose a date based solely on the occurrence of an eclipse at a given location. In the present work therefore, it is considered sufficient if an eclipse occurred, and not much weight is given to the exact location of visibility as per the simulation. Conversely, those works, which determine the date of the war solely on the basis of occurrence of a solar eclipse at Kurukṣetra should be accepted with caution. The extrapolated planetary positions on the other hand, are highly reliable.

Astronomical References in the Epic

It is well known that there are a large number of references to astronomical events, totalling to more than 150, scattered

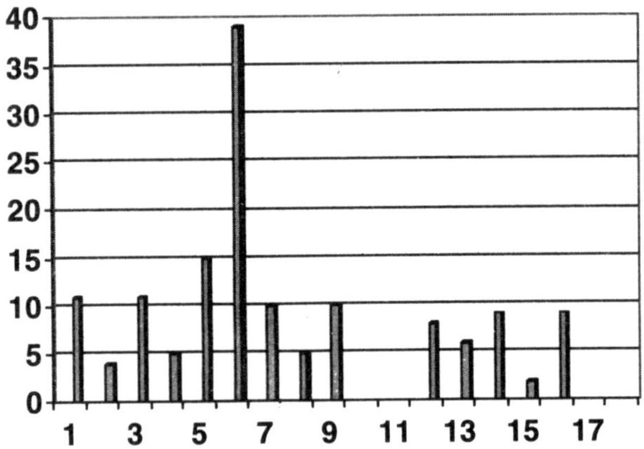

fig. 3: Distribution of the number of astronomical references among the eighteen Parvans of the epic. Udyoga (no. 5) and Bhīṣma (no. 6) contain the largest number of astronomical references pertaining to the war.

throughout the epic and have been catalogued.[15] *Fig.* 3 shows the distribution of the number of astronomical references among the different *parva*s of the epic. Admittedly most of the references are astrological in nature and the possibility that some of them may be later interpolations cannot be overruled. However, there must be a few genuine events that were observed and noted in view of the importance of the war. In fact, the majority of the astronomical references occur in Udyoga and Bhīṣma Parvas, pertaining to events just before or at the start of the war and will be examined in detail.

15. Sathe, Deshmukh and Joshi (1985), p. 1.

ASTRONOMICAL REFERENCES IN UDYOGA PARVA

There is a coherent chronology of astronomical events starting with Kṛṣṇa's departure for his diplomatic mission for peace to Hastināpura before the war and this mission must have been considered very important for recording the astronomical references.

(i) Kṛṣṇa leaves for Hastināpura on the diplomatic mission[16] for peace in the *maitrī muhūrtta* in the month of Kārttīka on the day of Revatī *nakṣatra*:

> *tato vyapete tamasi sūrye vimala udgate*
> *maitre muhūrtte saṁprāpte mṛdvaciṣi divākare* ||
> *kaumudemāsi revatyāṁ śaradante himāgame*
> *sphītasasyasukhe kāle kalyaḥ satvavatāṁ varaḥ* ||
> — *MB* V.81.6-7

> Then, when the *śarad-ṛtu* had ended and *hemanta-ṛtu* was just beginning, in the month of Kumuda (Kārttika), on the day of Revatī *nakṣatra* and in the *maitrī muhūrtta*, that ever-ready hero of heroes (set-off) in the tender rays of the sun (for Hastināpura).

It is to be noted that Kṛṣṇa leaves Upaplavya-nagara for Hastināpura on the day of Revatī *nakṣatra* in the month of Kārttika. It means that it is only a couple of days before the full moon of Kārttika, which should happen when the moon is near Kṛttikā *nakṣatra*.

(ii) On the way he halts at a place called Vṛkasthala and reaches Hastināpura on the day of Bharaṇī *nakṣatra*. That night happens to be the full moon and also a lunar eclipse takes place on this Kārttika full moon, which is referred to below by Karṇa and again by Vyāsa in his conversation with Dhṛtarāṣṭra in the next *parva*.

---

16. The Original Sanskrit *ślokas* are taken from the *Critical Edition of Mahābhārata*, Suktankar (1972).

(iii) Kṛṣṇa meets with various people to discuss the conditions of averting the war. On the day of Puṣya, Duryodhana rejects all offers of peace.

(iv) Kṛṣṇa leaves Hastināpura on the day of Uttaraphālguṇī. Karṇa accompanies him in his chariot and has a lengthy conversation with him. At the end of the conversation Kṛṣṇa sends a message through Karṇa to Bhīṣma and others that *amāvasyā* falls on the seventh day hence and that war rituals be started on that day:

saptamāccāpi divasād amāvāsyā bhaviṣyati
saṅgrāmaṁ yojayettatra tāṁhyāhuḥ śakradevatāṁ ॥
— *MB* V.140.18

Seven days from now falls the new moon day, with Indra as the deity for the *nakṣatra* of the day (i.e. Jyeṣṭhā *nakṣatra*). Let the war rituals be started on that day.

This is a very important piece of astronomical reference. Karṇa says there is going to be a solar eclipse on that day. Thus, there is a sequence of eclipses referred to here, first a lunar eclipse on the full moon of Kārttika followed by a solar eclipse at Jyeṣṭhā *nakṣatra*.

During this conversation Karṇa describes the positions of the planets at that time in the following verses while talking about the omens foretelling an impending disaster to the Kuru family:

prājāpatyaṁ hi nakṣatraṁ grahas tīkṣṇo mahādyutiḥ ।
śanaiścaraḥ pīḍayati pīḍayan prāṇinodhikaṁ ॥
— *MB* V.141.7

The noxious and much lustrous *graha* Saturn, which always harasses people extremely, is harassing the *nakṣatra* presided by Prajāpati.

kṛtvā cāṅgārako vakraṁ jyeṣṭhāyāṁ madhusūdana ।
anūrādhāṁ prārthayate maitraṁ saṁśamayanniva ॥
— *MB* V.141.8

Mars has performed a retrograde turn at Antares, O, Madhusūdana, and appears to be begging Anūrādhā's friendship, as if to pacify it.

nūnaṁ mahadbhayaṁ kṛṣṇa kurūnāṁ samupasthitaṁ ।
viśeṣeṇa hivārṣṇeya citrāṁ pīḍayate grahaḥ ॥
— *MB* V.141.9

Indeed a great danger awaits the Kuru family and is indicated by the *graha* afflicting Spica.

somasya lakṣma vyāvṛttaṁ rāhurarka mupeṣyati ॥
— *MB* V.141.10

The moon lost its lustre and Rāhu is approaching the Sun.

Here Karṇa is referring to the lunar eclipse that had already taken place and to an impending solar eclipse. It should be noted that Karṇa makes no reference to the number of days in the interval between the two eclipses. Furthermore, special attention should be paid to the message of Kṛṣṇa, which is sent to Bhīṣma and Droṇa, and not to Duryodhana. It cannot be a declaration of war, which can only be made either by Duryodhana or Yudhiṣṭhira to each other, and certainly not by Kṛṣṇa. Thus there is no reason to assume that the war started on the *amāvasyā* day. *Saṅgrāmaṁ yojayet* can only refer to the beginning of war rituals and not the war itself.

ASTRONOMICAL REFERENCES IN THE BHĪṢMA PARVA

As is well known, Vyāsa meets with Dhṛtarāṣṭra on the eve of the war and describes to him a whole set of ill omens he has seen. These descriptions of ill omens run over two chapters in the Bhīṣma Parva, and the astronomical references occur in four separate sections: *śloka*s 20-23 and *śloka* 32 in chapter 2, and *śloka*s 11-17 and *śloka*s 24-29 in chapter 3. The scholars who have studied these astronomical references have only seen the apparent contradictions, but have not appreciated how systematic Vyāsa is in his description. Just because the descriptions appear in four different sections, some[17] have suggested that they belong to different times. Or, what is worse, some scholars[18] have suggested that some of the *śloka*s belong to Sabhā Parva! However, the true situation is quite different. The astronomical references can be grouped in four different segments because they pertain to four different aspects of the ill omens as will be shown below. The tradition of recognizing astronomical ill omens can be traced to *Atharvaveda*[19] and its *pariśiṣṭa*s[20] and the ill omens described in the epic are consistent with the tradition.

The First Segment

*Śloka*s 20-23 of chapter 2 constitute the first segment. Here Vyāsa describes the omens foretelling the imminent war. Before describing the ill omens, he makes it clear that a great disaster is bound to occur just as indicated by the ill omens:

> *iha yuddhe mahārāja bhaviṣyati mahāṅkṣayaḥ* ।
> *yathemāni nimittāni bhayāyādyopalakṣaye* ॥
> — *MB* VI.2.16

> O King, a great destruction will occur in this war just as it is indicated by these omens, which are harbingers of great calamity.

> *ubhe pūrvāpare saṁdhye nityaṁ paśyāmi bhārata* ।
> *udayāstamane sūryaṁ kabandhaiḥ parivāritaṁ* ॥
> — *MB* VI.2.20

17. Sharma (1986, 2004).
18. Iyengar (2003), p. 77.
19. Saraswati (1992), vol. V, p. 1855.
20. Rai (1976), p. 288.

O Bhārata, I observe the sun everyday both morning at sunrise and in the evening at sunset and have seen him as if encircled by long arms (i.e. encircled by a comet).

śvetalohita paryantāḥ kṛṣṇagrīvāḥ savidyutaḥ ।
trivarṇāḥ parighāḥ saṁdhau bhānu māvārayantyuta ॥
— *MB* VI.2.21

I see the sun surrounded by halos on all sides, halos which are tri-coloured, dark in the middle and white and red towards the edges and accompanied by lightning.

jvalitārkendu nakṣatraṁ nirviśeṣa dinakṣapam ।
ahorātraṁ mayā dṛṣṭaṁ tatkṣayāya bhaviṣyati ॥
— *MB* VI.2.22

I have been watching days and nights the fierce sun, the moon and the stars shining incessantly and have been unable to distinguish between day and night. This surely forebodes utter destruction.

alakṣyaḥ prabhayā hīnaḥ paurṇamāsīṁ ca kārttikīm ।
candrobhūdagnivarṇaśca samavarṇe nabhasthale ॥
— *MB* VI.2.23

On the full moon night of Kārttika, the moon with fiery tinge was hardly visible, devoid of glory, and the horizons were also of the same hue.

It is clear that the intent of Vyāsa is to impress upon Dhṛtarāṣṭra that there is an imminent war, the armies are standing facing each other ready to fight and that war will bring about utter destruction. This has also been indicated by the ill omens.

Vyāsa begins by saying that he observes the sun everyday both in the morning at sunrise and in the evening at sunset. He has noted the appearance of halos and some comets, which appear to enclose the sun as if with long arms. The moon had become lustreless on the lunar eclipse day of Kārttika *pūrṇimā*. The class of omens thought to indicate an imminent war is quite consistent with the tradition going back to *Atharvaveda Pariśiṣṭa*.

Consistency with Tradition

The verses quoted above can be compared with similar verses (given below with a free flowing translation) from *Atharvaveda Pariśiṣṭa* describing *yuddhalakṣaṇa*, omens indicative of war.

arkebhra parighādīnāṁ pariveṣorka candrayoḥ ।
lākṣālohita varṇatvaṁ sarveṣāñca vicāraṇaṁ ॥
— *AP* 64.5.7

One should always consider the line of clouds and halos around the sun and the moon and observe whether they appear red or not in colour.

nīlalohita paryantaṁ kṛṣṇagrīvaṁ savidyutaṁ ।
— *AP* 61.1.4

Which are blue and red towards the edges and dark in the middle and accompanied by lightning.

trivarṇe parighevāpi trivarṇairvā balāhakaiḥ
udayāstamayamiyādyad sūryaḥ kadācanai ॥
— *AP* 61.1.15

pṛthivyāṁ rājavaṁśyānāṁ mahad bhayam upasthitaṁ ॥
— *AP* 61.1.15

Whenever the sun is surrounded at sunrise or sunset by tri-coloured clouds (the *balāhaka* clouds), it indicates great calamity to the earth and royal families.

tamro bhavati śastrāya . . . ।
dhūmravarṇo gnivarṇo vā grāmeṣu nagareṣu vā ॥
— *AP* 53.5.1-2

The colour of the moon (at the time of eclipse) indicates a

battle if it is red and disaster to cities and villages if it is smoky or fiery.

The omens described by Vyāsa are entirely consistent with the description in *Atharvaveda Pariśiṣṭa*. It may be noted that except for the Sun and the Moon, no planets have been mentioned in this segment.

The Second Segment

In the second segment, consisting of two *śloka*s, Vyāsa considers the ill omens foretelling the great harm to the Kuru dynasty and refers to the lunar eclipse, which occurred on the full moon day at Kṛttikā, followed by a solar eclipse. The earth experiences constant tremors. He also refers to Saturn afflicting Rohiṇī (Aldeberan) and Śvetagraha transgressing Citrā, which indicates the selective destruction of the Kuru clan.

rohiṇīṁ pīḍayanneṣa sthito rājañśanaiścaraḥ ।
vyāvṛttaṁ lakṣma somasya bhaviṣyati mahadbhayam ॥
— *MB* VI.2.32

O king, Saturn is harassing Aldeberan and the spot on the Moon has shifted from its position. Something terrible will happen.

abhīkṣṇaṁ kampate bhūmirarkaṁ rāhustathāgrasat ।
śveto grahastathā citrāṁ samatikramya tiṣṭati ॥
— *MB* VI.3.11

The Earth is experiencing tremors intermittently and Rāhu has seized the Sun. Śvetagraha has transgressed Citrā.

Consistency with the references in Udyoga Parva

These are almost identical to the omens described by Karṇa earlier in Udyoga Parva (Karṇa includes in addition the retrograde motion of Mars) at the time of his riding with Kṛṣṇa in *MB* (V.141.7) and *MB* (V.141.10) quoted earlier. This clearly shows that the second segment in Vyāsa's description to Dhṛtarāṣṭra in Bhīṣma Parva, of ill omens pertaining to the danger to the Kurus is consistent with the astronomical references in Udyoga Parva. It may be noted that there is a reference to a graha afflicting Citrā in both cases. Graha here refers to a comet and not to planet Mercury as is generally translated. In fact, it can be compared to the following verse from Varāhamihira[21] when he discusses the effect of comets when they "afflict" asterisms:

> *citrāsu kurukṣetrādhipasya maraṇaṁ samādiśettajñaḥ* ।
>
> — *BS* XI.57

> If the afflicted (by a comet) asterism be Citrā, a wise astrologer should predict the death of the ruler of Kurukṣetra.

It may further be pointed out that the second segment is the only segment, which includes true planetary positions in describing the omens.

The Third Segment

Vyāsa describes in the third segment further indicators of the calamity to the entire army (*senayoraśivaṁ ghoraṁ*). It is this segment that has caused so much difficulty to the scholars in that the planets appear to have been described as being at two or more locations at the same time. It is possible that the apparent ambiguity and confusion in the stated planetary positions arise because of the implicit interpretation that the word *graha* means a planet. The word *graha* (from the root √*grahṛ* to grasp or to seize) refers to any heavenly object, which can move and hence can grasp or seize a star. Thus, the word refers to a planet or comet, although in much later times in Indian astronomy, during the early years of CE, it came to be associated with only a planet.

---

21. Bhat (1981), p. 141.

But, Vyāsa leaves no doubt to the fact that here the word *graha* refers to a comet:

grahau tāmrāruṇaśikhau prajvalantāviv sthitau ।

— *MB* VI.3.24

The two *grahas* blazing with coppery and red hair.

It may be noted that the word comet itself derives from the Greek word for hair. The word *graha* with red hair in the context here can only refer to a comet. Furthermore, as noted by Varāhamihira,[22] the ancient astronomers Parāśara and Garga classified comets as sons of sun, sons of moon, sons of Mercury, sons of Venus, sons of Mars, children of Jupiter and children of Saturn, all of which indicate mainly impending calamities. This practice of considering a comet as *grahaputra* can be found in *Atharvaveda Pariśiṣṭa*[23] also. The astronomical references in the third segment can now be examined in this light and the words "son of" have been added to the translation to make it clear.

dhūmaketur mahāghoraḥ puṣya mākramya tiṣṭhati ॥

— *MB* VI.3.12

Deadly Dhūmaketu has overcome Puṣya.

senayo raśivaṁ ghoraṁ kariṣyati mahāgrahaḥ ।
maghāsvaṅgārako vakraḥ śravaṇe ca bṛhaspatiḥ ॥

— *MB* VI.3.13

The *mahāgraha* appears to bring about an awful destruction in both armies. (Son of) Mars is retrograde in Maghā, and (son of) Jupiter in Śrāvaṇa.

Some scholars have interpreted this to mean that the planet Mars and the planet Jupiter are the ones executing retrograde motion, implying total confusion and contradiction with other *ślokas* in this section.

22. Bhat (1981), p. 121.

23. Rai (1976), p. 288.

bhāgyaṁ nakṣatra mākramya sūryaputreṇa pīḍyate
śukraḥ proṣṭhapade pūrve samāruhya viśāṁ pate
uttare tu parikramya sahitaḥ pratyudīkṣate ||
— *MB* VI.3.14

The son of Sūrya has crossed the asterism pūrvāphālguṇī, and is vexing. O king (son of) Śukra has entered Pūrvā-proṣṭapada, going around Uttara-proṣṭapada and is rising in both.

śyāmo grahaḥ prajvalitaḥ sadhūmaḥ sahapāvakaḥ
aindraṁ tejasvi nakṣatraṁ jyeṣṭhāmākramya tiṣṭhati ||
— *MB* VI.3.15

Śyāmagraha is luminous and together with Dhūma and Pāvaka has crossed over to Jyeṣṭhā, the bright asterism ruled by Indra.

dhruvaḥ prajvalito ghoram apasavyaṁ pravartate |
citrāsvātyantare caiva dhiṣṭhitaḥ paruṣo grahaḥ ||
— *MB* VI.3.16

The luminous Dhruva has moved to the right of Ghora. The Paruṣa *graha* has established itself between Citrā and Svāti.

It is obvious that Dhruva cannot refer to the polestar.

vakrānuvakraṁ kṛtvā ca śravaṇe pāvakaprabhaḥ |
brahmarāśiṁ samāvṛtya lohitāṅgo vyavasthitaḥ ||
— *MB* VI.3.17

Pāvakaprabha has gone circumventing Śravaṇā, and Lohitāṅga has become steady after enclosing Brhmarāśi.

saṁvatsara sthāyinau ca grahau prajvalitāvubhau |
viśākhayoḥ samīpasthau bṛhaspati śanaiścarau ||
— *MB* VI.3.25

(Sons of) Jupiter and Saturn, which stay around for a year, are both luminous and are near the two Viśākhā stars.

kṛttikāsu grahastīvro nakṣatre prathame jvalan ।
vapūṁṣyapaharan bhāsā dhūmaketuriva sthitaḥ ॥
— *MB* VI.3.26

The *graha* Tīvra blazing in the first constellation Kṛttikā, and concealing forms with lustre resembles Dhūmaketu.

triṣu pūrveṣu sarveṣu nakṣatreṣu viśāṁ pate ।
budhaḥ saṁpatate 'bhīkṣṇaṁ janayan sumahadbhayam ॥
— *MB* VI.3.27

(Son of) Mercury is falling under all the three earlier constellations and causing a great terror.

Vyāsa names specifically twelve comets, Śveta, Dhūmaketu, Mahāgraha, Paruṣa, Pāvaka, Dhūma, Lohitāṅga, Tīvra, Pāvakaprabha, Śyāma, Ghora, and Dhruvaketu. All these names can be found in the list given by Varāhamihira.[24] Earlier scholars had translated some of these names as planets, for example, Śvetagraha as white planet (to refer to Venus), Śyāmagraha as dark planet (to refer to Mercury), and Paruṣagraha as cruel planet (to refer to Rāhu). Furthermore, Vyāsa refers to son of Sun, Sūryaputra, explicitly, but he also refers to some of the comets by the name of the parent planets. While this is quite according to the Sanskrit grammar, it is this notation that has caused so much confusion. The scholars have interpreted these references literally as referring to planets themselves. The net result is the confusion of conflicting planetary positions. When it is realized that comets are to be considered, there is no ambiguity or confusion of any kind. Moreover, comets have been considered to be harbingers of calamity since *Atharvaveda*.[25]

---

24. Bhat (1981), p. 121.

25. Saraswati (1992), vol. V, p. 1855.

The Fourth Segment: In the final segment, Vyāsa describes the omens which indicate destruction of the entire population; these include a pair of eclipses, a lunar and a solar eclipse occurring in the same month and within an interval of thirteen days, and at an *aparvaṇi* moment (i.e. not at the moment of exact conjunction or opposition of the sun and the moon).

> *caturdaśīṁ pañcadaśīṁ bhūtapūrvāṁ ca ṣoḍaśīm* ।
> *imāṁ tu nābhijānāmi amāvāsyāṁ trayodaśīm* ॥
> — *MB* VI.3.28

> *candrasūryāvubhau grastāvekamāse trayodaśīm* ।
> *aparvaṇi grahāvetau prajāḥ saṁkṣapayiṣyataḥ* ॥
> — *MB* VI.3.29

> I know new moon coinciding with fourteenth, fifteenth and also on the sixteenth day, but I have never known it coinciding with the thirteenth day. In one and the same month, both the Sun and the Moon are eclipsed on the thirteenth. These ill-timed eclipses indicate destruction of the people.

This is the famous reference to two eclipses occurring within a month with an interval of thirteen days. It may be remembered that there was already a reference to a lunar eclipse occurring on Kārttika *purṇimā* with a solar eclipse on the following new moon at Jyeṣṭha, but nothing had been said about the time interval between those two.

This can be compared with a description from *Atharvaveda Pariśiṣṭa*:

> *yadi tu rāhurubhau śaśibhāskarau*
> *grasati pakṣamanantaramantataḥ* ।
> *puruṣaśoṇita kardama vāhinī*
> *bhavati bhūrna ca varṣati mādhavaḥ* ॥
> — *AP* 53.3.5

It is clear that the omens described by Vyāsa in four different segments refer to different aspects: (i) an imminent war, (ii) calamity to the Kuru dynasty, (iii) destruction of the entire army, and finally, (iv) danger to the entire population. As such they involve different astronomical happenings. The truly planetary positions are indicated in the omens pertaining to the calamity to the Kuru family and in this case the descriptions given by Karṇa in Udyoga Parva are identical to the descriptions given by Vyāsa in Bhīṣma Parva. The alleged great confusion and ambiguity in "planetary" positions seen by scholars pertain to the third segment, which describes omens of a great danger to the entire army. This segment does not refer to planets, but to comets and has been made explicitly clear by Vyāsa, but scholars have not taken note of it. Explicit references by specific names to comets have been mistranslated as planets, leading to confusion. Compounding the confusion is Vyāsa's reference to comets as offsprings of planets, but denoting them by the names of the parent planets. But, once it is recognized that comets are implied here there is no confusion or ambiguity and every thing falls into place. There is no necessity for introducing adhoc hypotheses such as those advanced by Sharma[26] or Iyengar[27] to account for the ambiguity, because it is non-existent.

The description of omens turns out to be a coherent account. It is evident that criticism directed against the descriptions is unwarranted. It may be remarked in passing that other non-astronomical omens in these two chapters can also be found in *Atharvaveda Pariśiṣṭa*.

26. Sharma (1988), p. 88.

27. Iyengar (2003), p. 77.

Methodology of Determining the Date of the War

It is abundantly clear that the true planetary positions described are common to both Udyoga Parva and Bhīṣma Parva and represent a great calamity to the Kuru family.

It is regarded that planetary positions are most reliable and eclipses and comets are not so reliable. Thus Śani at Rohiṇī (Saturn at Aldeberan) is the most reliable configuration and has been stressed in both *parvas* The next is Aṅgāraka performing a retrograde motion just before reaching Jyeṣṭhā (retrograde motion of Mars just before reaching Antares). A lunar eclipse with the moon at Kṛttikā (Pleiades) followed by a solar eclipse at Jyeṣṭhā (Antares) are considered to be the next important events. For, the lack of lustre of the moon on the lunar eclipse of Kārttika *pūrṇimā* has been mentioned by both Karṇa and Vyāsa. The *amāvasyā* at *Jyeṣṭhā* (new moon at Antares) has been mentioned by Kṛṣṇa as the day for formal war rituals, and the solar eclipse has been mentioned by both Karṇa and Vyāsa. The rest of the astronomical references in Bhīṣma Parva pertain to comets as has been shown.

Thus the important references to planets consist of those that are common to both Udyoga and Bhīṣma Parvas and include the following:

(i) conjunction of Śani with Rohiṇī.

(ii) retrograde motion of Aṅgāraka just before reaching Jyeṣṭhā.

(iii) a lunar eclipse on the Kārttika *pūrṇimā*; followed by

(iv) a solar eclipse at Jyeṣṭhā.

These events lead to a unique year for the war as shown below. All other astronomical references in the epic are consistent with this date.

Simulations using Planetarium Software and the Date of the War

A search is made for the years in which there is a conjunction of Saturn (Śani) with Aldebaran (Rohiṇī) between 3500 BCE and CE 500. As Saturn takes an average of 29.5 years to go around the sun once, the event also repeats with the same period. There are 137 such conjunctions during the interval specified above. A search is then made for those years from among these 137 dates when Mars (Aṅgāraka) is retrograde before reaching Antares (Jyeṣṭhā). Since the retrograde motion of Mars repeats with the same period as its synodic period, a spread of two years on either side of each of the dates was considered in the search. The search reduced the set to just seventeen: 3271 BCE, 3067 BCE, 2830 BCE, 2625 BCE, 2388 BCE, 2183 BCE, 1946 BCE, 1741 BCE, 1503 BCE, 1299 BCE, 1061 BCE, 857 BCE, 620 BCE, 415 BCE, CE 28, CE 233 and CE 470, when Saturn was near Aldebaran and Mars executed a retrograde motion before reaching Antares. A search is then made for those years in which there is a lunar eclipse near Pleiades (i.e. on the Kārttika *pūrṇimā*). This reduces the set to just two, 3067 BCE and 2183 BCE. It turns out that in both of these years the lunar eclipse is followed by a solar eclipse at Jyeṣṭhā. A sequence of "two eclipses within a period of 13 days" also occurs in the two eclipse seasons and will be discussed later. When one considers the fact that Bhīṣma passed away on the Māgha *śukla aṣṭamī,* after the occurrence of winter solstice, a unique date results, for the winter solstice in 13 January 3066 BCE occurred on *śukla pañcamī,* where as the winter solstice in 2182 BCE occurred on *kṛṣna caturthī.*

Thus a unique date of 3067 BCE for the date of the war emerges. The author has shown that this date is consistent with all the other astronomical references in the epic in several publications with the help of copious illustrations of star maps generated by planetarium software. Some of them will be included as part of this article by way of illustration. In particular, the works of the authors and the dates shown in Table 1 will be considered for simulation. Four of these are older works based on manual calculations and the others are more recent ones using planetarium software. The simulations clearly bring out the deficiency of relying only on the occurrence of pair of eclipses.

Illustrations

Table 1 shows the list of works which have been chosen for verification by simulation using the planetarium software. The first four are by eminent astrophysicists and mathematicians, and all their calculations were made manually. The remaining ones in the table are more recent and also use planetarium software. On the whole these works cover the entire range of dates that have been proposed for the war.

Table 1: Authors and Projected Dates Selected for Simulation

Author	Work	Date of War
Kochhar	*The Vedic People* (1997)	955 BCE
Sidharth	*The Celestial Key to the Vedas* (1999)	1311 BCE
Sengupta	*Ancient Indian Chronology* (1947)	2449 BCE
Raghavan	*The Date of the Mahabharata War* (1969)	3067 BCE
Balakrishna	*Simulations Planetarium Software* (2004)	2559 BCE
Iyengar	*Simulations Planetarium Software* (2004)	1478 BCE

Sharma	*Simulations Planetarium Software* (2004)	3022 BCE
Achar	*Simulations Planetarium Software* (2000-04)	3067 BCE

Kochhar mentions that there are more than 150 astronomical references in the epic including "Saturn vexing Rohiṇī," but ignores all of them as nothing more than poetic imagery and regards that only a total solar eclipse seen in the north-west of India as significant. He gives two dates, 4 July 857 BCE and 4 October 955 BCE as the possible dates of the eclipse and hence the year of the War. The 857 BCE date can be ruled out as the eclipse takes place in the month of Āṣāḍha and quite far removed from the required month of Kārttika as per the epic. *Fig*. 4 shows the simulation for 4 October 955 BCE. It is a total solar eclipse, but occurs at Vaiśākha and not at Jyeṣṭha. Saturn is near Śrāvaṇa and not Rohiṇī as required. In fact, this date cannot match a single astronomical reference in the epic and has to be rejected.

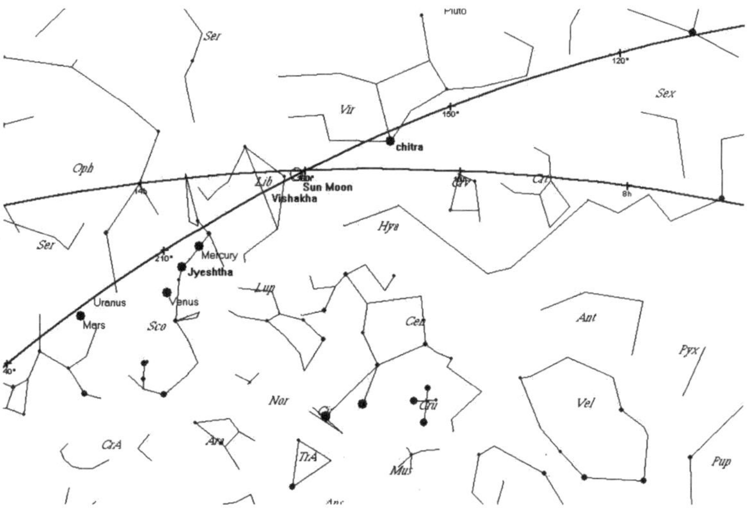

fig. 4: Star Map for 4 October 955 BCE (Kochhar's date).

Sidharth also considers a single solar eclipse to be important and gives the date of June 1311 BCE. *Fig.* 5 shows the star map for 14 June 1311 BCE. The eclipse occurs at Punarvasu, and the summer solstice is yet to occur. This cannot be the month specified in the epic. This date also fails to match any astronomical reference in the epic and is to be rejected.

Sengupta made extensive calculations all remarkably accurate, but the basic set of astronomical data he considered consist of (i) *amāvasyā* at Jyeṣṭha, (ii) Sun turned north in 80 days, and (iii) the war began when the moon was 13 days old and in Kṛttikā, and ended when moon was in Śrāvaṇa. He

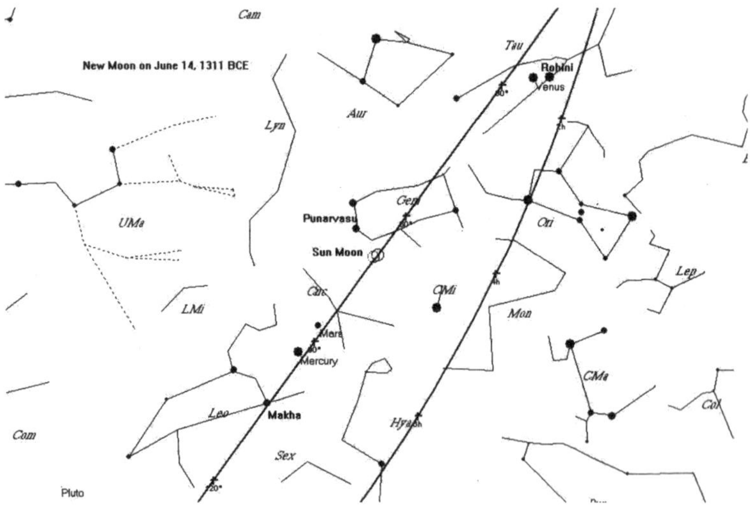

fig. 5: Star Map for 14 June 1311 BCE (Sidharth's date).

does not believe in any of the references given by Karṇa or Vyāsa. He vents out the harshest criticism of the astronomical references:

All this hopelessly inconsistent astrological effusion of evil omens fit for Mother Goose's tales only.

As to the occurrence of two eclipses one after another within 13 days, he says:

We cannot put any faith in any statement of this chapter.

Fig. 6 shows the star map for 21 October 2449 BCE, the date given by Sengupta.

There is indeed a new moon at Jyeṣṭha, but there is no solar eclipse on that day. Saturn is at Kṛttikā, and again there are no matches with the astronomical references in the epic. Like many scholars, Sengupta takes the view that the astronomical references in the epic is fiction and that he has made accurate calculations. His justification for the date is its alleged agreement with the so-called Varāhamihira tradition.

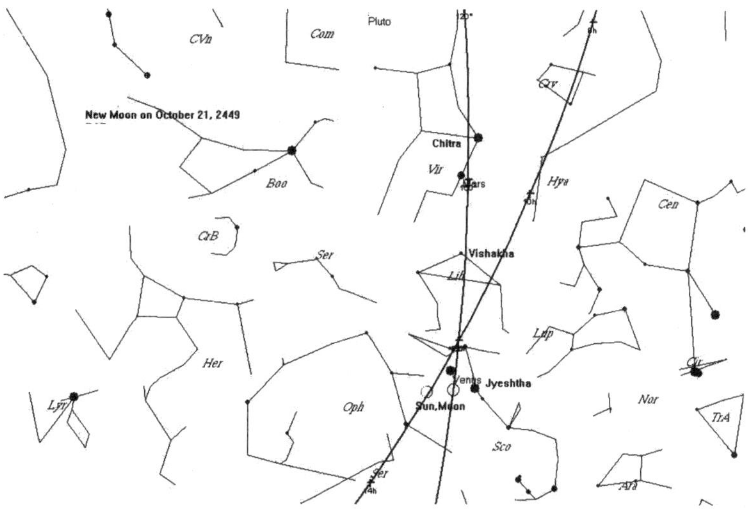

fig. 6: Star map for 21 October 2449 BCE (Sengupta's date).

This agreement is of no significance as will be shown later and Sengupta's date has to be rejected as not being in agreement with the astronomical references of the epic. Of the remaining authors, Raghavan's date will be discussed together with the author's work. Balakrishna and Iyengar both use planetarium software, but concentrate on eclipses.

Balakrishna searched through some 7000 solar eclipses and 4000 lunar eclipses to find possible pairs of eclipses occurring within 14 days and observable at Kurukṣetra, and identified the pairs of eclipses from 3088 BCE, 2950 BCE, 2907 BCE, 2559 BCE, 1966 BCE, 1876 BCE, 1666 BCE, 1211 BCE and 1084 BCE as clearly meeting the "13-day eclipse pair" requirement. He declared the 2559 BCE eclipse pair as the best and perhaps the nearest to the text in the epic and hence the year of the war. Iyengar was a little more general in his approach. He also considered the position of Saturn to be important and felt that there should be correlation with another pair of eclipse observed at Dvārakā, 36 years after the war. He has given a list of some 35 dates, in which pairs of eclipses occur at Kurukṣetra while Saturn is near Rohiṇī and found 11 pairs of these to be compatible with possible eclipse pairs observable at Dvārakā 36 years later. He chose 1478 as the best candidate for the date of the war. Both of the dates 2559 BCE, given by Balakrishna, and 1478 BCE given by Iyengar have to be rejected, because the lunar eclipse does not occur on Kārttika *pūrṇimā* and the solar eclipse does not occur at Jyeṣṭhā. In fact, none of the dates given by Balakrishna or Iyengar satisfies these requirements. Balakrishna has not paid much attention to planetary positions, which he regards as confusing and contradictory and perhaps later interpolations. Iyengar, taking inspiration from Sharma's earlier work regards that some *śloka*s in Bhīṣma Parva should belong to Sabhā Parva! Sharma advances his own hypothesis as to how many times Vyāsa meets with Dhṛtarāṣṭra and comes up with a date 3022 BCE. He is confused by the fact that Rohiṇī could refer to either Antares or Aldebaran, and in 3022 BCE, Saturn is near Antares. Sharma does not understand that while Rohiṇī may denote either one of those stars, there is a presiding deity for each *nakṣatra*. It is Prajāpati for Aldebaran and Śakra for Antares. It is perfectly clear where Saturn is by the statement: *prājāpatyaṁ hi nakṣatraṁ śanaiścaraḥ pīḍayati* Unfortunately, the extensive calculations made by these scholars using the planetarium software have been of little use as the basic premise of the true planetary positions is not considered. Moreover, the over emphasis on eclipses in order to determine the date is questionable.

Raghavan's date is identical to the date given in this article and he gives a chronology of events starting with Kṛṣṇa's diplomatic mission given in Table 2.

The star maps in *figs.* 7-14 show that the astronomical events are reproduced. In *fig.* 7, the day Kṛṣṇa starts on his diplomatic mission, it is clearly seen that moon is near Revatī, and Śani is at Rohiṇī. *Fig.* 8 shows the full moon in Kārttika, it also happens to be a lunar eclipse day. At this time, Kṛṣṇa is busy with the peace talks in Hastināpura.

Table 2. Chronology of events according to Raghavan

Kṛṣṇa's departure from Upaplavya nagara on the mission of peace	26 September 3067 BCE
Kṛṣṇa reaches Hastināpura	28 September 3067 BCE
Lunar eclipse	29 September 3067 BCE
Kṛṣṇa rides with Karṇa	8 October 3067 BCE
Solar eclipse	14 October 3067 BCE
War begins	22 November 3067 BCE
Fourteenth day of war continued till wee hours of morning	8 December 3067 BCE
Balarāma returns	12 Dec 3067 BCE
Winter solstice	13 Jan 3066 BCE
Bhīṣma's passing away	17 Jan 3066 BCE

In *fig.* 9, Kṛṣṇa rides with Karṇa after the failure of the peace mission; it is Uttarāphālguṇī. Seven days from that day, it will be *amāvasyā* at Jyeṣṭha. Kṛṣṇa sends the message to Bhīṣma and Droṇa to start the war rituals that day. *Fig.* 10 shows the star map for that day, which is also a solar eclipse day. The retrograde loop of Mars in that year is also shown in the figure. The retrograde motion of Mars before reaching Jyeṣṭhā had occurred several months earlier. *Fig.* 11 shows the day the war starts: moon is at Bharaṇī. *Fig.* 12 shows the fourteenth day, when the war continues until the wee hours of the morning and stops when the moon rises. *Fig.* 13 shows the last day of the war, it is Śravaṇā *nakṣatra* and Balarāma returns. *Fig.* 14 shows the day of Bhīṣma's death: *śukla aṣṭamī*, Rohiṇī *nakṣatra*.

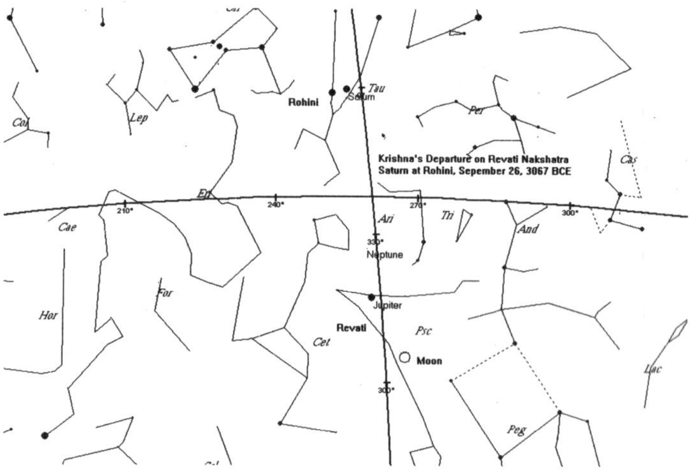

fig. 7: Kṛṣṇa's mission for peace: Departure on 26 September 3067 BCE.

It is clear that all the astronomical references listed are reproduced in the simulations. The sheer volume of astronomical data and the consistency of the astronomical references reinforce conclusively the traditional belief that the

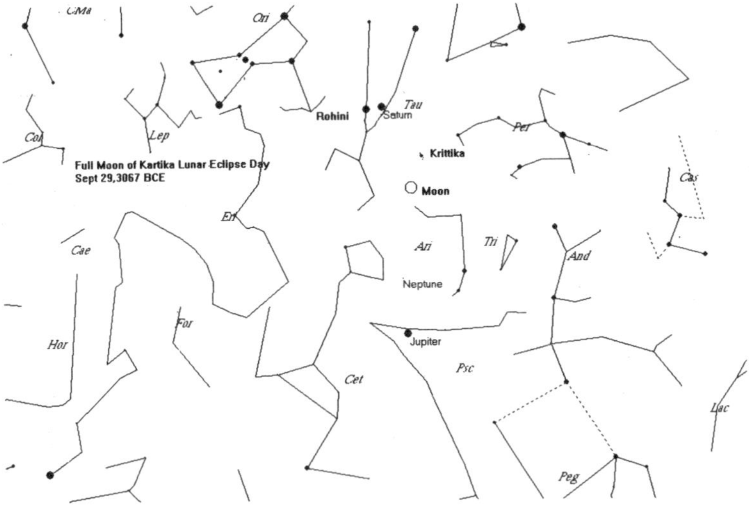

fig. 8: Full moon of Kārttika. Lunar eclipse day, 29 September 3067 BCE.

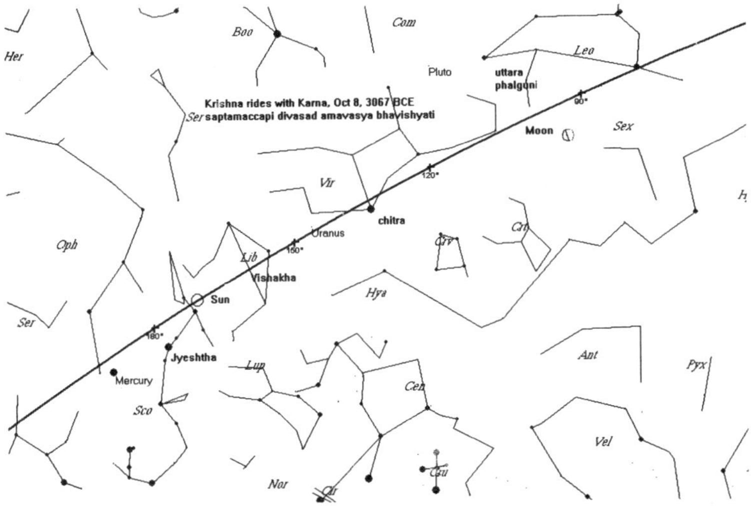

fig. 9: Karṇa rides with Kṛṣṇa Uttarāphālguṇī *nakṣatra* 8 October 3067 BCE.

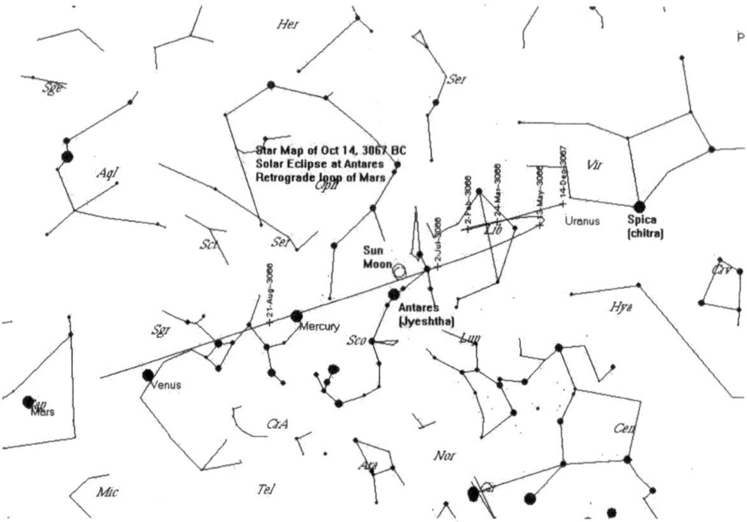

fig. 10: Jyeṣṭha *amāvasyā*, solar eclipse day; 14 October 3067 BCE.; Retro-loop of Mars.

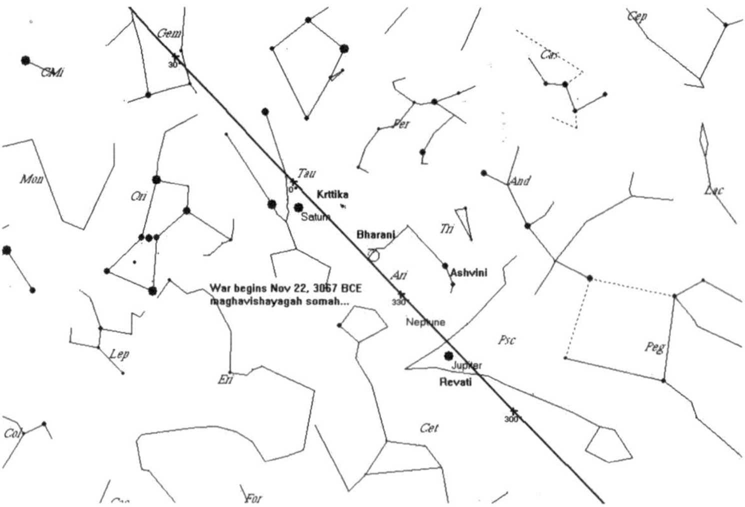

fig. 11: War begins 22 November 3067 BCE. It is Bharaṇī day

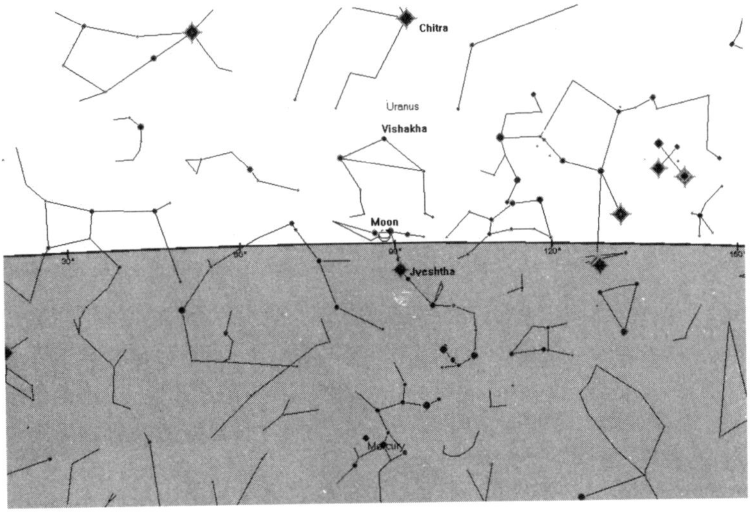

fig. 12: Fourteenth day of war. Moon rising at 2:30 a.m. seen just above the horizon.

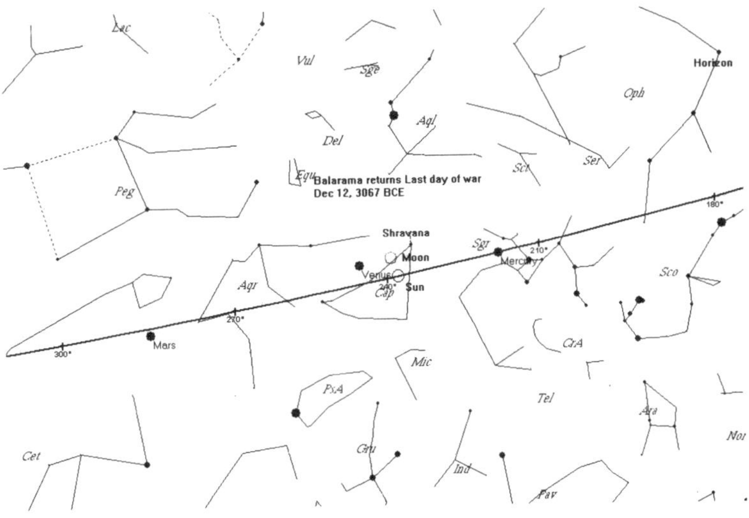

fig. 13: Last day of the war. Balarāma returns on the Śrāvaṇa day.

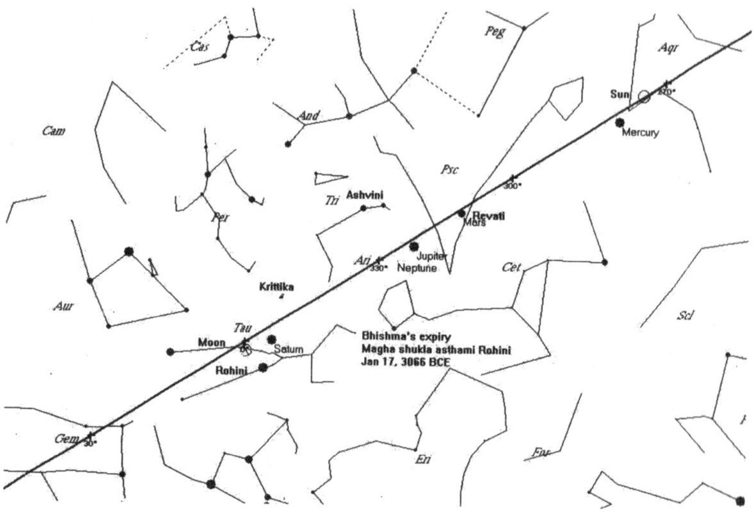

fig. 14: Bhīṣma's death. Māgha *śukla aṣṭami* Rohiṇī *nakṣatra.* 16 January 3066 BCE.

war took place about 3000 BCE and that the astronomical references are not clever interpolations of some later day astronomer. The date established by archaeo-astronomical reasoning, 3067 BCE, provides the "sheet-anchor" for the history of India.

The Uniqueness of this Date

It should be noted that the date of 3067 BCE has been derived entirely on the basis of astronomical information found in the epic alone. No information from any other outside source has been used. This date is identical to the date proposed by four other scholars. However, more than 40 scholars have proposed a date for the Mahābhārata war ~3000 BCE. Of these 17 have proposed 3102 BCE, 10 other authors have proposed 3101 BCE, seven authors have proposed 3139 BCE, some 3138 BCE, and 3137 BCE respectively. The question naturally arises which should be accepted and which should be rejected, if any. It is very easy to demonstrate that none of these dates can reproduce the astronomical events as described in the epic. For example, *fig.* 15 shows the star map for 19 October 3138 BCE, it is Jyeṣṭha *amāvasyā,* and according to Vedavyāsa, war began on that day. However, the day of Jyeṣṭha *amāvasyā* is required to be a solar eclipse day, as per the conversation between Kṛṣṇa and Karṇa: *rāhurārkamupeṣyati* . . . and . . . *saptamacchāpi divasād amāvasyā bhaviṣyati* . . . *tamāhuḥ śakradevatāṁ,* but 19 October 3138 BCE is not a solar eclipse day. The solar eclipse in that year had occurred on 21 August near Hastā and not near Jyeṣṭhā. Furthermore, Śani is at Mūla and not Rohiṇī, and Aṅgāraka is at Ārdrā (where he becomes retrograde later in the year) and not past Anūrādhā having become retrograde before reaching Jyeṣṭhā as described in the epic. In short, none of the astronomical events described in the epic are satisfied for this date. The author has demonstrated this non-compliance for a large number of other

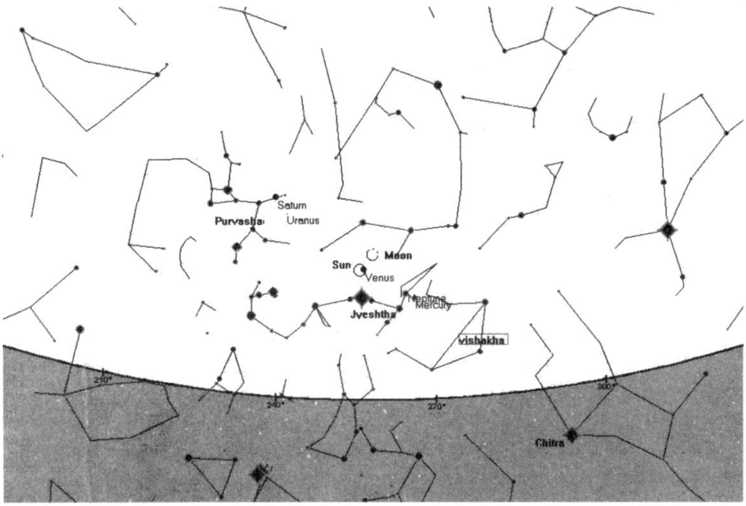

fig. 15: New moon day, 19 October 3138 BCE. Jyeṣṭhā *nakṣatra,* but no eclipse; Saturn at Mūla.

dates that have been proposed for the date of the war. Additional details can be obtained from several publications of the author.[28]

Consistency of the Date of 3067 BCE with Tradition

BEGINNING OF KALI YUGA AND INFORMATION FROM PURĀṆAS

According to Sengupta,[29] there are three traditions regarding the date of the Mahābhārata war, namely (i) the so-called Āryabhaṭṭa tradition,[30] according to which Pāṇḍavas lived at the beginning of the astronomical *Kali* age, 3102 BCE; (ii) 2449 BCE, based on the *Saptarṣi* tradition as allegedly recorded by Varāhamihira;[31] (iii) the tradition of the Purāṇas,[32] according to which from the birth of Parīkṣit to the accession of Mahāpadmananda, there was a time interval of 1500 years. Based on the Purāṇa tradition, modern historians who have identified Candragupta Maurya (who followed the Nandas) to have lived in 324 BCE, assign a date ~1900 BCE for the war. All these three will be examined for consistency. It is to be re-emphasized that the date of 3067 BCE has been derived independent of any of these traditions and is truly based on the internal evidence based on astronomical references found in the epic alone.

---

28. Achar (2004a, 2004b, 2005).
29. Sengupta (1947), p. 35.
30. *kāho manavo ḍha manuyugāḥ śkha gatāstemanuyugāḥchnāca* I
kalpāderyugapādāgaca gurudivasācca bhāratātpūrvaṁ II — A.I.5.
31. *āsanmaghāsu munayaḥ śāsati pṛthvīṁ yudhiṣṭhire nṛpatau* I
ṣaḍvika pañcadviyutaḥ śakakālaḥ tasyarājñasyāt II — *BrS*
32. *yāvat parīkṣito janma yāvat nandābhiṣecanam* I
evaṁ varṣa sahasrantu jñeyaṁ pañcaśatottaram II

Āryabhaṭṭa Tradition

Āryabhaṭṭa declares[33] that when he was 23 years old, 3600 years of *Kali yuga* had elapsed. This identifies the beginning of *Kali yuga* with 3102 BCE. At first sight there appears to be some question about the consistency of the date 3067 BCE for the war with the beginning of *Kali yuga,* which is traditionally thought to have started after the war. A large number of scholars who have proposed the date of ~3000 BCE for the war rely on the information regarding the beginning of *Kali yuga* in one way or the other. However, the epic itself does not explicitly give any information about the beginning of *Kali yuga.* It is generally accepted that the astronomical beginning of *Kali yuga* coincides with 17/18 February 3102 BCE. The date of the war is then tied to the beginning of *Kali yuga* (which according to some authors coincided with the end of the war and thus giving the date as 3102 BCE for the war). But there are others who take their clue from the Purāṇas, according to which *Kali yuga* began with the departure of Lord Kṛṣṇa from this world, an event occurring 36 years after the war. This results in the proposed date of 3138 BCE for the war. The spread of +/- 1 year on either side of these dates arises from slightly different modes of counting. Of course, the date 3067 BCE is posterior to 3102 BCE. Is there a conflict? Should not the war precede the beginning of *Kali yuga*? Not really. All that the epic says[34] is that the war occurred during the transitional interval between *Dvāpara* and *Kali yuga*s, and nowhere it says exactly when the *Dvāpara* ended or *Kali* began. The *antara* or the interval between the *yuga*s is quite extensive. According to *Viṣṇu Purāṇa,* the *sandhyā* for *Dvāpara* lasts for 200 (divine?) years and for *Kali,* it is 100 years. Thus there is a period of

33. *ṣaṣṭyabdānāṁ ṣaṣṭiryadā vyatītāstrayaśca yugapādāḥ* ।
tryadhikā viṁśatirabdāstadeha mama janmanotītāḥ ॥ — *A.,* III.10

34. See footnote 8 above.

some 100 years or so, which can be legitimately referred to as *sandhyā* and 3067 BCE falls within this interval of 3102 BCE. In fact, there is some indication that the *Kali yuga* had already started by the time of the war.[35] Even *Bhāgavata Purāṇa* acknowledges[36] that although *Kali yuga* had already started, because of the presence of Kṛṣṇa, *Kali*'s effect had been controlled. The full power of *Kali* became effective only with the departure of Kṛṣṇa, according to *Kali-rāja Vṛttānta*[37] Thus there is no conflict with the war occurring in 3067 BCE and the reckoning of *Kali yuga* from 3102 BCE.

The Alleged Varāhamihira Tradition

Varāhamihira states in his *Bṛhat Saṁhitā* that the *saptarṣis* were in Maghā when Yudhiṣṭhira was ruling and to get the epoch of Śaka Kāla one should add 2526 years to the epoch of Yudhiṣṭhira. Historians have assumed that the Śaka Kāla or Śakanṛpati Kāla refers to the Śālivāhana Śaka of CE 78. Thus arriving at the date -2448 (= 78-2526) or 2449 BCE for the Yudhiṣṭhira Era, the scholars declare that Varāhamihira gives this as the date of the Mahābhārata war. Kalhaṇa also assumes that the position of *saptarṣis* has been given by Varāhamihira, and makes the same mistake regarding the Śaka Kāla in his *Rājataraṅgiṇī*. However, he assumes that *Kali yuga* began in

35. *etad kaliyugaṁ nāma acirādyatpravartate* II — *MB* III.148.37

    The following remark is made when during the *gadāyuddha, Bhīma* hits *Duryodhana*'s thigh, the *adharma* act being the result of *Kali* having already entered.

    prāptaṁ kaliyugaṁ viddhi pratijñāṁ pāṇḍavasyaca — *MB* IX.59.21

36. *yadā mukundo bhagavānimāṁ mahīṁ jahau svatanvā śravaṇīya satkathaḥ* I
    tadāharevā pratibuddhacetasāṁabhadrahetuḥ kaliranvavartata II — *BP* I.15.36

37. *yāvat sa bhagavān viṣṇuḥ pasparśemāṁ vasundharāṁ* I
    tāvat pṛthvīṁ parākrāntuṁ samartho nābhavat kaliḥ II — Bhaga III, a. III

3102 BCE, hence declares that Pāṇḍavas lived 3102-2449 = 653 years after the start of the *Kali yuga*. This has only contributed to the confusion and some Indologists actually declare *Kali yuga* as a figment of imagination.

Varāhamihira simply quotes Vṛddha Garga's opinion regarding when Yudhiṣṭhira lived and how to get that period from Śaka Kāla and *this is not Varāhamihira's opinion.* Garga by all accounts lived before CE and the word Śaka Kāla of Garga cannot refer to Śālivāhana Śaka of CE 78. The Śaka Kāla or Śakanṛpati Kāla in Garga's words refers to the era of the Śaka king, Cyrus, beginning with 550 BCE. All this has been noted by many scholars,[38] and discussed in great detail by Kota Venkatachelam,[39] whose work may be consulted for further details. With the correct identification of Śaka Kāla, the date given by Varāhamihira is also consistent with the date of the war given here. It may be noted in passing that it was based on the wrong identification of Śaka Kāla that Professor Sengupta felt justified in his date of 2449 BCE for the war. Thus the so-called Varāhamihira tradition and the *Rājataraṅgiṇī* tradition of assigning a date of 2449 BCE to the war is based on a mistaken identity for the Śaka Kāla, compounded by the mistake in assuming that a mere quotation of Vṛddha Garga by Varāhamihira reflects the latter's own opinion. The date derived here is consistent with Āryabhaṭṭa tradition and the correct Śaka Kāla beginning in 550 BCE.

Saptarṣi Era and Genealogy List from Purāṇas

The saptarṣi-cycle is named after the seven sages and is allegorically associated with the Big Dipper, the easternmost star which is marked by Marīci followed by Vasiṣṭha, Aṅgīras,

38. Vaidya, C.V., (1983) *The Mahābhārata: A Criticism*, New Delhi: Cosmo Publications, p. 80.

39. Venkatachelam (1954), p. 1.

Atri, Pulastya, Pulaha and Kratu, respectively, in that order. The seven sages are thought to move through the 27 *nakṣatras* along the ecliptic at the rate of one *nakṣatra* per 100 years and to complete one cycle in 2700 years. This forms a convenient cycle for reference, but no astronomical significance[40] for the movement and the association of the stars of the Big Dipper can be ascribed. According to Purāṇas, it is accepted[41] that *saptarṣis* were in Maghā when Yudhiṣṭhira ascended the throne and that the time interval from Parīkṣit to the accession of the Nanda kings was 1500 years. Between Parīkṣit and the Nandas, there were three royal dynasties, Bṛhadratha, Pradyota and Śiśunāga families. The Nandas were followed by Mauryas, Śuṅgas, Kaṇvas and Āndhras. The *saptarṣis* returned to Maghā during the reign of the 24th king of the Āndhras. It was the 25th king, Gautamīputra Śātakarṇī who performed the *Aśvamedha yāga* and *Rājasūya yāga*. It is simply being recalled that the *saptarṣis* had returned to the position they had occupied during the time when these rituals had been performed earlier at the time of the Pāṇḍavas. The reason for this remembrance is that during this interval of 1500 years, there had been a decline of Vedic performances due to the ascendancy of Buddhism especially during the reign of the King Aśoka Maurya. Since 1500 years had passed till the time of Nandas, Aśoka Maurya's time must have been about 100 years later, i.e. 1500 BCE. The Āndhras were followed by the Guptas and the Paramāras. In the accounts given by historians there is a

---

40. This is the reason why Varāhamihira simply quotes *Garga* regarding the position of *sapta ṛṣis* and does not express his own opinion of it. It may also be noted that the two stars, *kratu and pulaha*, "the pointers," point towards the polestar polaris, now, but not in 3000 BCE. Then the pole star was Thuban (*dhruva*) and the entire *saptarṣi maṇḍala* was circumpolar.

41. A detailed discussion of these points are given by Kota Venkatachelam and summarized by Vedavyas.

mix-up of the Gupta king, Samudragupta, who was also known as Aśokāditya Priyadarśin and lived around 320 BCE, with Aśoka of the Maurya dynasty, which dynasty had ruled Magadha from 1535 BCE–1219 BCE. The celebrated inscriptions of Priyadarśin — Rock Edicts III and XIII mention Antiochus and Ptolemy as contemporaries of Priyadarśin, who is Samudragupta of the Gupta dynasty. The Gupta dynasty ruled Magadha from 328 BCE–83 BCE and not the Mauryas. This confusion is the reason for assigning the wrong date for the Mahābhārata war based on the Purāṇic genealogy lists. The confusion in the chronology of Bhārata is compounded by the historians, who misidentify King Vikramāditya of the Paramāra dynasty, who established the Vikrama Era in 57 BCE. The Vikrama Era together with the *saptarṣi* tradition will be discussed in greater detail later.

When proper identification of Aśoka is made, it is seen that all the traditions, namely, (i) Āryabhaṭṭa's *Kali yuga*, (ii) *saptarṣi* tradition, and (iii) the Purāṇic tradition are all consistent with the date 3067 BCE for the war.

INTERNAL CONSISTENCY IN THE EPIC OF THE DATE OF 3067 BCE

It is necessary to resolve some misconceptions that have been floating around the various events in the epic such as (i) the war started on an *amāvasyā* day, (ii) there was a conjunction of Śani and Bṛhaspati near Viśākhā and (iii) there were retrograde motions of Mars near Maghā and that of Jupiter near Śravaṇā. It is also necessary to assure the consistency of the chronology for various events as simulated in the year 3067 BCE (which is identical to the chronology given earlier by Raghavan) with those described in the epic. It turns out that this consistency requires an *adhimāsa* in that year and further brings up a question about the actual number of days between the fall of Bhīṣma and his final departure. According to the simulation, the interval appears to be 48 days (same as the number of days given by Raghavan) whereas all scholars proclaim that he spent 58 sleepless nights. All these issues have to be satisfactorily resolved.

The Question of Adhimāsa

The fact that for the months and dates to be consistent, the year 3067 BCE requires an *adhimāsa*, and according to some, this is not possible for the year 3067 BCE. However, this objection is raised on the use of the methodology based on the current Sūryasiddhānta and is not applicable to the date in question. At the time of Mahābhārata, the methods followed were based on Vedāṅga *jyotiṣa* (pre-Lagadha, in fact), and the method of determining the *adhimāsa* was based on observations and was called the Śunaḥṣepha method.[42] The author has shown that there was indeed an *adhimāsa* that year just as required.

How Many Sleepless Nights did Bhīṣma Spend?

Following the chronology given by Raghavan, which is identical to the chronology given in this article, then there are only 48 nights after the fall of Bhīṣma on the 10th day to his final departure after the arrival of winter solstice. Raghavan explains that the count of 58 (which is generally accepted as the number of sleepless nights that Bhīṣma suffers), includes the 10 days during which he led the Kaurava army and that he could not sleep because of the stresses involved. His argument is based on a somewhat different translation of the *śloka* in the epic than the one generally followed. This appears to be a reasonable explanation of this apparent discrepancy.

Did the War Begin on an Amāvasyā?

Scholars who insist that the war began on *amāvasyā* base their conclusion on the message sent by Kr̥ṣṇa through Karṇa:

42. Holay (2004), p. 24.

saptamāccāpi divasād amāvāsyā bhaviṣyati ।
sangrāmo yujyatāṁ tasyāṁ tāmāhuḥ śakradevatāṁ ॥
— *MB* V.140.18

Some scholars have interpreted this to mean that Kṛṣṇa declared the war to start on the *amāvasyā* day. According to the norms, the war could de declared either by Yudhiṣṭhira or by Duryodhana only and not by anybody else. Kṛṣṇa sends the message to Bhīṣma and Droṇa, and not to Duryodhana. Neither Bhīṣma nor Droṇa could start the war on their own. It is clear therefore, that this cannot be a declaration of war. The actual declaration of the war is made when Duryodhana sends brāhmaṇas to Yudhiṣṭhira. The proper translation of the above *śloka* is that war rituals or preparations for the war be started on that day and not the war itself. Furthermore, there is the graphic description of the war on the fourteenth day, when the battle continues into the night, breaking all rules; Ghaṭotkaca is killed and the battle stops only in the wee hours of the morning just as the moon rises. If the war had started on an *amāvasyā*, it would be *śuklapakṣa* on the fourteenth night and the moon would not rise early in the morning.

The Supposed Conjunction of Śani and Bṛhaspati

This conjunction has been considered to be an important planetary configuration by some scholars on the basis of the following:

saṁvatsara sthāyinau ca grahau prajvalitāvubhau ।
viśākhāyoḥ samīpasthau bṛhaspati śanaiścarau ॥
— *MB* VI.3.25

This is part of the third segment of the omens predicting the destruction of the two armies described by Vyāsa to Dhṛtarāṣṭra. As explained earlier, the *śloka* previous to this declares,

grahau tāmrāruṇaśikhau prajvalitāvubhau
— *MB* VI.3.24

"These two *grahas* with blazing coppery red hair," which can only refer to comets. Thus this is not a planetary configuration.

The Alleged Retrograde Motions of Mars and Jupiter

maghāsu aṅgārako vakraḥ śravaṇeca bṛhaspatiḥ ||
— *MB* IV.3.13

This verse in Bhīṣma Parva has been interpreted by many a scholar to indicate the retrograde motion of Mars at Maghā *nakṣatra* and that of Jupiter at Śravaṇā. In order for the stated retrograde motion of Mars, the Sun has to be near Śatabhiṣā and for Jupiter to be retrograde at Śravaṇā, the Sun has to be near Puṣyā. Of course, such configurations cannot occur at the same time and hence this verse has been considered a prime example of the inconsistency of astronomical references in the epic. As explained earlier, this verse is also part of the third segment of omens and this refers to comets, which belong to the families of Mars and Jupiter respectively, and not to planetary positions.

Date of Kṛṣṇa

According to the epic *Mahābhārata*, the character of Kṛṣṇa first appears at the time of Draupadī's wedding and his departure is exactly 36 years after the war. No information about his birth is available in the epic itself, although there is information about his departure. Kṛṣṇa observes omens[43] similar to the ones seen at the time of the Mahābhārata war, now indicating the total destruction of the Yādavas. Simulations show that in

43. *caturdaśī pañcadaśī kṛteyaṁ rāhuṇā punaḥ* |
tadāca bhārate yuddhe prāptacādya kṣayāya naḥ || — *MB* XIV.3.17

the year 3031 BCE, thirty-six years later than 3067 BCE, there was an eclipse season with three eclipses. A lunar eclipse on 20 October was followed by an annular solar eclipse on 5 November, followed by a penumbral lunar eclipse on 19 November, within an interval of 14 days and at an *aparvaṇi* time. Thus the date of departure of Kṛṣṇa is consistent with the popular tradition that he passed away after 36 years after the war. The information about his birth can be gathered from *Harivaṁśa* and *Bhāgavata Purāṇa,* according to which he was born in *kṛṣṇa pakṣa aṣṭamī* with Rohiṇī *nakṣatra,* but there is an uncertainty about how long he actually lived. Some believe that he lived for 125 years, while others take his life span to be only 105 years. Raghavan assigns only 81 years. The date of birth of Kṛṣṇa is calculated, apparently by extrapolation from the date of departure and so also are the several "horoscopes" of Kṛṣṇa. Simulations based on the dates yield results which only go to show whether the calculations had been done accurately and correctly by those who give such "horoscopes." As there is no clearly independent piece of information, which can be used for distinguishing the dates, one has to accept that date which suits the particular tradition. It should be understood, however, that the date of his departure from this world is established on the information in the epic and on the basis of simulations and it turns out to be 3031 BCE.

Pair of Eclipses Within Thirteen days

caturdaśīṁ pañcadaśīṁ bhūtapūrvāṁ ca ṣoṭaśīṁ ।
imāṁtu nābhijānāmi amāvāsyāṁ trayodaśīṁ ॥
— *MB* VI.3.28

candrasūryāvubhau grastāvekamāse trayodaśīṁ ।
aparvaṇi grahāvetau prajāḥ saṁkṣapayiṣyataḥ ॥
— *MB* VI.3.29

> I know new moon coinciding with fourteenth, fifteenth and also on the sixteenth day, but I have never known it coinciding with the thirteenth day. In one and the same month, both the sun and the moon are eclipsed on the thirteenth. These ill-timed eclipses indicate destruction of the people.

This is the famous reference to two eclipses occurring within a month with an interval of thirteen days. Everybody has interpreted this reference to mean that there was a lunar eclipse followed by a solar eclipse within thirteen days. Much effort has been devoted to this reference including the more recent work of Balakrishna.

Dikshit had examined this problem about hundred years ago. He had argued that the occurrence of two eclipses within an interval of thirteen days as a possibility is noticeable only by calculation and not by observation. Since one cannot get this occurrence through calculations adopting the mean motions of the luminaries, he concluded that Indians knew how to calculate the true positions of the sun and the moon as early as the date of *Mahābhārata*. There was already a reference to a lunar eclipse occurring on Kārttika *pūrṇimā* with a solar eclipse on the following new moon at Jyeṣṭha. Dikshit also argued that since in modern times it has not been possible to observe a 13-day *pakṣa* in which a lunar eclipse occurs first and is followed by a solar eclipse, the calculations of Vyāsa must have been inaccurate.

The epic refers to a lunar eclipse at Kārttika *pūrṇimā*, a solar eclipse at Jyeṣṭha, and a pair of eclipses within thirteen days. Kṛṣṇa was already in Hastināpura at the time of the lunar eclipse, and he leaves seven days before the jyeṣṭha *amāvasyā*. But, nowhere is it mentioned that the interval between the Kārttika lunar eclipse and the Jyeṣṭha solar eclipse is thirteen days. Only the scholars have assumed that the interval between these two eclipses is thirteen days. That there is another possibility, which has escaped the scholars, became evident while carrying out the simulations. It is based on the idea of eclipse season, well known in astronomy, that when the sun is near a node of the moon's orbit (say Rāhu) there is a period of about a month when eclipses can occur, and when conditions are right, three eclipses can occur in an eclipse season. There was such a situation before the war. The simulations show that the lunar eclipse on 29 September (*fig.* 8), is followed by a solar eclipse at Jyeṣṭha on 14 October (*fig.* 10). There occurred a third eclipse, a penumbral lunar eclipse on the following full moon on 28 October (*fig.* 16). According to Redshift, the lunar eclipse occurred within an interval of less than fourteen days after the solar eclipse, as the lunar eclipse occurred 5h 31m before the moment of full moon. Such an *aparvaṇi* occurrence (i.e. the eclipse occurring at a moment other than the moment of full moon) is possible only in the case of a penumbral eclipse. It must be the last pair of eclipses that Vyāsa was referring to, for he was the one who was observing the Sun both morning and evening daily:

ubhe pūrvāpare sandhye nityaṁ paśyāmi bhārata ।

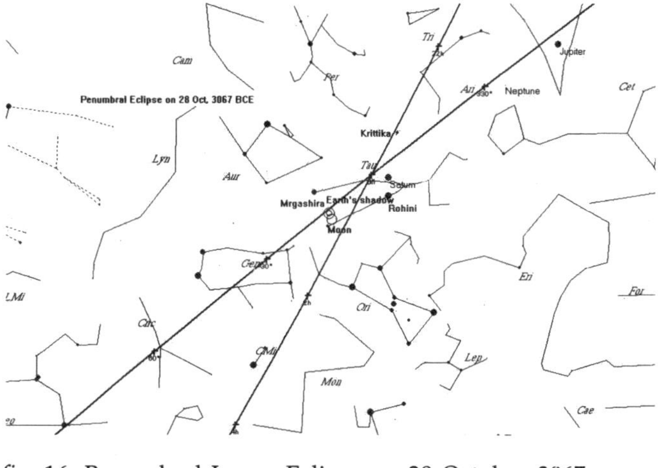

fig. 16: Penumbral Lunar Eclipse on 28 October 3067 BCE. This is the third eclipse in the eclipse season.

Thus, there is really a sequence of three eclipses that scholars should have been looking for, and not just two.

A further confirmation of this fact arises, for thirty-six years later, Kṛṣṇa sees the signs of destruction of the Yādavas and the sequence of three eclipses occurs with the last two within thirteen days as already mentioned earlier:

caturdaśī pañcadaśī kṛteyaṁ rāhuṇā punaḥ ।
tadāca bhārate yuddhe prāpta cādya kṣayāya naḥ ॥
— *MB* XIV.3.17

Conjunction of Śani with Rohiṇī

The conjunction of Śani with Rohiṇī which forms the major planetary configuration in deducing the date of the war is of course the prime indicator of disaster. It is well known in astrological works that conjunction known as *Rohiṇī śakaṭa bheda* where Saturn or Mars appears to pierce the "cart" of Rohiṇī indicates disaster in the world.

It is possible that the conjunction of Saturn with Rohiṇī probably had the same astrological significance at the time of *Mahābhārata*.

Conclusion

It has been conclusively demonstrated that the astronomical references in the epic lead to a unique date for the war, 3067 BCE. This date is consistent with all traditional reckonings of the date of the war and should form the anchor-sheet for the chronology of India.

References

Achar, B.N.N. (1999), "On Exploring the Vedic Sky with Modern Computer Software," *Electronic Journal of Vedic Studies*, 5-2.

——— (2004a), "Date of the Mahabharata War Based on Simulations Using Planetarium Software" in *The Date of the Mahabharata War Based on Astronomical Data,* ed. Suryanath U. Kamath, Banglore: Mythic Society, pp. 65-115.

Achar, B.N.N. (2004b), "Planetary Configurations in the Epic Mahābhārata: Revising an Exercise in Archaeoastronomy", in *Viewing the Sky Through Past and Present Cultures,* eds. T.W. Bostwick and B. Bates, published by City of Phoenix, pp. 433-49.

——— (2005), "Planetarium Software and the Date of the Mahabharata War" in *The Mahabharata: What is not here is Nowhere Else,* ed. T.S. Rukmani, New Delhi : Munshiram Manoharlal Publishers, PVt Ltd, pp. 247-63.

Basham, A.L. (1953), *The Wonder that was India,* New York: Grove Press Inc.

Balakrishna, S. (2004), "Two Eclipses in Thirteen Days Prior to Mahābhārata War" in *The Date of the Mahabharata War Based on Astronomical Data,* ed. Suryanath U. Kamath, Banglore: Mythic Society, pp. 1-23.

Bhat, M.R. (1981), *Varāhamihira's Bṛhatsaṁhitā,* Part I, ed. with English tr., Delhi: Motilal Banarsidass.

Dixit, S.B. (1966), *Bhāratīya Jyotiṣaśāstra,* Calcutta: Government of India Press.

Holay, P.V. (2004), "Year of the Kaurava Pandava War" in *The Date of the Mahabharata War Based on Astronomical Data,* ed. Suryanath U. Kamath, Bangalore: Mythic Society, pp. 24-54.

Kane, P.V. (1958), *History of Dharmaśāstras,* Pune: Bhandarkar Oriental Research Institute.

Kochhar, R. (1997), *The Vedic People,* Hyderabad: Orient Longman.

Iyengar, R.N. (2003), "Internal Consistency of Eclipses and Planetary Positions in Mahābhārata", *Indian Journal of History of Science,* : 77-115.

Pusalker, A.D. (1996), "Traditional History from the Earliest Time to the Accession of Parikshit", in *The Vedic Age,* R.C. Majumdar, A.D. Pusalker, and A.K. Majumdar (eds.), Mumbai: Bharatiya Vidya Bhavan.

Raghavan, K.S. (1969), *The Date of the Mahābhārata War,* Srinivasanagar: Srirangam Printers.

Rai, R.K. (1976), *The Pariśiṣṭas of Atharvaveda*, ed. with notes in Hindi of the original 1909 edn., ed. George M. Bolling, and J. von Negelein Varanasi: Chowkhambha Orientalia.

Saraswati, Svami Satya Prakash (1992), *Atharvaveda Saṁhitā* with English translation, New Delhi: Veda Pratishthan.

Sathe, S. (1983), *Search for thr Year of the Bharata War*, Hyderabad: Navabharati Publications.

Sathe, S., V. Deshmukh and P. Joshi (1985), *Bhāratīya Yuddha: Astronomical References*, Pune: Shri Babasaheb Apte Smarak Samiti.

Sharma, V.N. (1986), "Model of Planetary Configurations in the Mahābhārata: An Exercise in Archaeoastronomy", *Archaeoastronomy* 9: 88-98.

——— (2004), "On Astronomical References in the Mahābhārata — An Exercise in Archaeoastronomy", *Purāṇa* 46: 82-112.

Sidharth, B.G. (1999), *The Celestial Key to the Vedas*, Inner Traditions, Rochester.

Sky and Telescope Magazine (2001), "Other Resources for Amateur Astronomers", vol. 101, Sky Publishing Company.

Sukthankar, V.S. (1972), (Chair of the Editorial Board), *Mahābhārata, Text as constituted in its Critical Edition*, Poona: Bhandarkar Oriental Research Institute.

Vaidya, C.V. (1983), *The Mahabharata: A Criticism*, New Delhi: Cosmo Publications, p. 80.

Vedavyas, E. (1986), *Astronomical Dating of the Mahābhārata War*, Delhi: Agam Kala Prakashan.

Kota Venkatachelam (1954), *The Plot in Indian Chronology*, Vijayavada: Arya vijnana.

Yano, M. and M. Fushumi, Panchang2, a Programme based on the Sūrya Siddhānta, available by ftp://ccftp.Kyoto-su.ac.jp/pub/doc/sanskrit/

8

Patterns of Y-Chromosome Diversity in the Contemporary South Asian Gene Pool

Peter A. Underhill

SOUTH-WEST Asia, including modern-day India spans considerable geographic breadth that contains both substantial topological and climatic differences creating a regionalization of habitats encapsulating varieties of biological diversity. Included within this South-Western Asia biota, are of course, humanity with its recognizable phenotypic as well as ethnic cultural diversity. Correspondingly, the patterns of extant genetic diversity at the DNA level often reflect to some extent these geographic, linguistic and cultural landscapes (Cavalli-Sforza, Menozzi, Piazza 1994, Cavalli-Sforza & Feldman 2003, Underhill 2003).

While paleo-anthropology and archaeology have played important long-standing roles in the effort to recover episodes of human history, the more recent capability to decipher the genetic heritage passed down from ancestors to living peoples using modern molecular DNA analyses is providing an independent line of ever developing and independently reproducible empirical evidence. Ultimately, patterns of DNA variation should provide a dispassionate and comprehensive molecular genetic perspective that describes important human prehistoric movements as well as delineate the composition of modern populations. Ideally, the separate narratives given by the genes, languages, and material cultures should eventually harmonize when a common denominator of population heritage is involved. While it is unlikely that everything will fit together like a watch, this multidisciplinary approach is analogous to theology concepts where "many paths lead to one truth." In cases where gaps in the linguistic and/or archaeological records exist, the genetics of living populations may provide new insights.

Humans have the proclivity to classify things. Political groups in power often over-emphasize nationalistic tendencies and unfortunately manufacture collective, bounded and determinate identities for everyone. Identification by allegation rather than demonstration is often the game and ideology seldom equals reality. While groups with different geographic ancestry display some genetic differences, these differences are the exception. Rather the fundamental genetic structure of human populations is best viewed as a continuum emanating from Africa in a stepped clinal fashion caused by serial drift. The questionable desire by some ideologues to hijack discrete neutral genetic identifiers to classify groups of people is akin to the practice of having national flags.

The aim of this paper is to present perspectives regarding inferences of various migrations of anatomically modern humans within South-West Asia based upon the genealogy of the haploid non-recombining Y-chromosome (NRY).

Instructive examples are presented as well as some first principles concerning how to interpret patterns of genetic variability leading to deductions regarding potential geographic centres of the origins and directionality of spread of phylogenetic NRY haplogroups. Like its haploid maternally transmitted counterpart the mitochondrial DNA genome, the patterns of paternally transmitted NRY differentiation provide one representation of the evolution of modern populations and their migration pathways (Underhill et al. 2001a). The application of haploid molecular phylogenetics to human population genetics is now well established owing to substantive progress in defining the major architectural and hierarchical features of the haploid phylogenies, providing a different and instructive alternative to traditional genetic census surveys using either protein polymorphisms or DNA sequence variations based upon often less informative major and minor allele frequencies of various unlinked genetic polymorphic genomic constituents. Such frequency driven independent loci data while certainly important is often impoverished with regard to identifying the sources, directionality and timing of prehistoric migratory episodes.

Most of us are consumers of genetic facts as we currently understand them. This article attempts to address current shortcomings and limitations as well as provides insights regarding what we already know. Rapid technological progress in detecting genetic variation provides reasons to be optimistic that we will achieve a better dispassionate understanding of the biological forces such as natural selection, social customs and random chance that shape the genetic diversity in populations and thus help us transcend personal agendas and get our hands more fully around contested issues.

Human Genetics

Most research in human genetics is aimed at matters of function and malfunctions as they pertain to and elucidate certain traits and underlying metabolic pathways. However, genes are also records of past, and like ancient texts, records of past civilization or histories of people, the genetic heritage sequestered in living populations allows an independent outlet for the ancient ancestors to speak once more.

All data discussed here will focus on Y-chromosome diversification. It is an elegant powerful system to recover issues of patterns of gene, genetic diversity and provides an independent framework for interpreting an alternative data, whether it is cosmological, linguistic, archaeological, spiritual, etc.

One aim of this article is to inform readers of the current limitations of our ability to interpret the patterns of contemporary DNA diversity. All the data shown was obtained from people who live today on the planet. Ideally we would like to analyse DNA from people who lived thousands of years ago but such data is almost non-existent at this time as far as India is concerned. If and when in the future such ancient DNA is successfully analysed, the number of such data points, while obviously valuable, will be sparse. Contemporary DNA patterns will be critical to help interpret any potential future ancient DNA evidence as it provides context to the issue of continuity of the gene pool over time or discontinuity (replacement of an earlier gene pool with another).

We all harbour records of our ancestors in our contemporary DNA. Concerning the male perspective of human genetic heritage, I possess a replica copy of my father's Y-chromosome, that traces back to my paternal grandfather, that traces back to my paternal great grandfather and so on. Generations ago, somewhere along the line of succession we have lost track of the surnames of all of the previous persons. We will be talking about men who lived on earth thousands of years ago. We don't know who they were. They may not have been powerful or famous but they are important, as they may have left their genes behind.

A few cautionary words about using DNA from living populations to infer human history:

1. While ancient DNA obtained from preserved specimens would be an ideal source of information, such samples are exceedingly rare to obtain and study. Therefore we are mainly left with analysing contemporary DNA to provide proxy data for actual prehistoric events. Even when researchers are fortunate enough to get an occasional DNA profile from an ancient DNA specimen, it needs to be compared to contemporary data for context.
2. It is also important to recognize that there is no a priori reason for any direct 1:1 correlation between genetic evidence and non-genetic (e.g., archaeological, linguistic) evidence.

DISCUSSION

What about mitochondrial studies reflecting the maternal perspective?

Since the Y-chromosome provides just the male perspective of human genetic history and the mitochondrial DNA the alternative female narrative, it is not surprising that occasionally discordant patterns are revealed. However, I would say that, in general, both mitochondria and Y-chromosome data are more often in agreement than disagreement.

3. Different population histories can generate the same genetic landscape that we see genetically. Just because we see patterns on the planet today, we can imagine different scenarios that will lead to the same pattern.

4. Also it is possible that earlier demographic events or episodes may be hidden or replaced by more recent events.

An example is the agricultural expansion in Africa 3000 to 4000 thousands years ago catalyzed by Iron Age technology. We see Y-chromosome types that appear to originate in Cameroon area where it is generally attributed to be the starting point of the main expansion by agriculturalists, which then spread into the pre-existing hunter-gatherer African gene pool. The farming expansion did not completely erase previous varieties or what existed earlier but such demographic events surely have an impact, thus such impacts are important. Additional molecular resolution regarding the Y-chromosome needs to be detected and studied to better quantify the extent of the impact of expanding Iron Age farmers on the foragers. It could be that while the adaptation of farming was rapid and extensive, the spread of the genes of the first farmers may have been considerably less successful. Perhaps the pre-existing local hunter-gatherers just adopted farming.

Thus novel genes, which are new and have recently arrived at a new place that already has a larger pre-existing gene pool, may be considerably diluted and thus become relatively rare. An analogy would be throwing a few apples into a very large bag of oranges; the apples are there but they are hard to see. It is not that they don't exist, it is just that they are absorbed by a larger pre-existing signal. Major cultural innovations (e.g., farming) do not automatically lead to a large-scale replacement of the pre-agricultural gene pool.

A final word of caution: the molecular ancestry of the paternally inherited Y-chromosome may not always match the ancestry recorded in other components of the genome.

Some correlations may be demonstrated but caution must be exercised when making such inferences.

Phylogeny

It is a wide and powerful spatial and temporal record of the spread and molecular differentiation of anatomically modern humans. What we can recover from results of contemporary populations is the sequential pattern of the accumulation of mutations that happened on Y-chromosomes along the

Gene History: Time and Space

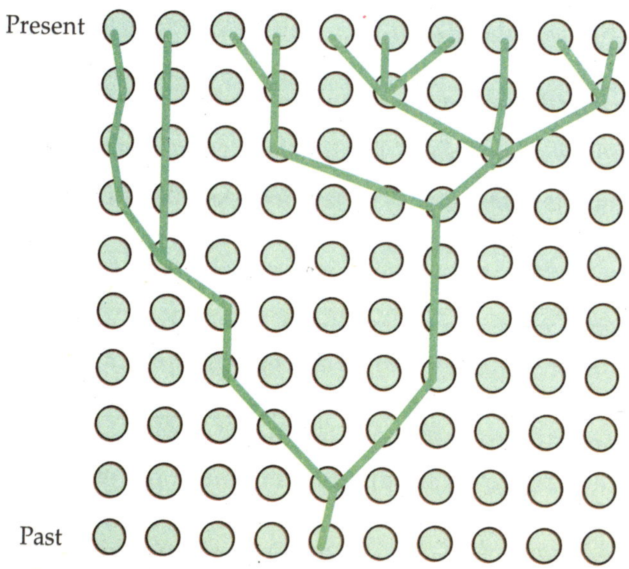

generations — an exquisite molecular record of the "line of descent." As long as man has a son(s) then his Y-chromosome is passed on to male descendents, just like surnames are today in many societies. Alternatively if he has only daughters, his Y-chromosome lineage will go extinct; however his other autosomal genes are passed on to the daughter and thus survive in the overall gene pool.

Because mutations occur during gametogenesis, albeit rarely, each time there is a father-son transmission there is a potential or possibility for a new molecular innovation or spelling change to happen within the inherited genome of the offspring, including the Y-chromosome. While such events are infrequent, it is the basis of the architecture that creates the gene tree.

The accumulation of mutations during the lineal lifespan of the Y-chromosome across the generations can be determined and displayed in a genealogy (tree). Such new harmless mutations represent branching points within the tree, creating its tree-like structure.

An Incompatible Mixture: Ideology and Phylogeny

1. While all politics is local, not all genetic signals are.
2. As scientists, dispassionate assessment of evidence is essential and required for progress.
3. Pre-conceived bias can prematurely support or reject one model or another since bias tends to unsystematically and incorrectly interpret the relevant literature of the other disciplines. As consumers of facts, we carefully evaluate what our current state of knowledge is about the contemporary genetics or DNA. All consumers of genetics, especially the non-specialists should resist the temptation to not just cherry pick what they want to see, to favour their point of view, but rather they should strive to see the data holistically, and recognize that the current understanding is incomplete and that it may become necessary to reappraise current models as new data modifies our current picture. Good science in the light of new good knowledge is characterized by self-correction.

4. Miscomprehension leads to misinterpretation. Again miscomprehension of facts may lead to mis-interpretation, which is not advisable.

Population Structure and Group Membership

1. Not all polymorphisms, markers or mutations are equally informative.
2. To distinguish between two populations, or two groups of people, the ideal locus (i.e. genetic marker) is one for which an allele is fixed in one group but is absent in another group.
3. In reality such loci or distinctions are very rare in comparisons between populations.
4. Y-chromosomes are however very peculiar with more power to harbour and more readily reveal such population-specific markers relative to the other genes.

Polymorphism or Markers

Consider for example a 241 base pair sequence of the 4 nucleotides GCT and A that represent particular address in every man's Y-chromosomes.

Every man has these 241 base pair sequences. You can use PCR technology to study this region in any man's Y-chromosome by amplifying these particular 241 base pairs, to make enough of material so we can do experiments on it. The fundamental question to ask is to determine if there is any variation or change in these 241 fragments between one man's Y-chromosome and that of any other man. While often no sequence difference is observed, occasionally a spelling variation is d.etected.

This variation is what we are looking for during our research efforts. In this example the variation is seen occurring as a C to T polymorphism at a very precise address

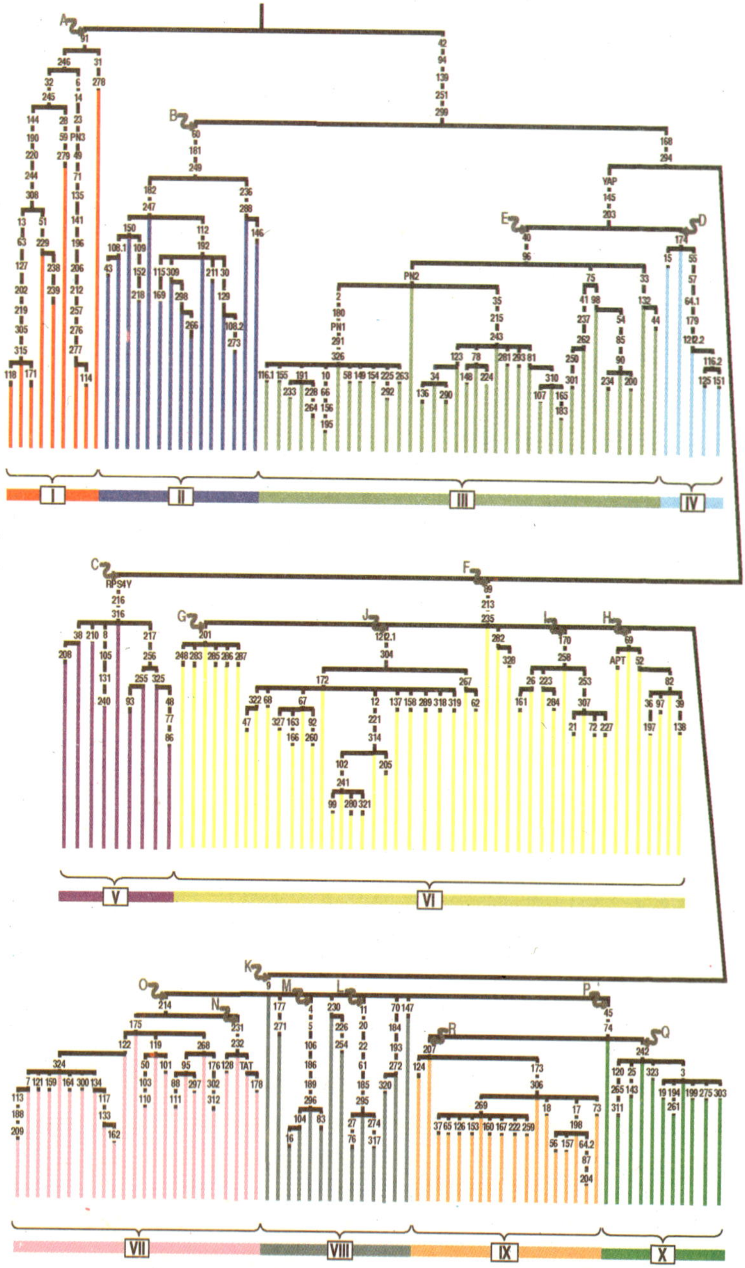

Stanford University, 17 June 2002

on a Y-chromosome. We can go to that precise nucleotide and ask the question, who is C and who is T and why is that simple harmless change important in understanding the genetic relationships between different groups of males?

Most men tested carry the C nucleotide rather then the T nucleotide. And even chimpanzees and gorillas are C, so we can use that fact to infer that C is the primitive ancestral variety.

But we see that some people in the world are T. Specifically a large majority of Native Americans have derived T at this position on their Y-chromosome. Thus when a Y-chromosome is shown to have a T nucleotide at this exact position we are looking at an individual whose paternity traces back to a single unique Native American paternal ancestor. This type of information is the localization of a genetic signature that the Y-chromosome does best. Not all Native Americans are T, but vast majority of them are. That means, probably in the early prehistoric colonization of North America, a man or a small group of people arrived and all the men were all C, because C is the ancestral nucleotide common to great apes and most men. Remember that humans share a very high level of DNA identity (roughly 98 per cent) with chimpanzees.

During the last Ice Age about 20,000 years ago, as sea level dropped and mega fauna migrated from North-East Asia across the exposed Beringian land bridge into North America, humans followed them. Some humans (or their descendents) eventually reach North America. Once here they survive and reproduce. Sometimes during this colonization of North America a healthy son is born who is nucleotide T at this specific position on his Y-chromosome. It is merely by luck, strictly by chance, that this boy survived to maturity and had a son or sons of his own. Thus it was the survival of the luckiest, (not necessarily survival of the fittest) which allowed such T-bearing Y-chromosomes to originate and gain a foothold in the fledgling Native American gene pool. This un-named son became the primogenitor of all the Native Americans who nowadays carry the T variety at this marker site. So these early Native American distant ancestors spread across the Americas developing into various ethnic groups with their own distinctive cultural attributes such as language and social custom. Thus if one talks for example with Native Americans from the Great Plains, they would say they are not related to other groups like the Eskimos, or indigenous people from South America. Their remote ancestry is real but so is their cultural uniqueness relative to other Native American groups.

So where is this T-mutation found in the global Y-chromosome tree? It is near one of the tips of the tree far from the root of the tree which is in Africa. Thus the tree starts in Africa and branches outwards. It is possible to position polymorphisms like the C to T mutation in the tree. Mutations that happened early in the molecular evolution of the Y-chromosome molecular position are closer to the root and subsequent mutations that have accumulated form new branches, some of which are most recent and are thus nearer the canopy of the tree. The two deepest (or most basal) branches of the tree are restricted to some men living in Africa. This is compelling evidence that all men trace their ancestry to a common ancestor who lived in Africa perhaps 100,000 years ago. The tree reflects the accumulation of molecular innovations (i.e. spelling changes) that create various branches. We see subsets of branches within Africans and evidence in the form of a deep branch in which some people left Africa and subsequently continued to accumulate their own sequential assemblages of molecular innovations displayed in the current structure of the Y-chromosome tree. Each of these mutations, including those that will be found in future studies of genetic variation, can be placed in the tree and thus further refine more precisely the actual phylogenetic relationships amongst the various branches.

We can try to take non-recombining haploid mtDNA and Y-chromosome data to attempt to answer some evergreen questions amenable to the phylogenetic approach like:

1. From which geographic areas has a region received its genetic elements?
2. When, how long, and in what sequence have these connections existed?

Approach Used

1. Are there informative sub-clades within an overarching monophyletic clade?
2. Do sub-clades display distinctive geography?
3. A well resolved phylogeny permits hypothesis testing and phylogeographic results can suggest alternative hypotheses to knotty problems.

DISCUSSION

Is it a quantitative method, in a statistical or hypothetic sense?

Yes, since such mutations and their frequencies can be experimentally observed and analysed for levels of statistical significance. Also computational simulations based upon chosen variables such as population size, growth rate, etc. can be conducted to evaluate the demographic parameters necessary to create the observed data.

Genetic Diversity in Populations: Result of Local Differentiation and Admixture

Genetic diversity in population results from both local differentiation in a population and also the input of existing variation from populations that merged to create the current population. An example of local differentiation is the molecular innovation, T nucleotide in Native Americas that originated early in the pioneer colonization of North America in descendents of migrating ancestors from Asia. Such local differentiation creates genetic distance between groups. Within the membership of Native Americans with the T mutation on their Y-chromosome are additional markers that create geographically distinctive subsets of such overall T-chromosomes. Some have markers that are more restricted to Mesoamericans, some have markers restricted to South America and some have other markers restricted to North America. Since much of the variation on the Y-chromosome has yet been discovered, we can anticipate getting additional refined resolution within any current branch. Finally the genes that arrived that are not indigenous also influence the gene pool of a region. These are brought in by additional gene flows that eventually merge into the amalgamation we see in today's various populations. So these are the two main components that contribute to the contemporary gene pool population.

Interpreting Gene Phylogenies

1. Temporal and geographic patterns in Y and mtDNA data must be viewed through the opposing dual lenses of migration and drift. This is the duality of isolated indigenous innovation that creates unique patterns of variants and migration that contribute genes that originated at some external place.
2. Drift leads to isolation and the development of distinguishing markers.
3. Migration creates geographic affinity, as it often tends to blend converging previously distinctive populations.

The deep background framework of a gene tree like the

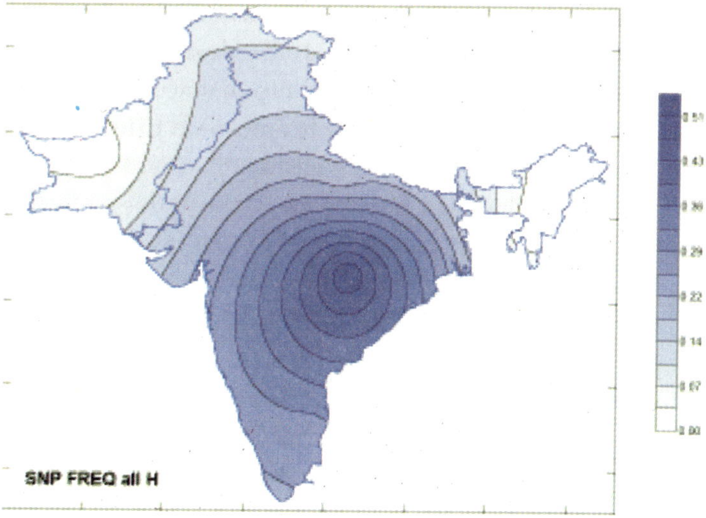

Am. J. Hum. Genet. (2004) 74: 1023-34

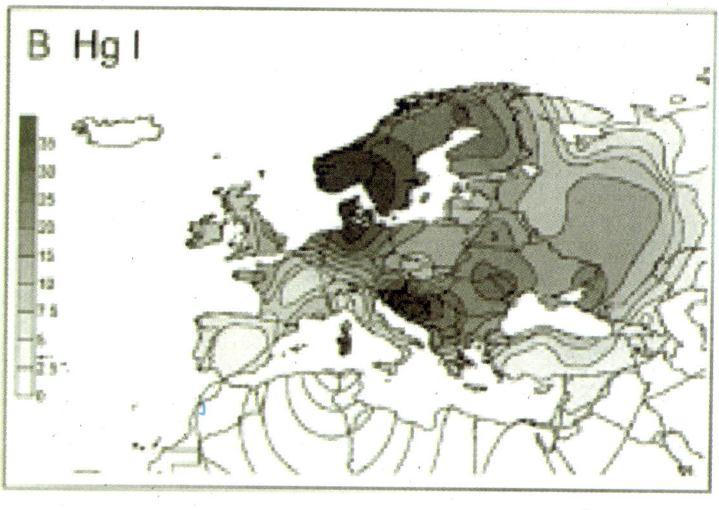

Am. J. Hum. Genet. (2004) 75: 128-37

Y-chromosome locus displays both ancient shared common ancestry, from which all individuals descend, as well as subsequent regional differentiation into distinctive geographic varieties. For example, basic Y-chromosome categories like haplogroups G, I, J, F reflect the characteristics of geographic regionalization. The deep framework of the Y-tree shows that mutations that define the F branch of the genealogy arose very early in diversification of humans after they departed Africa and successfully settled in Asia. We can infer that European specific haplogroup I is a descendent of the haplogroup IJ precursor who had a paternal ancestor who had derived mutations that define the F branch but was ancestral for mutations that define the H, G and K branches. Some descendents of an F ancestor evolved into IJ descendents whose offsprings eventually evolved in independent European specific haplogroup I and Middle Eastern (Levantine) specific haplogroup J representatives. Conversely, other individuals who had derived haplogroup F defining mutations but ancestral for I, J, G, defining mutations became the primogenitor for haplogroup H individuals who are common in South-West Asia including modern India. That's why we see the dramatic regionalization of haplogroup H representatives in South-West Asia, haplogroup I in Europe and haplogroup J in the Middle East. But notably they all descend from an ancient common haplogroup F bearing common ancient ancestor that defines a deep interior node within the Y gene tree. The discovery of mutations that uniquely link haplogroup I and J clearly show that these chromosomes are closer to one another evolutionarily speaking than to haplogroup G, H and K members. And we can anticipate that other markers will eventually be found that will join currently independent major haplogroups like F*, G and H adding further resolution to the deep evolutionary relationships amongst these core haplogroups. The process of recombination characteristic of the autosomes such as chromosomes 1 through 22 breaks apart and erases such ancient relationships. Since haploid genomes do not recombine they are a stable record that preserves these ancient evolutionary relationships.

The sub-structure within the various clades provides a relative time scale between clades. When one is looking at specific haplogroup genetic data one needs to have some sense of what phylogenetical level (genetics) the data is reflecting. While haplogroups (e.g. haplogroup C) that position deeper within the core tree structure can certainly still be involved in more recent gene flows, the mutations that define sub-clades reflect lineages which have evolved more recently relative to earlier branches, and thus these sub-haplogroups position closer to the canopy of the tree and provide a more direct line of molecular evidence suitable for tracing more recent demic expansion and gene flow events. The more sophisticated consumer of haploid molecular phylogenetic data is a person who appreciates the significance of understanding the level of molecular resolution of the data within the phylogeny that is being used in any population history narrative that is being attributed to such data. Also the sophisticated consumer will recognize that not all the diversity sequestered within the phylogeny is known, despite its bushy appearance. The possibility exists that currently held interpretations may require significant reappraisal when the hidden branches are subsequently exposed as new markers are discovered, especially using samples from populations of interest given the strong geographic signal inherent in the Y-chromosome gene tree. Thus if one wishes to understand the genetic landscape of populations in India, it is best to analyse such

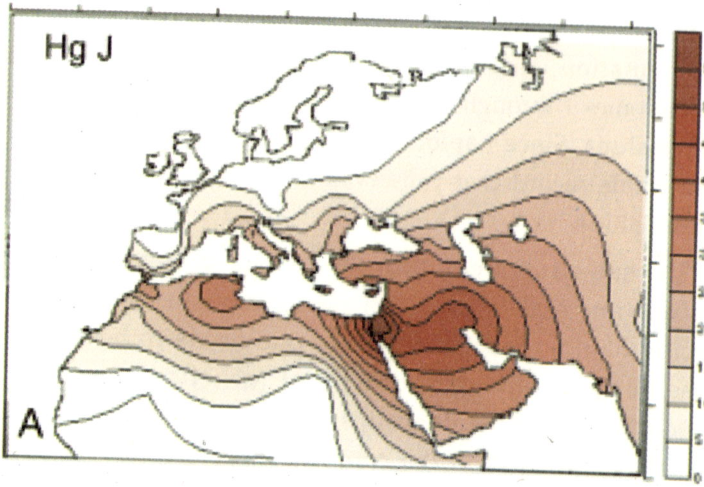

Am. J. Hum. Genet. (2006) 78: 202-21

Regionalization of Y-chromosome binary haplogroups.

data using markers that have the hallmarks originating in India, such as haplogroup H.

Given that many Y-chromosome markers are geographically localized, such data can be visualized using spatial frequency maps in which frequency surfaces are interpolated between actual sample collection data points. The more densely sampled, the better such interpolated maps reflect the actual genetic picture. For almost all data sets, the density of sampling is still too sparse to provide data suitable for actual geo-statistical analyses. Nonetheless, such maps provide insight into the net spread pattern of a particular haplogroup.

When the maps show data at a level of molecular resolution that is typical of current data set, these interpolated maps of the genetic landscape today are reflecting not just necessarily one expansion or migration or movement of people but perhaps a composite of multiple demographic results. We cannot see those at this level of resolution, we see only an overall net trend. It is prudent not to rush a judgement and say that the

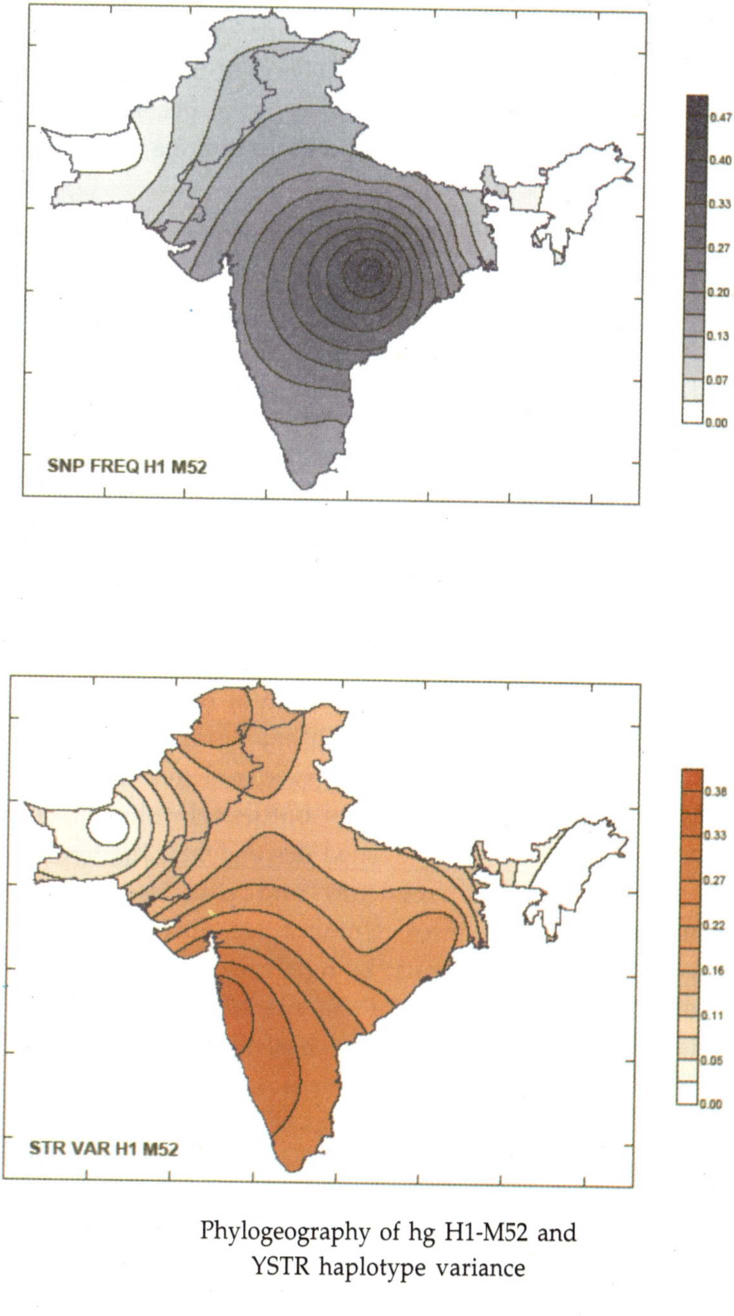

Phylogeography of hg H1-M52 and
YSTR haplotype variance

frequency distribution is due to a specific event. Such maps most often actually reflect the consequences of multiple events. However as sub-haplogroups are mapped it becomes more feasible to untangle the mixture into more discrete individual events.

While the area of highest SNP (or haplogroup frequency) is often viewed as its actual point of origin, this may not always be true. For example, a few descendents of the original founders could migrate from their homeland into un-populated territory and then experience a population increase that would create a zone high frequency that could exceed the frequency in the actual homeland. One way to control this possibility is to also study the degree of Y-short tandem repeat (YSTR microsatellite) linked to the particular binary (SNP) defined haplogroup. If an area has both characteristics of high haplogroup frequency plus the highest associated haplotype variance, then the likelihood increases that this is the geographic area of origin of the haplogroup. Conversely, if an area has very high haplogroup frequency, but low associated YSTR variance averaged over multiple STR loci, then this area is a recent bottleneck followed by very rapid increase in closely related descendents. The figures of haplogroup H-M52 frequency and associated YSTR variance suggest a complex demography. However, such highly interpolated maps must be recognized as preliminary and rather more as examples of concept than actual specific population histories since they are based on relatively few data points. Again, as more sub-haplogroup resolution is deployed along with more well characterized and denser population sampling, such maps and their interpretation will improve.

DISCUSSION

Can we put a time bracket with the present technology?

Only approximately. It is likely that haplogroup H originated before the Holocene era but begin to increase in numbers considerably and spread *c.* 10,000 years ago. However some of the spreads could be more recent. What we can have is a continual movement of people or succeeding punctuated episodes of migration. Thus we have to be careful about interpreting a picture like this and saying that it reflects a single event attributed to a particular sliver of time, or maybe a composition of many events.

Status of Y-Chromosome Phylogenetics

1. What is required? The current framework of the Y-chromosome phylogeny has afforded the opportunity to take a long and synthetic view of global human migration and population origins. It is very deep and global; many of the themes and interest are recent (three to four thousand years) than very old (about 35,000 yrs).

   So how do we get to the tips of the tree (three to four thousand years)? Add more molecular innovation and place them accurately within the gene tree. But we have just started to scratch the surface to discover them.

2. To a larger extent however, what remains to be exposed are informative levels of sub-clade diversification patterns that permit assessments of migrations and colonization of events associated with subsequent human micro-evolutionary episodes.

If we have to find Native American markers or any population of choice then we have to be looking for those markers in populations of specific interest. This is the concept of ascertainment. In order to detect a genetic signature restricted to particular regions you need to be searching for such markers in the appropriate populations.

A shortcoming that can influence our view (in a potentially misleading way) of India is that most of the markers currently applied to India by reseachers were actually detected in non-Indian samples. Such data can create a bias in our perspective. So we have to be careful. The shortcoming with India is that there is not much effort made to discover markers on Indian populations though that's not intentional. It is very hard for scientists like myself who look systematically for new markers to get Indian DNA to use in such new marker discovery efforts.

Phylogenetics and Pitfall of Paraphyletic Haplogroups

While progress associated with ever increasing resolution of the Y-chromosome phylogeny continues to offer much promise in the future to applying genetics to particular debates and hypotheses regarding human prehistory, there are also pitfalls associated with such data beyond the limitation that just the male perspective is being represented. Some key concepts are involved.

1. Consideration of the level of phylogenetic hierarchy represented in the data sets. Are we looking at phylogenetic data based upon either just deep, intermediate or more recent branch tips of the tree?
2. And if we are interested in relatively recent history events, are we sure that we are making inferences using data defined by sub-haplogroup branches that position near the tips of the tree. How likely is it that the sub-haplogroup we are discussing is near the tip of the actual gene tree? Are we are talking either about an interior node in the tree or terminal node at the tips?

3. HgL is presented as a conceptual example.
4. HgL population membership spans Turkey, Iran, Pakistan and India (= 10 per cent) which not only cover considerable geographic space but also considerable cultural, linguistic diversity.
5. Viewpoint of the strength of the conclusions is best dictated by the degree of molecular resolution used Haplogroup L is one of the major haplogroups defined by its own set of multiple distinctive mutations.

It was first defined by mutation M11, an A to G change. Members of haplogroup L all carry the derived G allele, while members of all the other major haplogroups carry the ancestral A allele. We know that A is ancestral state since the Great Apes like gorilla and chimpanzees are also A. Since haplogroup L defined chromosomes predominantly occur in India, Pakistan, and Turkey and very rarely in Europe and Central and East Asia it is likely that this haplogroup arose somewhere between Turkey and India. When the centroid of all haplogroup L frequency data from Turkey, Pakistan and India is drawn with a radius of one standard deviation, its centre position is near the Indus Valley.

However as haplogroup L phylogenetic resolution is improved by fractionating L chromosomes in various sub-haplogroups, each with their own unique defining binary (SNP) marker, we see that virtually all the chromosomes studied (98 per cent) actually partition into three distinctive sub-clades, each with its own centre of gravity. At some time following the initial localized geographic origin of haplogroup L its members persisted and accumulated mutations that they all shared. Then subsequently, they were compelled to disperse to other geographic regions. As they became physically separated their descendents accumulated their own unique mutations (i.e. molecular innovations) increasing the genetic distance amongst themselves. It is possible that in the past some undifferentiated L chromosomes entered India and then evolved into the halogroup L1-M27 variety with frequency and then participated in its own range expansion(s) independent of the other L2-M317 and L3-M357 varieties. Hence when someone is just talking about the haplogroup L-chromosomes one must ask how might the interpretation be changed when the L data are viewed in terms of their various sub-haplogroups. Lastly, it is also worth pointing out that the likelihood is high that other as yet undiscovered mutations exist that will unite two out of the three known haplogroup varieties since the phylogenetic trend is always towards two offsetting haplogroups.

Hg R1a-M17 Frequency in EurAsia

Several lines of evidence exist to indicate that north India is different from the south. Understanding the origins and factors shaping these differences is a perennial question amongst both scholars and ideologues in South Asia. In this regard I think from Y-chromosome perspective, the haplogroup that's probably going to have the most impact in illuminating this topic in a dispassionate manner will be hg R1a1-M17. Such chromosomes distribute from south India across West Asia all the way to Scandinavia (Norway). The current of interpretation of what M17 represents is based upon viewing M17 as a terminal tip mutation. However such viewpoints typically do not realize that its current terminal position in the tree is an artifact since phylogeographic subdivision within currently defined R1a1-M17 chromosomes must exist unless we presume that all R1a1-M17 are very recently descended

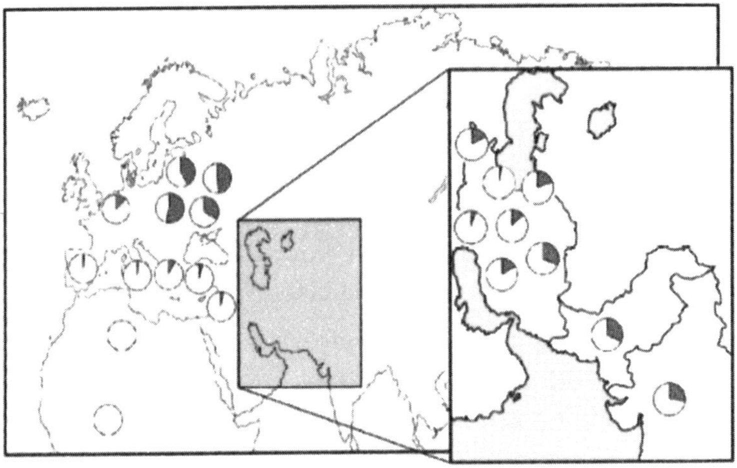

Hg R1a-M17 frequency in EurAsia

Quintana-Munci 2001 *AJHG* 68: 537-42

from a common ancestor. If however enough time has elapsed for subdivision to take hold in a manner similar as the haplogroup L-M-11 situation has shown, we expect to see some local geographic sub-haplogroup division emerge at informative frequencies with haplogroup R1a1-M-17. If that occurs then we can get some independent new evidence to provide insights on where the various sub-haplogroups originated and which is the general net trajectory of movement in one way or the other of such sub-haplogroups. Also when YSTR haplotype data are considered we can obtain some insights into the age of the last detectable bottleneck of such sub-haplogroups. Such phylogenetic approaches using Y-chromosome haplogroup R1a1 phylogenetics (and other haplogroups as well) — while it will not have all answers for all the questions but such genetic data will provide a platform or key source for progress — provide more dimensions to explore the basic topic of the relationships between north and south India as well as north India and West Asia.

DISCUSSION

1. Although we are looking at the DNA that is available today, we interpret the observed genetic variation to recover the deep genetic memory retained in this molecular record.

2. A technical question: Would you be happy to have an opportunity to compare your data and conclusions with HLA — class A and class B?

   Yes, such a synthetic approach is worth doing. In fact with the recent availability of highly parallel autosomal mapping arrays, such work is being done by other laboratories. If genetic relationships are recent between geographical distinct populations (not adjacent villages) then haplotype blocks of shared segments of autosomal chromosomes should emerge. The longer the time since separation between geographic areas, the older are their historical relationships.

   Two forces are at play that can influence the diversity observed on genes in a population:

   a) *Natural selection or fitness.* HLA diversity is certainly shaped by natural selection. Other autosomal loci sometimes are also shaped by natural selection. However some diversity observed at other autosomal loci can also be caused by another force.

   b) *Survival of luckiest.* This is drift or random change where the genetic change has no bearing on success, outcome, superiority or inferiority of a genetic element. The prevailing view is that classic natural selection on the Y-chromosome would have happened very early in the speciation of anatomically modern humans or even earlier. Once they get to that stage (fitness), then drift or survival of luckiest is a major chance event shaping the observed patterns of diversification, like the harmless C to T mutation in Native Americans especially when population sizes were small. However, culturally catalyzed sexual selection by women for a certain man (e.g. best hunter, provider) could also by chance influence the level of success of a Y chromosome haplogroup.

HLA is involved with immune response. It is very polymorphic because HIV or other pathogens are challenging it. While HLA polymorphism is driven mainly by the requirement that it can respond to new threats — pathogens — by having a subset of its HLA genes already in place to respond to a new pathogen, not all variation in the genome is maintained by selective forces.

Thus different genes can reflect different perspectives. Haploid mitochondria and Y- chromosome are, in part, records of sex bias during mating while other genes like HLA are influenced by natural selection. If a gene gives fitness, it maintains itself in the gene pool. It may not be reflecting the history of the overall population, but just reflecting the history of the gene.

3. When is genetic variation reflecting the history of population, origin, movement, and people?

   This is when the Y-chromosome, as well as perhaps the mitochondria, and some other neutral autosomal gene that are not under strong selection, also have the same general geographic structures or diversity patterns because they are assumed to be neutral elements that we carry along with us and they don't have a role in fitness but do have this recorded history, mutual changes that occurred. When we see one gene variant that manifests in a peculiar way when compared to others that is a strong clue of a particular gene under selection. When five or six independent genes display evidence of serial drift then we are seeing the movement of people and perhaps the culture of the population. It is important not to just cherry pick elements of a genetic system that seems to confirm our own preconceptions. It is always good to ask, can other explanations be possible. Just try to flip things over and consider the other perspective also.

4. Present state of knowledge is often not useful yet for relatively recent historical periods.

   We have to recognize that as we explore these sub-clades, as we get closer to the tips and study them at the population level our current perceptions may require alteration. Is there differentiation beyond the current level of molecular resolution of haplogroup R1a1-M17? Yes, it is very like there hidden in the gene pool but just not revealed yet.

5. Haplogroup R1a1-M17 is commonly observed in India and elsewhere. Can you put the geographic presence in different regions in chronological order?

   Not yet with any satisfying certainty. It is observed in India, rare in western Europe and common in eastern Europe and Scandinavia. While we can reasonably speculate that its area of origin might be somewhere between eastern Europe and south Asia it remains difficult to make further progress since we currently know little regarding the phylogeographic nature of informative sub-clades within haplogroup R1a1-M17. The true set of hierarchical relationships amongst R1a1-M17 chromosomes both within India and external to India remains very incomplete. Thus we have to be careful in saying anything conclusive based upon our current understanding of the phylogeography of R1a1-M17. We have to make those discoveries, namely identify subsets of M17 varieties and deduce their geographic origins and spread in geographic time and space. Just recently a European specific R1a1-M17 related sub-haplogroup defined by the M458 A to G SNP has been described (Underhill et al., 2009). However much remains unanswered for now but some day will have the answers. Given the rapid pace of genetic sequencing, new markers should be discovered and new genotyping technologies will make it feasible to type the new markers in more and more samples. So we can anticipate significant progress in just a few years.

References

Cavalli-Sforza, L.L., P. Menozzi, A. Piazza (1994), *The History and Geography of Human Genes*, Princeton: Princeton University Press.

Cavalli-Sforza, L.L., M.W. Feldman (2003), "Biology as History: Population Genetic Approaches to Modern Human Evolution", *Nat. Genet. Suppl.* 33: 266-75.

Underhill, P.A., G. Passarino, A.A. Lin, P. Shen, R.A. Foley, M. Mirazón Lahr, P.J. Oefner, L.L. Cavalli-Sforza (2001), "The Phylogeography of Y-chromosome Binary Haplotypes and the Origins of Modern Human Populations", *Ann. Hum Genet*, 65: 43-62.

Underhill, P.A., 2003, "Inferring Human History: Clues from Y-chromosome Haplotypes", in *The Genome of Homo Sapiens*, Cold Spring Harbor Symp. Quant. Biol., 68: 487-93.

Sengupta, S., L.A. Zhivotosky, R. King, S.Q. Mehdi, C.A. Edmonds, C-ET Chow, A.A. Lin, M. Mitra, S.K. Sil, A. Ramesh, M.V.U. Rani, C.M.

Thakur, L.L. Cavalli-Sforza, P.P. Majumder, P.A. Underhill, 2006, "Polarity and Temporality of High Resolution Y-chromosome Distributions in India Identify Both Indigenous and Exogenous Expansions and Reveal Minor Genetic Influence of Central Asian Pastoralists", *Am J Hum Genet*, 78: 202-21.

Underhill, P.A., 2006, "Interpreting Patterns of Y-Chromosome Diversity: Pitfalls and Promise, A case study from SW Asia", in "Proceedings of the Pre-Symposium of RIHN and the 7th ESCA Harvard-Kyoto Roundtable" (ed. Toshiki Osada) Research Institute for Humanity and Nature (RIHN) Kyoto, Japan; pp. 214-19.

Underhill P.A., N.M. Myres, S. Rootsi, M. Metspalu, L.A. Zhivotovsky, R.J. King, A.A. Lin, C.-E.T. Chow, O. Semino, V. Battaglia, I. Kutuev, M. Järve, G. Chaubey, Q. Ayub, A. Mohyuddin, S.Q. Mehdi, S. Sengupta, E.I. Rogaev, E.K. Khusnutdinova, A. Pshenichnov, O. Balanovsky, E. Balanovska, N. Jeran, D.H. Augustin, Marian Baldovic, R.J. Herrera, K. Thangaraj, V. Singh, L. Singh, P. Majumder, P. Rudan, D. Primorac, R. Villems, T. Kivisild, 2009, "Major Y- chromosome founder effect in early Holocene Eastern Europe identified through a novel branch of haplogroup R1a1", *Eur J Hum Genet* Nov 4.

1. With conch blowing the conference begins

2. Marcie Williams, Vice President of University Massachusetts inaugurating the Conference

3. Bal Ram Singh introducing the Conference

4. Yvette Rosser presents to attentive audience, including Michael Witzel (right corner) who takes careful notes

5. N.S. Rajaram presents as the audience, including ambassador C. M. Bhandari, Piotr Eltsov, and Divya Tripathi look on, and Michael Witzel takes notes.

8. Attentive audience listening to the lectures

9. Peter Underhill, Nicholas Kazanas, and VD Misra

10. Delegates on a break

9

Aryan Gene Pool in Indian Populations: Myth or Reality

Genetic Evidences from the Subcontinent

V.K. Kashyap, R. Trivedi* and *S. Sahoo

IT probably all started with the quest to understand how Indo-European (IE) family of languages came to occupy such a broad region from Europe and western Asia to parts of the Indian subcontinent. Invasions and migrations were seen as the most likely, fastest and easiest mediator for spread of languages, culture (agriculture and technology) and people (or genes). There are two alternate hypotheses that describe the pre-historic spreading of the IE language group. One proposed by Gimbutas (1980) assumes that invading migrants ("Kurgan" culture) had spread the languages out from a common point of origin through conquest of relatively passive farming populations. The other more recent alternative view (Renfrew, 1989) held that these languages spread with the farmers that swamped out the languages of hunter-gatherer groups, speaking non-IE languages. In context to the Indian subcontinent, this has been linked to the "Aryan Invasion" which led to the destruction and extinction of the Haṛappan Civilization (Wheeler, 1946). Since the homeland of the IE languages was already placed outside India, it was proposed that a group of IE speakers invaded India around 3000-1500

BCE and imposed their language on the "Draviḍian" or other non-Aryan aboriginal inhabitants of India by force.

We have examined the certainty of this hypothesis by analysing the genetic component in the present-day populations of India, which harbour signatures of pre-historic events in their gene pool. Linguistically, the four main language families spoken in India have strong regional patterns, with the largest group, IE, prevalent in northern India. Draviḍian language family is the second largest and covers the majority of the languages in the south. Most of the IE speakers belong to caste groups, while the majority of the tribal populations (over 450) speak languages from the other three i.e. Draviḍian Sino-Tibetan and Austro-Asiatic families (Singh, 1997). However, the existence of both IE-speaking tribal groups and Draviḍian-speaking castes indicates the complexity of historical interactions between Indian populations. In spite of these overlaps, it has been generally presumed that the IE languages were brought in by the "Aryans" who came from Central Asia CE ~3500 and invaded the subcontinent, subjugating the Draviḍian-speaking tribes and pushing them down south. In addition, the trend of finding farming castes and IE languages grouped together (Renfrew, 1989) has also led to the belief that invading Aryans introduced the caste system and agricultural technology to the people of South Asia.

These pre-conceived notions given by a host of philologists, archaeologists, and historians were supported by several geneticists, who led to find a genetic link between Indians and Europeans. Several studies have argued that, in contrast to the relative uniformity of mtDNA, the Y-chromosomes of Indian populations display relatively small genetic distances to those of West Eurasians, linking this finding to hypothetical migrations by Indo-Aryan speakers. Bamshad et al. (2001) suggested that IE-speaking people from West Eurasia entered

India from the north-west and diffused throughout the subcontinent. They purportedly admixed with or displaced indigenous Draviḍic-speaking populations and subsequently, established the Hindu caste system and placed themselves primarily in castes of higher rank. Another study by Wells et al. highlighted M17 (R1a1) as a potential marker for this spread of IE speakers and the "Aryan" migration, as it demonstrates decreasing frequencies from Central Asia towards south India. It has also been associated with the Kurgan culture, domestication of horses and spread of IE languages, all of which supposedly originated in southern Russia/Ukraine and subsequently extended to Europe, Central Asia around 3000 BCE (Wells, 2001). Aryan migration has also been linked to appearance of iron and Painted Grey Ware culture in north-west frontier of India (Cavilli-Sforza, 1994). The Indo-Aryan migration scenario advocated by Cordaux et al. was based on the suggestion that all Indian caste groups are similar to each other and significantly different from the tribes and defined, heuristically, a package of haplogroups (J2, R1a1, R2, and L) to be associated with the migration of IE people and the introduction of the caste system to India, from Central Asia.

We have examined this hypothesis by significantly increasing the available sample size for India by typing 936 individuals from 77 populations, representing 32 tribal and 45 caste groups from all four major linguistic groups of India; IE (n=470), Draviḍian (n=323), Austro-Asiatic (n=83), and Sino-Tibetan (n=60). This study included thirty-eight highly informative single nucleotide polymorphisms (SNPs), including M168, M89, M9, RPS4Y711, M216, M217, YAP, M174, M201, M69, M52, Apt, M82, M170, p12f2, M172, M70, M147, M20, M11, M27, M5, M214, M231, M175, M95, M88, M122, M134, M242, 92R7, M45, M207, M173, SRY1532, M17, M269, and M124, which are typed to permit more detailed resolution of geographic patterns, and the identification of region-specific subsets of lineages, if any. These new Y-chromosomes are analysed in the context of available data from West, East, South-East, and Central Asia, Europe, the Near East, and Ethiopia. Measures of genetic distance, admixture, and factor analysis drawn from the Y-chromosome data are used to investigate the genetic relationship between castes and tribes and demographic links to Europe, West and Central Asia.

Our data on 936 Indian Y-chromosomes revealed a total of eighteen paternal lineages, out of which, haplogroups R1, R2, L, O, H, J2, and C together, characterize more than 90 per cent of the Y-chromosomal variation in all socio-linguistic groups of India (Sahoo et al. 2006). Both IE and Draviḍian-speaking populations show a high combined frequency of haplogroups C*, L1, H1, and R2, which has a marginally low frequency outside India. On the other hand, haplogroups E, I, G, J*, and R1* have a combined frequency of 53 per cent in Near-East, and 24 per cent in Central Asia, and haplogroups C3, D, N, and O specific to Central (36 per cent) and South-East Asian populations, are rare or virtually absent in India. Overall the distributions of Y-chromosome lineages between India and West and Central Asia, display a clear geographic pattern. Only haplogroups R1a1 (M17) and J2 have inter-regional frequency patterns west of India: R1a1 occurs at the highest frequencies in populations of India, East Europe, and Central Asia, while J2 is most common in Afro-Asiatic and IE-speaking populations of Near and Middle East.

One of the main features of Indian society is that it is highly structured by social factors such as caste system, in which birth determines the position in the society, mode of subsistence (occupation), and choice of marriage partners. However, genesis of caste system in India is ambiguous, since Kosambi (1964) suggested that many of the caste groups have tribal origins. The measures of genetic distances between regions based on haplogroup frequencies revealed that the caste populations of "north" and "south" India are equidistant from the tribal groups and not particularly more closely related to each other (average Fst=0.06). The multidimensional scaling plot also demonstrated that the tribes (excluding those from east and north-east) were positioned mid-way between those for northern and southern castes, whilst the Austro-Asiatic and Tibeto–Burman-speaking tribal populations of the east and north-east formed as a separate category. When the individual haplogroup frequencies within each of the four geographical regions were considered, it could be asserted with 95 per cent CI that no consistent pattern was detected in the distribution of the Y-chromosome lineages to distinguish either the castes from the tribes, or Draviḍians from IE, confirming display distinct regional concentrations of Y-chromosome lineages in India. Using a much more representative dataset — numerically, geographically, and definitively — it was not possible to confirm any of the purported differentiations between the caste and tribal pools. Although differences could be found to occur within particular regions, between particular caste and tribal groups, consistent and statistically significant variations at the subcontinental scale were not detected. While it could be argued that assimilation of tribal populations into the caste system could have skewed distributions of Y-chromosome haplogroups in any particular region, this cannot explain the persistence and prevalence of those lineages put forward as being typical of incoming IEs (J2, R1a, R2, and L) among many of those populations who are still designated as tribals. Although appeals to language change are plausible for explaining the appearance of supposedly tribe specific Y-lineages among incoming IE speakers, it is much harder to conceive of a systematic movement of external Y-chromosome types in the opposite direction, via the uptake of Draviḍian languages. Rather, the existence of R1a1, R2, L1 male lineages which occur together with strictly Indian specific haplogroups and paragroups (C*, F*, H) both among caste and tribal groups, more parsimoniously supports a predominantly pre-IE, pre-Neolithic presence of the majority of these lineages in India. A pre-Neolithic chronology for the origins of Indian Y-chromosomes is also supported by the lack of a clear delineation between Draviḍian and IE speakers.

Higher frequency of J2 and R1a1 among caste populations have been linked by Quintana-Murci et al. (2001) and Cordaux et al. (2004) to a simplistic assumption that agriculture was brought along with caste system by the IE speakers as a result of demic diffusion of early farmers from south-western Iran, Fertile Cresent and Anatolia. However, the absence of other Neolithic markers of early farmers, M35 and M201 that have been reported by Semino et al. (2000) and Underhill et al. (2001) to be prevalent in Europe, Anatolia, South Caucasus and Iran, and the persistence of J2 in Draviḍian speakers and tribal groups of southern and western India questions the validity of this hypothesis. The distribution of R2, with its concentration in eastern and southern India, is not consistent with a recent demographic movement from the north-west. Instead, its prevalence amongst castes in these regions might represent a recent population expansion, perhaps associated with the transition to agriculture, which may have occurred independently in South Asia as suggested by Fuller (2003), which, unlike J2, does not show evidence of a recent diffusion throughout India from the north-west. It has been proposed by both Fuller (2003), and Diamond and Bellwood (2003), that agriculture in India probably arose as two independent events; one that was a consequence of earliest migration that brought the Draviḍian speakers and another much later through spread of rice cultivators from SE Asia. In fact, archaeo-botanical evidences (variety of rice) from recent excavations at archaeological sites of Lahura-Deva from northern India reveal regular farming and developed cultures dating back to sixth-seventh century CE. Our study clearly reveals that there is no one-to-one correlation between lineage, language and mode of subsistence, or social system, at least in the Indian subcontinent.

Analysis of admixture proportions evaluates the potential parental contributions of Central Asia to north-western and southern castes. The findings of admixture analysis confirmed the results obtained from the Fst analyses; that southern castes and tribals were very similar to each other in their Y-chromosomal haplogroup compositions, and that their gene pool was no different from the castes of north-west India. It also revealed that the contribution from West and Central Asia to the Indian Y-chromosomal pool is minor. These observations suggest if R1a1 (M17) is indeed linked to the "Aryanization" of the Indian gene pool, then the proposition that the observed high frequency of R1a1 in India is due to admixture with populations of Central Asian origin is difficult to substantiate. Although a decreasing frequency of M17 Y-chromosomes from Central Asia towards south India has been observed (Wells et al. 2001), the proposed source region (Russia/Central Asia) does not meet the expectation of containing high frequencies of the other components of haplogroup R, with no examples of R* and generally low incidence of R2. Also, if the source of R1a1 variation in India comes from Central Asia, as claimed by Wells et al. and Cordaux et al., then, under a recent gene flow scenario, one would also expect to find the other Central Asian derived NRY haplogroups (C3, DE, J*, I, G, N, O) in north-west India at similarly elevated frequencies, but that is not the scenario.

One could also argue that the other haplogroups were lost during a hypothetical bottleneck leading to lineage sorting amongst the early Indo-Aryans arriving in India. But this reason can be argued, for we have observed dramatically higher genetic variation amongst Indian R1a1 lineages, as opposed to lower STR diversity, which should be expected in case of population bottlenecks. In fact, Kivisild et al. (2003) reported that the STR haplotype diversity on the background of R1a in Central Asia and Eastern Europe is lower than that found in India. Rather, the high incidence of R1* and R1a throughout Central Asian and East European populations (without R2 and R* in most cases) is more parsimoniously explained by gene flow in the opposite direction, possibly with an early founder effect in South or West Asia. A study carried out by Majumder and Dey (2001) on HIV resistance of Indians showed that Indians virtually lack the HIV-1 — protective δ CCR5 allele that is frequent in Europe, Western Asia, and central Asia, implying either that the resistance allele arose very recently in Europe or that there has not been substantial gene flow to India from the north-west. This report provides additional support to our theory that although the Indian subcontinent may have acquired agricultural techniques and languages — but it absorbed few genes — from the west, but none can be linked to the "Aryan migration."

References

Bamshad, M., T. Kivisild, W.S. Watkins, M.E. Dixon, C.E. Ricker, B.B. Rao, J.M. Naidu, B.V. Prasad, P.G. Reddy, A. Rasanayagam, S.S. Papiha, R. Villems, A.J. Redd, M.F. Hammer, S.V. Nguyen, M.L. Carroll, M.A. Batzer, L.B. Jorde "Genetic evidence on the origins of Indian caste populations", *Genome Res* 11(2001): 994-1004.

Cavalli-Sforza, L.L., P. Menozzi, A. Piazza, *The History and Geography of Human Genes* (1994), Princeton: Princeton University Press, pp. 208-13.

Cordaux, R., R. Aunger, G. Bentley, I. Nasidze, S.M. Sirajuddin, M. Stoneking, "Independent Origins of Indian Caste and Tribal Paternal Lineages", *Curr Biol* 14 (2004): 231-35.

Cordaux, R., E. Deepa, H. Vishwanathan, M. Stoneking, "Genetic Evidence for the Demic Diffusion of Agriculture to India", *Science* 304 (2004): 1125.

Diamond, J., P. Bellwood, "Farmers and Their Languages: The First Expansions", *Science* 300(2003): 597-602.

Fuller, D., *Examining the Farming/Language Dispersal Hypothesis*, Cambridge: The McDonald Institute for Archaeological Research (2003).

Gimbutas, M., "The Kurgan Wave Migration (*c.* 3400-3200 BCE) into Europe and the following Transformation of Culture", *Journal of Near Eastern Studies*, 8 (1980): 273-315.

Kivisild, T, S. Rootsi, M. Metspalu, S. Mastana, K. Kaldma, J. Parik, E. Metspalu, M. Adojaan, H.V. Tolk, V. Stepanov, M. Golge, E. Usanga, S.S. Papiha, C. Cinnioglu, R. King, L. Cavalli-Sforza, P.A. Underhill, R. Villems, "The Genetic Heritage of the Earliest Settlers Persists both in Indian Tribal and Caste Populations". *Am J Hum Genet* 72 (2003): 313-32.

Kosambi, D.D., *The Culture and Civilization of Ancient India in Historical Outline*, New Delhi: Vikas (1964).

Majumder, P., B. Dey, "Absence of the HIV-I Protective Delta ccr5 Allele in most Ethnic Populations of India", *Eur J Hum Genet* 9 (2001): 794-96.

Quintana-Murci, L., C. Krausz, T. Zerjal, S.H. Sayar, M.F. Hammer, S.Q. Mehdi, Q. Ayub, R. Qamar, A. Mohyuddin, U. Radhakrishna, M.A. Jobling, C. Tyler-Smith, K. McElreavey, "Y-chromosome Lineages Trace Diffusion of People and Languages in Southwestern Asia", *Am J Hum Genet* 68 (2001): 537-42.

Renfrew, C., "The Origins of Indo-European Languages", *Sci Am* 261(1989): 82-90.

Sahoo S., A. Singh, G. Himabindu, J. Banerjee, T. Sitalaximi, S. Gaikwad, R. Trivedi, P. Endicott, T. Kivisild, M. Metspalu, R. Villems, V.K Kashyap "A prehistory of Indian Y-chromosomes: evaluating demic diffusion scenarios." *Proc Natl Acad Sci USA*, 103 (2006): 843-48.

Semino, O., G. Passarino, P.J. Oefner, A.A Lin, S. Arbuzova, L.E. Beckman, G. De Benedictis, P. Francalacci, A. Kouvatsi, S. Limborska, M. Marcikiae, A. Mika, B. Mika, D. Primorac, A.S. Santachiara-Benerecetti, L.L. Cavalli-Sforza, P.A. Underhill, "The Genetic Legacy of Paleolithic Homo-sapiens sapiens in extant Europeans: A Y-Chromosome Perspective", *Science* 290 (2000): 1155-59.

Singh, K.S., *The Scheduled Tribes*, vol. III (1997), Oxford: Oxford University Press.

Underhill, P., G. Passarino, A.A. Lin, P. Shen, M. Mirazḍn Lahr, R.A. Foley, P.J. Oefner, L.L. Cavalli-Sforza, "The Phylogeography of the Y-Chromosome Binary Haplotypes and the Origins of Modern Human Populations", *Ann Hum Genet*, 65 (2001): 43-62.

Wells, R.S., N. Yuldasheva, R. Ruzibakiev, P. Underhill, I. Evseeva, Blue-J. Smith, L. Jin, et al., "The Eurasian heartland: A continental perspective on Y-chromosome diversity", *Proc Natl Acad Sci USA*, 98 (2001):10244-249.

The Contributors

Bajpai, Shiva G., served as Professor of History and Director of Asian Studies at the California State University, Northridge, and Los Angeles from 1970 to 2003. As a Professor Emeritus, he still continues to teach courses in Indian history and culture at that institution. He has also taught at the Banaras Hindu University, India (1958-68) and worked at the University of Minnesota (1967-70). He has published many articles on various aspects of Indian history and culture and contributed dozens of articles to the *Hindi Viśvakośa* (Encyclopedia) and to the *Encyclopedia of Asian History*. He co-authored a major reference work — *A Historical Atlas of South Asia* (1978: University of Chicago Press & updated 2nd edition 1992: Oxford University Press; 2005: The Digital Library of South Asia, Chicago University Press). Following the California textbooks' controversy, he has collaborated with the Hinduism Today in their publications of Hindu History Lesson Supplements in three parts, (2007 & 2009) to the World History School textbooks [*address*: 670 Wildomar Street, Pacific Palisades, CA 90272, USA; *e-mail*:<hchis006@csun.edu>].

Eltsov, Piotr, grew up in Russia where he studied Sanskrit, Hindi and ancient History in Saint Petersburg University and the Institute of Oriental Studies of the Russian Academy of Sciences. After moving to the US in 1994, he first completed an MA in South Asian Studies at the University of California at Berkeley, and then received a Ph.D. in anthropological archaeology at Harvard (2005). From 2006 to 2008, Eltsov held a position as an Alexander von-Humboldt Post-Doctoral Fellow at the Institute for the Languages and Cultures of South Asia in Berlin, Germany. His current position is a Kluge Research Fellow at the John W. Kluge Center at the Library of Congress. Piotr Eltsov's most important publication is a monograph *From Harappa to Hastinapura: A Study of the Earliest South Asian City and Civilization* (Boston/Leiden: EJ Brill 2008). He has excavated in Pakistan (Harappa), Tadjikistan (Penjikent), Crimea (Solkhat), Jordan (Wadi Fidan), and Dagestan (Velikent and Syugut) [*address*: The John W. Kluge Center at the Library of Congress,

101, Independence Ave, Washington, DC 20540, USA; *e-mail*: <eltsov@zedat.fu-berlin.de>].

Kashyap, V.K., is an eminent molecular geneticist whose main interest has been to analyse diversity in the genome of tribal and caste population of India. He has studied the diversity in genome of about 400 tribes of India which has provided deeper insight into the origin, evolution, migration, history, susceptibility and resistance to various diseases of these people. His work has contributed in identifying the suitable autosomal Y-chromosome and mitochondrial DNA markers for human identification and populations in the Indian subcontinent which has been the foundation stone of DNA technology in criminal justice delivery system. He has published more than 115 peer reviewed papers in international journals. He has been decorated with several prestigious awards. He has headed CFSL, Kolkata and National Institute of Biologicals, Noida, the prestigious health science institutions of India. Presently he is working in the capacity of Director at Directorate of Forensic Science, Ministry of Home Affairs, Government of India and is entrusted with the task of setting up a large number of forensic institutions in the country [*address*: A-123; Gaur Green Avenue, Indrapuram, Gaziabad – 201 010 (UP); *e-mail*: <vkk2k@hotmail.com>].

Kazanas, Nicholas, born in Greece in 1939, studied English Literature at University College, Economics and Philosophy at the School of Economic Science and Sanskrit at the School of Oriental and African studies — all in London; also post-graduated at SOAS and at Deccan College in Pune (India). He taught in London and Athens and since 1980 has been Director of the Omilos Meleton Cultural Institute. In Greece, he has published treatises of social, economic and philosophical interest. He has many publications in Western and Indian journals and some other books. He is on the Editorial Board of *Adyar Library Bulettin* (Chennai). He has also introduced a three-year course of learning Sanskrit for Greeks and translations of the principal Upanishads [*address*: Director, Omilos Meleton Cultural Institute, 15, Archimedous Str., Nea Ionia/14232, Athens, Greece; *e-mail*: <nkazanas@omilosmeleton.gr>].

Lal, B.B., a world-renowned archaeologist, was the Director-General of the Archaeological Survey of India for a number of years and was also the President of the World Archaeological Congress. His excavations cover a very wide range — from Palaeolithic times to the early historical. Notable of the excavations were the ones done at

Kālībaṅgan, Rajasthan (Indus Civilization), Hastināpura (*Mahābhārata*), Ayodhyā (*Rāmāyaṇa*) and in Egypt (Egyptian Prehistory). Prof. Lal was the recipient of several prestigious honours – including D.Litt. (Honoris causa), Mahāmahopādhyāya and Padma-Bhushan. His publications include numerous books on archaeology and excavations, and over 150 seminal research papers [*address*: F-7, Hauz Khas Enclave, New Delhi – 110 016; *e-mail*: <bblal3@yahoo.com>].

Narahari Achar, B.N., originally from Bangalore, India, is currently a Professor of Physics at the University of Memphis, Memphis, TN, (USA). He has a PhD from the Pennsylvania State University. He pioneered the use of Planetarium Software in exploring the sky described in the Vedic texts. In his article on the date of the Mahābhārata War using Planetarium Software, he clearly demonstrates how a unique date for the Mahābhārata War can be arrived at. He argues that the Mahābhārata war should be taken as the sheet-anchor for the chronology of Bhārata [*address*: Professor of Physics, University of Memphis, Memphis, TN-38119 (USA); *e-mail*: <nachar@memphis.edu>].

Rajaram, Navaratna, is a scientist and historian who turned to history after spending more than twenty years as an academic and industrial researcher in the United States of America. He pioneered the study of ancient Indian, Egyptian and Babylonian mathematics and their relationship to Harappan archaeology. Along with David Frawley and the late Natwar Jha, he has authored important books on Ancient India including on the Harappan writing [*address*: F2 Rajatha Manor, 30/7 Patalamma Temple Road, South End Circle, Basavanagudi, Bangalore – 560 004; *e-mail*: <nsrajaram@airtelmail.in>].

Rosser, Yvette Claire, is the co-founder of the International Day Without Violence designed to infuse conflict resolution in schools. She holds a PhD degree from the University of Texas at Austin. Her specializations are teaching, studies of curricula meant for instruction and comparison of secondary level social studies textbooks. Her publications include *Indoctrinating minds: Politics or Education in Bangladesh* and *Islamization of Pakistani Social Studies Textbooks.* She has to her credit several articles published in renowned newspapers and journals [*address*: 2403 Trafalgar Drive, Austin, TX 78723, USA; *e-mail*: <ranirosser@gmail.com>].

Sahoo, Sanghamitra S., is postdoctoral associate in the University of Texas, USA, in Health Science. She has extensively studied Y-chromosome marker to understand the genetic structure of Indian population *vis-à-vis* global population as an associate of Dr Kashyap at CFSL, Calcutta. Her studies contributed significantly in deciphering the migration of population across the Asian continent. As a part of technology development, she has developed a number of multiplex reactions to analyse genetic variation of Y-chromosome [*address*: Postdoctoral Associate, Health Science Center, University of Texas at Tyler, Tyler, TX. (USA); *e-mail*: <sanghamitra_sahoo@hotmail.com>].

Singh, Bal Ram, is the Director of Center for Indic Studies at UMass Dartmouth, where he teaches a course on Science of Kriyayoga. Dr Singh as a Professor of Biophysical Chemistry and Henry Dreyfus Teacher-Scholar at University of Massachusetts Dartmouth, and the Director of Botulinum Research Center, has been conducting research for 20 years at UMass Dartmouth on the molecular mode of action of botulinum and tetanus neurotoxins, and lately also on yoga, mind, and consciousness. His research on biodefence and biotechnology is internationally recognised, and he has served on many national and international scientific panels. Dr Singh has published about 175 research articles; three dozen scholarly articles on issues related to Indian tradition, culture, and philosophy; has edited three books, including *India's Intellectual Traditions and Contributions to the World* (DKPW, 2010); and has obtained 3 patents. Dr Singh has been honoured with awards by several reputed institutions in India and abroad [*address*: Director, Center for Indic Studies, University of Massachusetts, Dartmouth, 285 Old Westport Road, Dartmouth, MA 02747 (USA); *e-mail*: <bsingh@umassd.edu>].

Trivedi, Rajni has been a Cytogeneticist by training. Her main interest has been analysis of chromosome and genome in different diseases. She has studied polymorphic region in genome of a large number of Indian caste and tribal population. These studies have greatly assisted in appreciation of history and origin of caste population in India. She has also developed technology of carrying genetic study by single genome. She has been trained at Lucknow University, India and Harvard University, USA. She has published over 40 papers in various peer reviewed journals and acted as a mentor of Ph.D students. She is working as Deputy Director, CFSL, Kolkata presently on deputation from Ministry of Finance, Government of India [*address*: Deputy Director, CFSL, Kolkata; *e-mail*: <trivedi_r@hotmai.com>].

Underhill, Peter A. has worked as a staff researcher at Stanford University School of Medicine since 1990. His research involves the molecular analysis of human DNA sequence variation in human populations. He has been doing pioneering research on human Y chromosome diversification since 1992 that has led to the development of a robust gene tree that elegantly defines numerous Y-chromosome varieties with distinctive geographic localization. The main focus of his research involves deciphering population affinity, substructure and history in contemporary populations using Y-chromosome compound SNP and STR lineages. He has co-authored numerous peer-reviewed publications on the subject [*address*: Child and Adolescent Psychiatry and Child Development Hallmayer Laboratory, Stanford University, 1201 Welch Roa, MSLS Building Room P 120-Lab 6, Stanford, California 94304-5485 (USA); *e-mail*: <under@stanford.edu>].

Index